*Studies in American Biblical Hermeneutics 11* •

# Making Sense of New Testament Theology

## *"Modern" Problems and Prospects*

• *Studies in American Biblical Hermeneutics 11* •

# Making Sense of New Testament Theology

## "Modern" Problems and Prospects

▫ ◻ ◻ ◻ ▫

by
A. K. M. Adam

MERCER

ISBN 0-86554-459-X

BS
2397
.A33
1995

MUP/P114

□ □ □

The paper used in this publication meets
the minimum requirements of American National Standard
for Information Sciences—Permanence of Paper
for Printed Library Materials, ANSI Z39.48-1984.

□ □ □

*Library of Congress Cataloging-in-Publication Data*
Adam, A. K. M. (Andrew Keith Malcolm) 1957–      .
Making sense of New Testament theology :
"modern" problems and prospects / by A. K. M. Adam.
x+240pp. 6x9" (15x23 cm.).
(Studies in American biblical hermeneutics ; 11).
Includes bibliographical references and index.
ISBN 0-86554-459-X (pbk.; alk. paper).
1. Bible. N.T.—Theology.  2. Bible. N.T.—Hermeneutics.
3. Bible. N.T.—Criticism, interpretation, etc.
I. Title.  II. Series.
BS2397.A33                      1995
230—dc20                   95-21953
                                                    CIP

# Contents

# Editor's Preface

Hegemony is not a concept that sits well with the American character. Much of American history reflects various attempts to disperse hegemonies in many areas of human endeavor. A. K. M. Adam has written a book that attacks the problem of hegemony in the field of New Testament theology.

Adam's theme is simple. In his own introduction, he writes: "New Testament theology *need not* be founded on warrants derived from historical-critical reasoning" (my emphasis). As such, Adam's book is not to be taken as an attack upon the historical-critical method. Rather, it is directed toward the problem of hegemony itself in New Testament studies. The target is historical criticism because of the pretentious role it plays in modern biblical studies, not because it has no legitimate role to play.

This volume of the Studies in American Biblical Hermeneutics series is especially for those interested in an analysis of the philosophical underpinnings of this pretentiousness, or hegemony. It is also for those who are interested in suggestive exploration of alternative ways that New Testament theology might be addressed. Adam liberally gives reference to American New Testament scholarship on both sides of the "historical-critical problem" throughout this text. It is not a far reach from his analysis to comprehend that the hegemony problem is one of European import—a problem that begs for redress in the American setting.

Adam has skillfully crafted here a critical study that does not kill the patient as he destroys the disease. Adam's analysis is designed to teach both historical critics and those of alternative persuasions. The former will gain a better sense of the underlying presuppositions of their methodological principles. Those of alternative persuasion will find the philosophical, or ideological, context in which they set their work renewed and refreshed. It seems clear to many of us that the pressing need now is to study historical analysis itself if we are to move to a richer and fuller Bible. We need, in other words, a kind of hermeneutics of theology. In this volume Adam has taken an important first step in that direction. The contemporary erosion of church involvement from the old Protestant mainstream that has traditionally supported the banner of intellectual freedom (read, historical-critical analysis) is an important indicator that something has gone very wrong in our theological house. Increasingly, people seem to feel this historical analysis lacks some very basic pieces of what interested them in the Bible in the first place.

It is a difficult thing this business of dehegemonizing. Hegemonies are underwritten and legitimized by institutions and the armies of personnel that inhabit them. New Testament theology is a product of such an institution—an institution that is specifically the child of the Enlightenment, the modern university. Within the hallowed halls of the major intellectual centers in American life during the last several generations—Adam shows us—we have severed the fundamental ties of the Bible to the believing communities that produced it. In the university, the *primary* way the Bible is now studied is through the lens of historical-critical scholarship. Alternate paradigms of scholarship tend to be discounted or trivialized as eccentric or nonmainstream. How ironic that the mainstream of liberal arts education in the university is out of touch with the mainstream of the culture itself, and has become, in effect, subject to the same forces of trivialization.

In short, in historical-critical scholarship, the university has found a way to wrest the Bible from the control of the church, but it has done so at the purchase of giving up any real significant meaning to the architects of the culture itself.

It would be comfortable for the church if it were indeed the case that the academy was simply serving the church's own interests by backing up its faith claims with historical scholarship, proving in an analogous way that "Troy was a real place and not a figment of the poet's imagination." Many no doubt believe such is indeed the case. But all too few in the faith communities have adequately considered that the "historical Troy" perspective when applied to the Bible is really a genie who no longer lives in the bottle. The believing patrons of our academies (wealthy or otherwise) who naively have believed and continue to believe that history would prove the Bible have in fact been taken for a long joyride. The situation is not unlike that of tourist agents who gladly continue to take their patrons to "authentic" historical biblical sites in the Holy Land itself. It was all, if Adam is correct, a house of cards from the beginning.

Adam here helps us understand what to keep of the historical-critical perspective when the realization hits that we have been sold a bill of goods that no longer makes good on its promises. In that sense, Adam's book is far more friendly to the historical-critical method as such than unfriendly.

As I conclude this invitation to Adam's text, let me refer to a rather strange image drawn from nature. In this scenario, historical criticism appears as a herd of great beasts devouring every other species in the field. Gradually those other species begin to dwindle until they in fact become endangered. Many such species are lost, never to be heard from again. The danger is that soon there will be nothing left in the field but that one herd of great beasts. Who knows what has been lost? Who knows what will be lost in the future if we don't address the hegemony of the great beasts themselves?

Ecumenical Theological Seminary, Detroit          *Charles Mabee*

# Acknowledgments

This work owes much to many sources. I am indebted for advice and inspiration to Dan O. Via, Jr., Stanley Hauerwas, Mary McClintock Fulkerson, and Dale Martin of Duke University; to Stephen Fowl of Loyola College in Maryland; and especially to my colleagues Philip D. Kenneson (Milligan College), David Cunningham (University of St. Thomas), L. Gregory Jones (Loyola College of Maryland), Jonathan Wilson (Westmont College), and Michael Cartwright (Allegheny College), whose friendship has sustained and challenged me at every step.

The Episcopal Church Foundation and the James B. Duke Foundation provided material support for the research for this project. I am deeply grateful for their generosity.

However generous my benefactors, however helpful my colleagues, however insightful my advisers, I would not have been able to write this book without the encouragement, criticism, and daily support of Margaret Bamforth Adam. Her commitment to this book belies the (modern) notion of individual authorship, for her contributions sustain and pervade the whole text. Her wholehearted dedication to following truly in God's ways continues to teach me, day after day, about God's good news of love.

With Margaret, I dedicate this book to Nathaniel, Josiah, and Philippa Adam, our beautiful, wonderful children; and to Delores Adam (whose constant grace has touched me more deeply than she can know); and to Ruth Pennington, who, one night in Minnesota, asked the question that eventually provoked this book.

*A. K. M. Adam*

# Introduction

"Biblical theology is a subject in decline"—so says John J. Collins.[1] Collins is not alone when he makes this claim. Indeed, there have come many and plaintive cries over the past fifty years, cries for some sort of biblical theology that recaptures the power and vision of the biblical theologies of ages past. Such works ought to be all the more readily available in an age that has distinguished itself for the vigor, scope, and disciplinary precision with which it has undertaken the task of biblical interpretation. Still the laments continue, and the biblical theologies (or, more typically, the "Old Testament theologies" and "New Testament theologies") that modern biblical studies has produced seem unable to satisfy the desiderata of the discontents.

In *Making Sense of New Testament Theology*, I seek to establish one simple premise: that New Testament theology need not be founded on warrants derived from historical-critical reasoning. I argue that the perceived necessity of historical foundations grows not from insights into the nature of interpretation or understanding, but from the cultural situation of modernity, whereby instrumental reason, chronological determination, the myth of progress, and the cult of expertise imply that New Testament theology must be derived scientifically—with an eye to the historical origins of the text—by experts who continually surpass their predecessors. I do not argue that this way of conceiving New Testament theology is invalid; indeed, it is precisely the right way for *modern* New Testament theologians to conduct their studies. The modern

---

[1]"Is a Critical Biblical Theology Possible?" the keynote essay in *The Hebrew Bible and Its Interpreters*, Biblical and Judaic Studies 1, ed. William Henry Propp, Baruch Halpern, and David Noel Freedman (Winona Lake: Eisenbraun's, 1990) 1.

approach is not, however, exclusively correct or universally binding.

My argument against the universality or exclusivity of modern criteria ought not to be perceived as an effort to establish a new and improved way of doing New Testament theology—the *post-modern* way. Such an interpretation of my work would inscribe it into the vast circular leapfrog game of modernity, in which the only way to get somewhere is to surpass someone else. I neither seek nor repudiate the label "postmodern"; it is simply irrelevant to my aspirations. My goal is to help undermine the hegemonic control on interpretation that historical criticism currently exercises. The chosen site for my effort is the field of New Testament theology, though (as I have argued elsewhere, under other circumstances) that field is chosen simply as a strategic point; I do not see historical criteria as any more necessary for interpretation in general than for theological interpretation in particular.

In order to defend my claim, I will solicit testimony concerning the qualities of modernity, the modern ways of thinking that have come to seem natural to academic intellectuals. For it was not always thus; the category of the "modern" was invented in the Renaissance, in the conflict between the "Moderns" and the "Ancients" (initiated when the Moderns were at the margins, and the Ancients held a cultural hegemony). I will collate these testimonies concerning modernity into a physiognomy, a composite sketch of the suspected face of culture. Some witnesses will disagree with others, some will outrightly contradict one another; still, I will add their testimony to the sketch. The point is not to distill the true essence of modernity, nor even to come up with the most adequate account of this subtle and pervasive cultural phenomenon. It is rather to provide a basis for recognizing modernity in the particular field of New Testament theology.

Once I have put together a composite sketch of modernity, I will try to persuade my readers that the theoreticians whose work has decisively influenced contemporary New Testament theology—Johann Philipp Gabler, William Wrede, Krister Stendahl—all reflect presuppositions and interests that correspond to the presuppositions and interests of modernity. I will label the Gabler-Wrede-

Stendahl tradition "modern New Testament theology," but without implying that New Testament theology has deliberately adopted modernity, or even that New Testament theology shares in some posited "essence" of modernity. I simply point to the match between the discourse of contemporary New Testament theology and the broader discourse of modernity, because an increasing number of observers have spotted serious problems in the project of modernity. The correspondence between the discourses of New Testament theology and modernity suggests that there may be a like correspondence between their problems.

Indeed, even a casual observer of the disputes over biblical theology will recognize that the path of New Testament theology that can be charted with reference to the claims of William Wrede, which find their precedents in the work of Johann Philipp Gabler and their culmination in that of Krister Stendahl, simply does not lead where many critics want to go. You can't get there from here. The *Wredestrasse* is the path of *modern* New Testament theology, a road entirely satisfactory to most theologians, but nonetheless quite unsuitable for others. The *Wredestrasse*, however, bills itself as the *only* road to New Testament theology. Its contented travellers often argue that all other paths lead either to a chaotic realm where nothing is as it seems, or to an authoritarian hierarchy in which independent thought is outlawed.

The exclusive legitimacy of this approach may reasonably be questioned. Much of the weight behind arguments for the exclusive validity of modern New Testament theology comes from assumptions that seem natural in the cultural context of modernity, but which are manifestly dubious to critics who recognize no allegiance to modernity and its presuppositions. If the arguments in favor of modern New Testament theology are compelling only on internal presuppositions, the way is clearly open for exploring alternative avenues to New Testament theology.

If, however, the broadly recognized criteria that modern New Testament theology has sponsored no longer govern the evaluation of New Testament theologies, it might seem that I thrust the would-be theologian into a twilight world without critical guidelines. This is not so. There are (and behind the scenes of modern biblical interpretation always have been) more canons than the strict historical yardstick. Theological and ecclesial criteria, aesthetic criteria, and ethical criteria provide three starting points for critical evaluation of New Testament theologies; but there will always be more specific local criteria that apply to evaluating New Testament theologies in contexts with particular interests (interests such as defending the inerrancy of the Bible, or the liberation of women from structures of oppression, to name but two). On this account, the validity of any interpretation is measured not against the transcendent criterion of historical accuracy, but against criteria that vary depending on the situation of the interpreter and his or her audience.

An interpretation does not derive its authority from transcendent rules of legitimacy, but from immanent social, institutional, and political circumstances. This is just as true of my interpretation of the discourse of New Testament theology as it is of theological interpretations of the New Testament. Readers who resist my account of New Testament theology will be better able than I am to locate the social and political determinations of my thesis. I am in no position to dodge their critique. I conclude my introduction, therefore, with an avowal of some of my own interpretive interests and goals.

I envision three audiences for my claims. The first is the diverse assortment of Christians for whom theology, politics, and daily life are not distinguishable; these may remind me (more or less cordially) that they don't need my theory, since they are enacting New Testament theology daily without my assistance. The second is the audience of determined advocates of historical-critical priority, most of whom will probably be unmoved by my arguments. The third audience, and that to which this book is especially addressed, is the collection of interpreters who feel acutely the difficulty of linking the Bible (which they have been taught to read in a modern way) with their theological and political practice. I hope these perplexed interpreters may recognize their dilemma in these pages, and find in my thesis reassurance that there is more than one road to New Testament theology.

I am likewise concerned that the class of academic biblical critics (of which I am a member) not try to insulate its industry from the searching questions of those excluded from the guild—the "noncanonical" interpreters of Barbara Herrnstein Smith's recent work.[2]

If my thesis is persuasive, we may imagine New Testament theology more as perpetuating the New Testament traditions than as "the history of early Christian religion." We may think of New Testament theology as a variety of family trades, handed down from generation to generation of the disciples of Jesus, rather than as the esoteric academic province of licensed historical practitioners. Some among these disciples will want to seek out historical foundations and original meanings; some others will listen more attentively to interpreters whose warrants are the evidence their lives provide. My own sympathies are especially with the latter mode of undertaking New Testament theology.

---

[2]See her *Contingencies of Value* (Cambridge MA: Harvard University Press, 1988) 24-27.

# Chapter 1

# A Physiognomy
# of Modernity

*Il faut être absolument moderne.*          —Rimbaud

Though the term "postmodern" is notoriously elusive, the term "modern" is every bit as slippery. On the one hand, "modern" means up-to-date, contemporary, recent. On the other hand, it may refer to a particular manner, a period, a style, a set of assumptions; "modern" no longer ensures recent vintage. Modern philosophy began with Descartes, or Kant;[1] modern art, with any of several nineteenth-century painters. But just as these moderns were not especially recent, neither are recent thinkers or painters necessarily "modern." That is not all, though—for there can be considerable debate over whether Descartes was *really* modern; rival definitions of this modern manner contest the validity of applying the label "modern" to any particular object.

Since the thesis of this monograph rests upon distinguishing one current of New Testament theology as "modern," it is crucially important to make clear the interpretation of "modern" with which I am working, its characteristics and its basis. Since there is no consensus definition of modernity to which one can appeal for a

---

[1]Jean-François Lyotard suggests in one essay that Augustine was the first "modern" (a "modern" before the term even existed, as the historical survey below will show); "Rules and Paradoxes and Svelte Appendix," trans. Brian Massumi, *Cultural Critique* 5 (1986): 215.

simple meaning, in this first chapter I will propose a working interpretation with reference to various alternatives for understanding
and defining "modernity."

My characterization of modernity will not be exhaustive, and
it will at many points deviate from the testimony given by the witnesses whose analyses of modernity I will discuss. Though I will
marshall evidence from theorists who participate in the debate of
modernity against postmodernity, my aim here is not to take the
side of one of these parties, or to explore the postmodern at all
(except to the extent to which the opposition of "modern" and
"postmodern" clarifies my interpretation of modernity). The point
of this section is to draw upon the various discourses of modernity
to provide an interpretation which grows from the work of
preceding theorists of modernity, but which also is cut to fit its
potential application to the practice of New Testament theology.

The aspects of this modernity are intertwined in such a way
that it is finally impossible to consider one of them in isolation; as
I consider one facet of modernity, other aspects that are implied by
that modernity will continually weave in and out of the analysis.
Thus the cardinal characteristic of modernity—its relation to novelty—implies another mark of modernity, the repudiation of tradition. At the same time, novelty cannot endure more than a
moment before it becomes passé, so that modernity also implies a
precarious relationship with the present moment; in order to be
modern, one must paradoxically *get ahead* of the present, so that
when the present arrives one will be ready for it. This endless
cycle of catching up with and surpassing the present mirrors
modernity's commitment to the ideal of progress, which always requires that one overcome the past and establish a new, improved
present.

The particular way in which Western culture has undertaken
the effort to embody this ideal of progress is through applying
purposive rationality to the world; and as the world is pro-
gressively rationalized, various value-spheres attain autonomy over
against others. These value-spheres, now autonomous, develop
according to their own inner logics, which are articulated by
experts whose fields are increasingly specialized (which specializa-

tion recapitulates the process by which value-spheres attain autonomy). All this rationalization and specialization provides more and
more new commodities, both intellectual and material—which both
satisfies the need of modernity for the new and provides broader
fields for innovation.[2] None of these features of modernity can in
the end be separated from the others; still, I will endeavor to emphasize one aspect of modernity at a time in order to illuminate
the role each plays in the greater conglomeration.

There will at the same time be contradictions internal to the
given interpretation of modernity; any treatment of modernity that
avoids such contradictions does so at the cost of excluding certain
characteristics that other theories have understood as typical of
modernity.[3] For example, the division of the world into value-
spheres in modernity is counterbalanced by a continual effort to
find a discourse that grounds a theory of the whole. Indeed, at
least one account ascribes to modernity just this need to break
down the divisions between the value-spheres, in order then to
restore to the life-world (from which the value-spheres have been
separated) the benefits that specialization has brought.[4] Such a self-
contradictory character of modernity is likewise emphasized in
Terry Eagleton's description of modernism:

---

[2]The relation of modernity to capitalism (implied by this sentence) is
critically important in a number of respects. First, an analysis of the
material dimensions of modernity's emergence would banish the possible
inference that modernity is a purely intellectual, ideal phenomenon.
Second, an economic analysis of modernity would prepare the way for
an economic examination of the industry of biblical interpretation. These
endeavors would be intensely interesting, but they fall outside the scope
of this essay.

[3]In *All That Is Solid Melts into Air* (New York: Simon & Schuster, 1982),
Marshall Berman contends that "modernism contains its own inner
contradictions and dialectics" (171), and his depiction of modernity amply
bears out that claim.

[4]This goal of dedifferentiation is expressed by Jürgen Habermas,
among others. See "Modernity versus Postmodernity," *New German
Critique* 22 (1981): 3-14.

[It] suggests at one and the same time an arresting and denial of history in the violent shock of an immediate present, from which vantage point all previous developments may be complacently consigned to the ashcan of "tradition," and a disorienting sense of history moving with peculiar force and urgency within one's immediate experience, pressingly actual yet tantalizingly opaque.[5]

Granted, then, that there are contradictory tendencies within modernism, I choose to include these conflicting elements in the interest of approaching New Testament theology with a more comprehensive depiction of modernity. My stipulated modernity should show a powerful attraction among its constituent elements despite the tensions its contradictions entail.

The foregoing discussion has hinted at certain characteristics of modernity that I will use as a benchmark in the succeeding chapters. While the result will fall short of being a comprehensive "theory of modernity," that is not inappropriate; the drive to develop a totalizing view of a given subject, particularly the subject of modernity, is itself a characteristically modern enterprise. Instead of defining all of modernity, I will sketch a composite portrait, taking testimony from some witnesses here, and others there. I will concentrate on modernity's family traits; individual traits may be absent from any given member of the family, but the presence of several of the traits will be taken as prima facie evidence of some significant relation to the project of modernity.

The first and most obvious characteristic of modernity is its commitment to the *new*. The association of modernity with this drive is obviously one fruit of the *querelle des Anciens et des Modernes*. Modernity first struggled to establish its own legitimacy over against the traditional canons drawn from antiquity, and then took the offensive to argue for its superiority to those models. The defense of novelty as an inherently favorable quality begins with Baudelaire ("au fond de l'Inconnu pour trouver du *nouveau*") and

---

[5]"Capitalism, Modernism, and Postmodernism," *New Left Review* 152 (1985): 66.

continues through Vattimo's emphasis on modernity as an endless cycle of *Überwindung*. In American consumer vernacular, "modern" and "new" are virtually synonymous: a refrigerator that is not "modern" will not sell. The case is much the same in scholarship, wherein theories may rely upon only the most up-to-date sources, and where the process of obtaining academic credentials involves not simply the mastery of one's chosen field, but the production of "original" scholarship.

The converse of the modern commitment to the new is its continual rebellion against the past. This is once again a characteristic to be found already in the *querelle*, but in this case the theme remains virtually constant through the discourse of modernity. As Weber pointed out, modern intellectual endeavors need to be self-authenticating (as opposed to projects that are legitimated by appeal to tradition, for example); such endeavors are conceived and take shape as the further rationalization of an incomplete project. The modern scholar views the history of previous work in his or her field as the story of a series of inadequate attempts to answer problematic questions he or she at last has solved.

A case in point is Habermas's own narrative of the history of modernity, wherein one philosopher after another misses the point of intersubjective rationality, which Habermas has finally brought to our attention as the key to a fruitful fulfillment of the promise of the Enlightenment. In this, however, Habermas's efforts differ little from the conventional form of scholarly work, which first reports the history of all relevant previous work and explains why it went wrong, then offers a new synthesis that straightens out all the snarls introduced by preceding errors.

Since modernity is committed to the new and repudiates the old, it has coexisted quite comfortably with (and at times has depended upon) the myth of perpetual progress. Indeed, if it could be argued that modernity had not introduced significant progress into the world, but that on the whole the world was no better off now than before the Enlightenment, the image of modernity would be greatly weakened. The principle evidence on behalf of modern progress has been founded on science and technology; one might be hard-pressed to defend the work of modern painters as an obvious sign of progress over their predecessors.[6] The impact of the myth of progress in the field of scholarship (which is, of course, included under Weber's rubric of science, *Wissenschaft*) has been extensive; among other things, it has provided one strong motive force for the increasing specialization of knowledge and the proliferation of journals and technical works, which the scholar is then obliged to read (and contribute to) in order to maintain one's reputation.

Second, modernity will persistently call attention to time, to the compulsory force time exerts upon modern people. Time may obligate people to think in particular ways (in order to be taken seriously as "modern"), or it may forbid certain moves ("one can no longer . . . "). The modern scholar will strive always to acknowledge the most recent works, and will feel little or no obligation even to mention works that are now conventionally seen as outdated. History, time's accomplice, will constitute an unfathomable gap that, according to modernity, ruptures the relation of the contemporary to the past.

Third, modernity will appeal to distinctive warrants to legitimate its products. Legitimate scholarship will respect the autonomy and specialization of the value-spheres, lest a truth-claim bounce free and unsettle the equilibrium of the lifeworld (Habermas). Modern scholars will use the correct method, which method is itself proper to the given field of study; the results will therefore be guaranteed without regard to the character of the scholar, since one's personal and professional thoughts are entirely distinct. The same reliance upon formal methodological criteria guarantees that any rational, well-informed scholar may participate in any given enterprise.

---

[6]Progress in the sphere of morality would be even harder to assess, but there are clearly forceful arguments to the effect that modern ethics is virtually a contradiction in terms; cf. Alasdair MacIntyre's vivid parable at the beginning of *After Virtue*, 2nd ed. (Notre Dame: University of Notre Dame Press, 1984). While moderns frequently assume that contemporary mores are evidently superior to those of the past, it is not clear what criteria they would advance to defend that claim.

Fourth, modern studies are so founded on this culture of expertise that the modern scholar is always in a position authoritatively to mediate esoteric conclusions to the mass of nonexperts. The modern expert perceives, and reinscribes, an essential distinction between what is at a popular level, and what can be evaluated only by a suitably trained scholar.

## • Modernity and Newness •

The most prominent aspect of "modernity" is its association with "newness": as Richard Wolin observes, in modernity *"newness itself has become traditional."*[7] The word was in fact determined by opposition to the past from its origins. *Modernus* (meaning "nowness," "currency") was coined in the late fifth century from the adverb *modo* ("just now," "recently") to contrast with "ancient."[8] Though the word was used in various ways—Shakespeare knew it as a synonym for "everyday"[9]—its sense of "newness" came into prominence as a mark of positive value in the seventeenth and

---

[7]"Modernism vs. Postmodernism," *Telos* 62 (1984/1985): 16. Other testimonies: Gianni Vattimo states that we discover "the essence of modernity as the epoch in which Being is reduced to the *novum*" (*The End of Modernity*, trans. Jon R. Snyder, Parallax: Revisions of Culture and Society [Baltimore: Johns Hopkins University Press, 1988] 168). Leszek Kolakowski asks, "Is our civilization based on the belief . . . that what is *new* is good by definition? In expressions like modern technology and modern science, there is a strong suggestion that what is modern is thereby better" ("Modernity on Endless Trial," *Encounter* 66 [March 1986]: 9).

[8]Matei Calinescu, *Five Faces of Modernity*, 2nd ed. (Durham NC: Duke University Press, 1987) 13-14.

[9]In lines most appropriate for the topic of this study, Shakespeare writes: "They say miracles are past, and we have our philosophical persons, to make modern and familiar, things supernatural and causeless" (*All's Well That Ends Well* 2.3.2). So likewise Leszek Kolakowski: "The world became soulless, and only on this presupposition could modern science evolve. No miracles and no mysteries, no divine or diabolical interventions in the course of events, were conceivable any longer" ("Modernity on Endless Trial," 10).

eighteenth centuries. It became an object of particular attention as the self-identification of one of the parties to a particular debate: the Ancients against the Moderns, *la querelle des Anciens et des Modernes*, the Battle of the Books. Since then—from Baudelaire through Habermas ("the distinguishing mark of works, which count as modern, is the 'new'"[10])—novelty has remained at the heart of modernity.

In the centuries-old battle between Ancients and Moderns, the Ancients maintained allegiance to classical ideals; for them, the notion of progress was an empty illusion, and the highest point of artistic achievement had come in classical antiquity. We ought not, they argued, presume to insight superior to that of the artists and writers of ancient Greece and Rome. Indeed, the achievements of the ancient writers were unsurpassable and so constituted the models for all subsequent efforts. To this end, the Ancients held as binding upon contemporary poets standards drawn from classical literature. Such standards might include the familiar unities of action, time, and place in drama, or the insistence that the subject matter of ancient literature was the only appropriate material for contemporary works. It was not considered extravagant to suggest that "there is no one learned, whether physician, politician, mathematician, theologian, jurist, who has not taken shelter and lodged in the Homeric tent."[11] While there were relatively few reasoned arguments for the Ancients—their most common tactic was simply to question the possibility of surpassing the sublime

---

[10]"Modernity versus Postmodernity," 4.

[11]André Thevet, quoted in Hubert Gillot, *La Querelle des Anciens et des Modernes en France* (Nancy: Crépin-Leblond, 1914) 68n.1. Thevet goes on to list orators, grammarians, poets, and geographers as other beneficiaries of Homer's tutelage. Swift, on the other hand, mocks those who attribute Homer with universal competence, arguing that Homer had grievously ignored such crucial topics as English Common Law, Christian doctrine, and tea. See Swift's "A Digression of the Modern Kind," from *A Tale of a Tub*, in *The Writings of Jonathan Swift*, ed. Robert A. Greenberg and William B. Piper, Norton Critical Editions (New York: W. W. Norton & Co., 1973) 326-27.

Homer, Cicero, Sophocles, Euripedes, et al.—they often pointed out that most of the Moderns knew their Greek classics only at second-hand (via translations into Latin, if indeed they were not relying on French translations). It seemed to the Ancients that their opponents were not only mocking the great artists of the past, but doing so simply on the basis of an uninformed prejudice in favor of the present.

*Les Modernes*, on the other hand, insisted that progress in artistic insight justified their demands for the liberty to compose according to their own standards, to treat the subject matter they chose. The poets of antiquity were generally conceded to have done well *for their day*, but in a more intellectually advanced time, the primitive character of the ancient poets could not be taken as a model for modern works.[12] If Homer permitted Odysseus's dog to survive the full twenty-odd years of the Odyssey, if he allowed his heroes to employ gross invective in addressing hostile kings, he could hardly be considered greater than seventeenth-century French poets who knew that a dog could live no more than thirteen or fourteen years, and who honored the necessary *bienséance*. The Moderns enlisted the increasingly popular assumption of progress to underline the absurdity of recourse to ancient rules and models for modern literature. Each generation of poets has learned from the previous generation; how then could Corneille be subordinate to Sophocles, or Voltaire to Plautus?[13]

---

[12]As Jürgen Habermas points out, the first move of these first moderns was to deploy historical criticism. See *The Philosophical Discourse of Modernity*, trans. Frederick Lawrence (Cambridge: MIT Press, 1987) 8.

[13]As both Gillot and Rigault testify, the Moderns were motivated not only from these laudable theoretical considerations, but also (to a great extent) from the conviction that France could hardly come in second to Greece in artistic achievement. The chauvinism of many of the documents of the *Querelle* betrays a social determination which several current accounts soft-pedal. See Rigault, *Histoire de la Querelle des Anciens et des Modernes*, in *Oeuvres Complètes*, vol. 1 (Paris: Librairie de L. Hachette et Cie., 1859).

The impetus for the *querelle* came to the realm of æsthetic argument by way of the sciences, where Baconians and Aristotelians had been debating the issue for almost a century.[14] Whereas the Ancients in the scientific *querelle* maintained that the cosmos was aging and decaying, the Moderns argued that Nature always remains constant. The scientific accomplishments of the Moderns—including printing and gunpowder, to name but two—lent considerable weight to their argument in the field of æsthetics. Of course, the argument from science was by no means universally persuasive; in England, the Baconians were closely associated with the Puritans, which fact diminished the positive rhetorical force of appeals to experimental science in the Restoration.[15] On the other hand, the period of Puritan ascendancy in which the modern scientific movement was encouraged made problematic any direct return to scientific ideas drawn from the ancient writers.

Calinescu sees one turning point of the *Querelle* in the familiar metaphor of the far-seeing dwarf standing on the shoulder of the giant, which evidently dates to Bernard of Chartres in the early twelfth century.[16] With this figure, Bernard both admits the overwhelming superiority in stature which the ancient enjoys over the modern, and ultimately upholds the modern's claim to greater vision. The Moderns are not better than the Ancients—indeed, they are dwarfed not only by the titans of antiquity, but even by

---

[14]Indeed, the full title of Perrault's *Parallèles* was *Parallèles des Anciens et des Modernes en ce qui regarde les arts et les sciences*; the volumes on the sciences were quite as voluminous as those on the arts. Hans Baron traces the roots of the *Querelle* as far back as the early fifteenth-century consideration of historical relativism in Italy. Though the participants in the *Querelle* were often influenced by such sources, they did not draw the connection between these influences and the question of modernity. See Hans Baron, "The *Querelle* of the Ancients and Moderns as a Problem for Renaissance Scholarship," *Journal of the History of Ideas* 20 (1959): 3-22.

[15]On the conflict of Ancients and Moderns in the field of science as an aspect of the *Querelle*, see Richard Foster Jones's *Ancients and Moderns*, 2nd rev. ed. (St. Louis: Washington University Studies, 1961).

[16]Calinescu, *Five Faces of Modernity*, 15-18.

"normal humans" of unspecified times—but are more advanced by virtue of their predecessors' accomplishments. The figure has persisted in discussion of the relation of the present to its past, though (as Calinescu notes) the deprecatory characterization of the contemporary as lilliputian has diminished.[17] Indeed, it became a commonplace among the Moderns that "it is we who are the ancients."[18] After all, Homer wrote in humanity's infancy, whereas the moderns were alive in humanity's maturity.

In the context of the *querelle des Anciens et des Modernes*, modernity's association with the new acquired several enduring nuances. First, modernity became entwined with the concept of progress—"modernization." "Modern" had hitherto simply indicated contemporaneity; there was no implication that this was a particular virtue. After the *querelle*, however, "modern" was conventionally associated with the argument that the Moderns had progressed, had indeed surpassed their predecessors; once again, "It is we who are the ancients." The *querelle* also contributed the contestatory character to the notion of modernity. "Modern" would no longer be a simple chronological marker, but one pole of a dichotomy distinguishing the modern from the ancient (or of the tripartite division of history into "ancient," "middle ages," "modern"), placing the "modern" at the uttermost pole of novelty and progress. That which was newest—and therefore, least trammelled with obsolete survivals from antiquity—was modern, desirable, admirable.

Baudelaire accented this mark of modernity in his critical essays. His understanding of modernity was in some respects quite familiar. He characterized modernity positively as seeking always what is novel, "those aspects of nature and those human situations which the artists of the past disdained or didn't know."[19] When in "The Painter of Modern Life" Baudelaire extolled Constantin Guys

---

[17]Ibid., 18.

[18]Descartes as cited in ibid., 25.

[19]Le Salon de 1846," *Œuvres Complètes*, ed. Marcel A. Ruff (Paris: Éditions du Seuil, 1968) 230.

for his modernity, one of the qualities he singled out for attention was Guys's childlike vision: for "the child sees everything as a novelty; he is always intoxicated."[20] In the same way, Baudelaire sketches the trajectory of modernity with the closing lines of "Le Voyage," the last poem in *Les Fleurs du Mal*:

> Nous voulons, tant ce feu nous brûle le cerveau,
> Plonger au fond du gouffre, Enfer ou Ciel, qu'importe?
> Au fond de l'Inconnu pour trouver du *nouveau*.[21]

Of course, such novelty can only be momentary; once it has had its moment of novelty, it falls into familiarity. A modernity that seeks "above all to know the aspects of nature and the human situation which the artists of the past have disdained or not even known,"[22] will have built "the transitory, the fugitive, the contingent,"[23] into its self-definition. In the war of the present against the past, Baudelaire stakes everything on the side of the present.

The modern could not rest content with what had been known before, it always pressed on to transgress the boundaries of what was possible. Thus Baudelaire also applied the principle of novelty to the domain of imagination: modern art should be characterized not by those skills that were handed down from the past, which anyone with a steady hand could develop, but by insight and creativity. "Whoever has only skill is a beast, and the imagination which wishes to pass that way is mad."[24] The modern artist is not a copying machine, but a visionary.

Such prophetic modernity cannot in the nature of the case be justified with reference to a tradition, nor is it recognized by the present; it is finally recognized and justified by its future reception. By introducing this characteristic of modernity, Baudelaire twists

---

[20]"Le Peintre de la Vie Moderne," *Œuvres Complètes*, 552.

[21]"We want, so much does this fire burn our brain, / To plunge to the source of the abyss, Hell or Heaven, who cares? / At the source of the Unknown to find the *new*." *Œuevres Complètes*, 124.

[22]"Le Salon de 1846," 230.

[23]"Le Peintre," 553.

[24]"Le Salon de 1859," *Œuvres Complètes*, 393.

the attention of the artist away from antiquity (which can neither legitimate nor serve as source for an authentically modern work) and from the present (which generally cannot distinguish what is transient from what will endure) to the future. Baudelaire's advocacy of a position that sees the past as dead and useless, the present as not yet mature, and which anticipates vindication from the future, is yet another characteristically modern stance.

Jean Baudrillard has likewise pointed out the contradictions that characterize modernity's peculiar elevation of novelty to normative status. "Neither a sociological concept, nor a political concept, nor properly a historical concept. It is a characteristic mode of civilization which opposes itself to tradition, that is, to all other preceding or traditional cultures."[25] It is an unstable condition, which nonetheless presents itself as a unifying cultural imperative.

> Since it is not an analytical concept, there are no laws of modernity; there are only traits of modernity. There is likewise no theory, but rather a logic and an ideology of modernity. A canonical ethic of change, it opposes the canonical ethic of tradition. . . . It is "the tradition of the New."[26]

Modernity embraces crisis, but at the same time flees it continually in a relentless charge into the future. "Thus, inasmuch as it is an idea where an entire civilization recognizes itself, it takes on a culturally regulative function and thereby surreptitiously rejoins the tradition."[27] Baudrillard summarizes the ideology of modernity as a conservatism of change. "It is not the transvaluation of values, but the destructuration of the traditional values without their being replaced. There is no more good nor evil, but we are not 'beyond good and evil.'"[28] For modernity, "liberty is formal, people become masses, culture becomes fashion."[29]

---

[25]"Modernité," in the *Encyclopædia Universalis*, vol. 11 (Paris: Encyclopædia Universalis France, 1968) 139.

[26]Baudrillard is here ("Modernité," 139) citing Harold Rosenberg.

[27]"Modernité," 139.

[28]"Modernité," 141.

[29]"Modernité," 141.

Baudrillard's claim that modernity rejoins the cultural tradition "surreptitiously" (*subrepticement*), and his dystopic picture of a culture of unfree amoral consumers, implies some illegitimacy in modernity's self-understanding. This theme of modernity's legitimacy is addressed at length in Hans Blumenberg's massive treatise *The Legitimacy of the Modern Age*.[30] Though Blumenberg does not supply any particular definition of "modernity," the principal characteristic of modernity that he is concerned to justify is the "progress" ideal. Blumenberg undertakes his study in reaction against the claim—articulated by Karl Löwith and of widespread currency since—that modernity (as reflected in commitment to an intelligible pattern to historical events and unquestioning adherence to the assumption of "progress" that may be found in the philosophies of history set forward by Voltaire, Hegel, Marx, et al.) had no legitimacy of its own, but was rather the illegitimate product of secularized Judeo-Christian eschatology.[31] Löwith had shown one philosopher after another arguing that he had finally uncovered the pattern of history, which pattern provides a clue to the nature of the future; the very repetition of this gesture undermined its credibility for Löwith, and the events that turned out to be in the future of the philosophers in question (the increasing exploitation of labor, the two World Wars, Auschwitz, and Hiroshima) belied their theories.

Blumenberg's defense of modernity refutes Löwith's argument on a variety of bases. Most important in this context is his derivation of the modern belief in progress from actual expansion of scientific knowledge. (The case in point is the advance from Ptolemaic cosmology through Copernicus and Galileo to Johannes Kepler.) In this case, Blumenberg argues, the sense of progress came not from a supposed transfer of Christian teleology to the realm of culture; instead, the intellectual developments themselves

---

[30]*The Legitimacy of the Modern Age*, trans. Robert M. Wallace (Cambridge MA: MIT Press, 1983).

[31]Löwith's argument is made principally in *Meaning In History* (Chicago: University of Chicago Press, 1949).

warranted the perception that humanity was advancing from relative ignorance to sophistication. The legitimacy of human self-
assertion (the fundamental characteristic of modernity, according
to Blumenberg) is the basis for the legitimacy of the modern age.
Blumenberg argues that medieval Christianity had governed
intellectual inquiry by restricting the scope of the questions that
might be asked and the answers that might be supplied. This
eventually led to the argument that God's infinite power and
unsearchable will implied that there was no necessary order to be
detected in nature, and that it was left to humanity to detect what
order it might find.

> If one proceeds from the assumption that human autonomy
> can henceforth articulate its positive character only outside the
> Middle Ages, then it becomes clear that only two fundamental
> positions remain open to it, if it wants to throw off its supposed-
> ly 'natural' role: hypothetical atheism, which poses the question
> of man's potential under the condition that the answer should
> hold 'even if there is no God'; and rational deism, which employs
> the 'most perfect being' to guarantee this human potential. . . .
> The double face of the Enlightenment, on the one hand its
> renewal of a teleological optimism and on the other hand its
> inclination to atheism, loses its contradictory character if one
> places it in the context of the unity of the onset of human self-
> assertion and the rejection of its late-medieval systematic role.[32]

The case of astronomy, in which theoretical arguments enabled
the transmutation of Ptolemy's imaginative art to Kepler's mathe-
matically precise science, provided an example for the introduction
of hypothetical/theoretical method into other enterprises (and
thence to establishing experimental science as a model for all fields
of inquiry).[33] Modernity took this sort of progress as paradigmatic

---

[32]*The Legitimacy of the Modern Age*, 179.

[33]*The Legitimacy of the Modern Age*, 181-226. Blumenberg also makes
passing reference to an odd but important aspect of the *querelle des
Anciens et des Modernes*. One of the issues at stake in the *querelle* was
whether the population was larger in antiquity than it is in modern times.

for humanity in general (rather than drawing the more modest conclusion that it is usually possible to come up with a better answer to a vexing question), and projected the explosive advances in technical capacity onto the field of life in general.[34] To this extent the modern attachment to an ideal of limitless progress is not justified. But modernity *is* justified in holding to an ideal of progress, on Blumenberg's account, which corresponds to the more limited project of human self-assertion.

Giovanni Vattimo is as firm an opponent of modernity as Blumenberg is its defender. Vattimo specifies, as one of the critical problems with modernity, the modern necessity of constantly *overcoming* preceding and contemporary conversation partners. The urge to overcome is reflected in many aspects of modern discourse; most obviously, it is part and parcel of the myth of progress:

> From the point of view of Nietzsche and Heidegger, which we may consider to be a mutually held one in spite of the considerable differences between the two philosophers, modernity is in fact dominated by the idea that the history of thought is a progressive "enlightenment" which develops through an ever more complete appropriation of its own "foundations." . . . The idea of "overcoming," which is so important in all modern philosophy, understands the course of thought as being a progressive development in which the new is identified with value through the mediation of the recovery and appropriation of the foundation-origin.[35]

In order to legitimate truth-claims under these conditions, one must demonstrate in what way these truth-claims entail progress over previously accepted knowledge; but success in overcoming another position immediately reinscribes the victorious truth-claim in the discourse of modernity. Vattimo's work provides a valuable

---

Montesquieu weighed in on the side of antiquity; Hume argued that modernity must have a higher population. This discussion prompted the development of the discipline of theoretical statistics (222).

[34]*The Legitimacy of the Modern Age*, passim, esp. 25-36.
[35]*The End of Modernity*, 4.

caution that one cannot escape modernity by overcoming it;[36] any effort to work under conditions different from those prescribed by modern discourses must deploy more subtle tactics.

This progressive modernity implies another aspect of modernity: the obverse of the valorization of newness in the repudiation of tradition. From the *querelle* on, moderns have felt the need not only to uphold the value of their own work, but at the same time to undermine the validity of their predecessors' work. The *querelle* involved as much depreciation of the ancients as it did appreciation of the moderns. "Ruthless denial of the past was . . . an essential component of the modern movement."[37] The relentless conflict between the modern and all that went before is encapsulated in the manifestoes of the Futurists, who screamed such battle cries as

> Comrades, we tell you now that the triumphant progress of science makes changes in humanity inevitable, changes that are hacking an abyss between those docile slaves of tradition and us free moderns who are confident in the radiant splendor of our future.[38]

Fredric Jameson stresses the antagonism of the modern and the traditional in an article that contrasts modern architecture with postmodern. Whereas the monumental skyscrapers and distinctive styles of high modernism stand over against architectural tradition by expressing the "high-modernist imperative of stylistic innovation,"[39] postmodern architecture borrows freely and explicitly from the past. Jameson finds this pattern in various other cultural fields

---

[36]Vattimo is here drawing on insights from Nietzsche, particularly from *Human, All-Too-Human* and *The Dawn*.

[37]Andreas Huyssen, "Mapping the Postmodern," *New German Critique* 33 (1984): 14.

[38]"Manifesto of the Futurist Painters, 1910," by Umberto Bossioni et al., trans. Robert Brain, in *Futurist Manifestos*, ed. Umbrio Apollonio (New York: Viking, 1973) 25. Cited from *All That Is Solid Melts into Air*, 24-25.

[39]"Postmodernism, or the Cultural Logic of Late Capitalism," *New Left Review* 146 (1984): 54. Huyssen echoes these assessments in "Mapping the Postmodern," 12.

as well; while postmodernism flourishes under conditions of infinite reproducibility, which undermine the very notion of "originality," "modernism was predicated on the achievement of some unique personal style that could be parlayed out to the subject of genius. . . . All the great modernists invented modernism in their own fashion."[40]

The modern resistance to tradition is not only concerned with æsthetic styles, but involves at the same time a struggle for hegemony in material and political terms. Peter Sloterdijk points out that the Enlightenment—the paradigmatic modern intellectual movement—had to perform an unprecedented cultural task: the replacement of tradition, not with a refurbished or rediscovered alternate tradition, but with a self-legitimating project that looked only *forward*.[41] The political and intellectual ruling powers, as well as the general population, would resist anything that presented itself as new: "Enlightenment as critique recognizes in everything which is 'already there' in people's heads its inner archenemy; it contemptuously designates these contents: *'prejudices'*."[42]

Since modernity is dominated by the ideal of progress, an ideal that necessarily takes the shape of diachronic narrative, Jean-

---

[40]Quoted from an interview with Anders Stephanson: "Regarding Postmodernism—A Conversation with Fredric Jameson," in *Universal Abandon? The Politics of Postmodernism*, ed. Andrew Ross (Minneapolis: University of Minnesota Press, 1988) 21, 27.

[41]At this point, analyses of modernity which cite the Protestant Reformation as an early impetus for the "modern" need to reckon with the strongly restorative character of that movement; in this sense (oddly enough), the Counter-Reformation might be a better example of a modern direction.

[42]Peter Sloterdijk, "Cynicism—The Twilight of False Consciousness," trans. Michael Eldred and Leslie A. Adelson, *New German Critique* 33 (1984): 200. Of course, the *topos* of the Enlightenment's "prejudice against prejudices" is familiar from Gadamer's *Truth and Method*, trans. G. Barden and J. Cumming (New York: Seabury, 1975) 239ff. Sloterdijk is valuable for enriching Gadamer's account by specifically locating the necessity of this prejudice in the character of the Enlightenment.

François Lyotard calls attention to the particular accounts that have told the story of modern progress, the metanarratives of liberation. The idea of progress, whose origins Lyotard locates very generally in the Enlightenment, is the backbone for modern understandings of the natural sciences and technology (especially), and of the arts, the human sciences, liberal politics, economics, and philosophy—to specify but a few of the fields Lyotard surveys. The metanarratives that have justified the major movements in Western culture of the last two centuries—Marxism, liberalism, scientism, romanticism, capitalism—adopt the assumption of human progress toward a telos attainable through human effort; but Lyotard wants to call the notion of progress into question, and thereby to attack the modern metanarratives at their concealed common root.

## • Modernity and Chronology •

The interest of modernity in the relative temporal distinction between "ancient" and "modern" forms only one aspect of a modern fascination with chronology.[43] When being modern becomes a desirable end in itself, countless chronological difficulties crop up. When did modernity begin, and can it ever end? If in every age there is a modern moment, were the ancients in fact modern, too? If the current moment is modern, what distinguishes its modernity from yesterday's state of affairs? Among the symptoms of modernity's distinctive relation to time are an incurable anxiety concerning whether one has "kept up with the times," and an equally insatiable desire to get ahead of the times; a historical consciousness that constructs an abyss separating "now" from "then," such that modernity enforces its laws with the phrase "one can no longer"; a hunger for historical knowledge for its own sake; and the discovery of time as a commodity. In all of these cases, modernity characteristically enforces notions of what time *is*, there-

---

[43]Anthony Giddens suggests in passing that the widespread distribution of the clock in postfeudal Europe may be the root of modernity ("Modernism and Postmodernism," *New German Critique* 22 [1981]: 15-16).

by creating the illusion that time actually is something apart from socially mediated experiences of time.

The characteristically modern stance in favor of the novel, opposed to the traditional, has formed two versions of modernity since the *querelle*. On the one hand, the modern has remained simply the most recent fruits of the continuing march of progress. It is this sense of the modern that Calinescu characterizes as "bourgeois modernity":

> The doctrine of progress, the confidence in the beneficial possibilities of science and technology, the concern with time (a *measurable* time, a time that can be bought and sold and therefore has, like any other commodity, a calculable equivalent in money), the cult of reason, and the ideal of freedom defined within the framework of an abstract humanism, but also the orientation toward pragmatism and the cult of success—all have been associated in varying degrees with the battle for the modern and were kept alive and promoted as key values in the triumphant civilization established by the middle class.[44]

On the other hand, another modernity has constantly sought to outrun this bourgeois sort; it has tried to be so up-to-date that it escapes not only tradition, but also mere conformity with the moment. This avant-garde modernity aims to uncover the hidden true quality of the contemporary moment. In both versions of modernity, however, time itself has become the canon of what may be acceptable; the work itself is secondary to its relation to one or another period. In the bourgeois modernity that Calinescu identifies, the critical time is the immediate present; that which is adequately modern is what is up-to-date, what is chronologically unsurpassed. For those who resist this position, modernity entails establishing a relation of hypothetical futurity toward the bourgeois-modern, so as to be able to diagnose and correct it. Baudrillard notes, though, that while æsthetic modernity continues to seek to disrupt the social modernity of the bourgeois, the impression that this subversion conveys through the media is not finally sub-

---

[44]Calinescu, *Five Faces of Modernity*, 41-42.

versive; instead, the media's presentation of the avant-garde, the decadent, the surreal, transmits the urgency of keeping ahead of the times and the irrelevance of whatever seems to be "traditional." As novelty becomes a criterion of value, the novelties themselves lose their content, and novelty itself—without regard for the character of the novelty, what it radicalizes or reimagines—simply becomes the mode of being modern.

Calinescu associates the beginning of the impetus toward anti-(bourgeois)-modern modernity in the definition of romanticism that nineteenth-century French novelist and critic Stendhal proposed in *Racine et Shakespeare*. Romanticism, according to Stendhal, "is the art of presenting to the people literary works that, in view of the present-day state of their customs and beliefs, affords them the utmost possible pleasure."[45] The force of Stendhal's argument is not to defend mass-market art, but to uphold criteria specific to a given moment as having greater importance for romanticism than criteria inherited from tradition. Moreover, Stendhal sets himself at the opposite pole from the *Ancien* assumption that beauty transcends time: Stendhal's formulation puts time—more specifically, *presentness*—at the very heart of modern beauty. It is soon clear, however, that the criteria specific to a given "present" are not always clear to most people at that moment; so that the artist or writer undertakes a diagnostic task as well as the task of entertainment.

This, however, implies a discrepancy between the artist's diagnostic task and the popular reception of the artist's work. If the public were ready for, or sympathetic with, the modern artist, it would not need the diagnosis the artist offers. Yet the very untimeliness of the artist's vision antagonizes the public whose needs the work of art addresses. As the discrepancy between the accuracy of an artist's judgment of the time and the popular acclaim the artist

---

[45]Quoted by Calinescu, in *Five Faces of Modernity*, 39; translation altered.

could expect increased, greater emphasis was put upon the former and the latter was belittled, and eventually rejected outright.[46]

Baudelaire captured this shifting situation in æsthetic assumptions under the heading of "modernity" in "The Painter of Modern Life" and of "romanticism" in "The Salon of 1846."[47] Baudelaire emphasizes the presentness of the work of art; but this does not, of course, imply a blanket endorsement of the contemporary moment. For there has always been a present, and the highest achievements of the artists of antiquity have come when they attained to what was then "modern." Modernity is therefore a quality quite distinct from what is currently popular. The latest hero of the public is by no means certain to be modern; Calinescu points out that Baudelaire despised Victor Hugo as a mere technician, an academic before he was even born, in whom even eccentricity took symmetrical forms. But Delacroix, Hugo's contemporary, was creative, imaginative, and truly *modern*. Whereas acclaim comes naturally to a workman like Hugo, the greatness of a genius like Delacroix comes much later.

---

[46]As Stendhal suggests, "One needs courage to be a romantic [sc., "a modernist"] . . . a writer needs almost as much courage as a soldier" (quoted in Calinescu, *Five Faces of Modernity*, 39-40).

[47]Though there are surely nuanced distinctions that a more detailed treatment of Baudelaire would bring out, the "romanticism" of "The Salon of 1846" and the "modernity" of "The Painter of Modern Life" will be treated as interchangeable in this context. Of course, Baudelaire discusses modernity separately and explicitly in the final section of the "Salon," entitled "On the Heroism of Modern Life"; but these passages (which deal principally with dandyism) actually complement his conception of romanticism more than they stand apart from it. Baudelaire authorizes this conclusion both implicitly and explicitly. Implicitly, when he concludes the "Heroism" section of "The Salon of 1846" with a paean to Balzac, whom he declares "The most *heroic*, the most singular, the most *romantic*, the most poetic of all the characters drawn from your breast!" (my emphasis). Explicitly, when he declares, "Whoever says 'romanticism' says 'modern art'" ("Salon," 230).

The evident complexity of these accounts of modernity points to a pivotal point in the theory of this concept. We are no longer dealing here with a simple opposition between "ancient" and "modern" (though as we have seen, even that opposition turned out to be more complicated than it appeared); the temporal and qualitative criteria implicit in the original ancient/modern distinction have developed in ways that verge upon contradicting one another. Modernity entails a ceaseless quest for novelty, but once it attains novelty, it is no longer modern; the quest must continue. Modernity is fleeting, but the modern can be found to have endured for centuries in the great works of antiquity (each of which, according to Baudelaire, has its own particular sort of modernity). Modern artists ought to be historically aware, but they ought not be too interested in the historical conditions of the past; and their interest in the past should be motivated by an interest in the universal, the transhistorical element they might express in their own work. Modernity is the present moment, as in the title "The Painter of Modern Life"; yet it is at the same time the distinguishing quality of ancient art.

Finally, Calinescu notes that on the one hand Baudelaire rejects the past as an authority for or even a relevant influence upon the modern artist; yet on the other hand, he "nostalgically evokes the loss of an aristocratic past and deplores the encroachment of a vulgar, materialistic, middle-class present."[48] Such tensions remain characteristic of the theory of modernity and account in no small part for the controversies over just what constitutes modernity. Moreover, as more developed ideas of modernity travel from æsthetics to other fields, some will claim that the definitive characteristics of modernity become field-specific.[49]

Nietzsche attacks the relation of modernity to time on a different basis.[50] His discussions of modernity, particularly in *The Uses*

---

[48]Calinescu, *Five Faces of Modernity*, 58.

[49]Of course, just this construction of various field-specific modernities is a very modern tendency, in keeping with Weber's division of rationality into autonomous spheres (as will be shown below).

[50]The Nietzsche of this thesis will be more the Nietzsche of con-

*and Disadvantages of History for Life*,[51] treat the modern person as suffering from a "historical sickness." Though Nietzsche's discussion is not systematic ("modernity" appears here to designate contemporaneity, there to designate a period of art, there again in the sense of a cultural/philosophical attitude), he marks several characteristics of modernity which both resound the notes played by his predecessors and presage the points which his successors will stress.

Nietzsche scorned "modern man" for weakness of character, for hostility to life itself. This invidious modernity is manifest in the modern fascination with history.

> Let us now picture the spiritual occurrence introduced into the soul of modern man by that which we have just described. Historical knowledge streams in unceasingly from inexhaustible wells, the strange and incoherent forces its way forward, memory opens all its gates and yet is not open wide enough, nature travails in an effort to receive, arrange, and honor these strange guests, but they themselves are in conflict with one another and it seems necessary to constrain and control them if one is not oneself to perish in their conflict. Habituation to such a disorderly, stormy, and conflict-ridden household gradually becomes a second nature, though this second nature is beyond question much weaker, much more restless, and thoroughly less sound than the first. In the end, modern man drags around with him a huge quantity of indigestible stones of knowledge, which then, as in the fairy tale, can sometimes be heard rumbling about inside him.[52]

---

temporary French theory—that is, an antagonist of modernity—than the Nietzsche who originated modern philosophy (as he is portrayed in Robert Pippin's thoughtful and powerful article, "Nietzsche and the Origin of the Idea of Modernity," *Inquiry* 26 [1983]: 151-80).

[51]In the *Untimely Meditations*, trans. R. J. Hollingdale, Texts in German Philosophy (Cambridge: Cambridge University Press, 1983) 57-123.

[52]"On the Uses and Disadvantages of History for Life," 78.

At the same time that this intellectually overweight subject internalizes historical knowledge, he utterly neglects considering the consequences of what he has learned.

> Knowledge, consumed for the greater part without hunger for it and even counter to one's needs, now no longer acts as an agent for transforming the outside world but remains concealed within a chaotic inner world which modern man describes with curious pride as his uniquely characteristic "subjectivity."[53]

The consequence of this absorption into history is a debilitating reliance upon abstractions; whatever is not already an abstraction, a modern person must convert into abstraction in order to assimilate. These abstractions, having none of the messy connectedness-to-life of concrete particulars, underwrite the illusion of objectivity which Nietzsche execrates. With regard to the modern historian,

> it is a matter of indifference what they do so long as history itself is kept nice and "objective," bearing in mind that those who want to keep it so are for ever incapable of making history themselves. . . . [Those who are 'historically educated' through and through] are neither man nor woman, nor even hermaphrodite, but always and only neuters or, to speak more cultivatedly, the eternally objective.[54]

Finally, it should be observed to the extent that Nietzsche's work (pursued in the teeth of a modernity that made his meditations untimely[55]) was antirationalist and antiemancipatory, it was so not on the basis of transcendent principles of Reason or Judgment, but with relation to the sensibility of the judge (whoever that might be at any given moment). The perspectivism that marks Nietzsche's philosophy allows no room for the kinds of criteria to

---

[53]"On the Uses and Disadvantages of History for Life," 78.
[54]"On the Uses and Disadvantages of History for Life," 86-87.
[55]A recent translation of "On the Uses and Disadvantages" and its companion essays renders the book's title, *"Unmodern Meditations"* (New Haven: Yale University Press, 1990).

which modern thinkers naturally appeal. Such criteria can on Nietzsche's account always only reflect a concealed manifestation of the will to power. Instead, Nietzsche appeals to arational criteria founded in the discourse of art, "experiences of self-disclosure of a decentered subjectivity, liberated from all constraints of cognition and purposive activity, all imperatives of utility and morality."[56] Where modernity imposes *"the demand that history should be a science,"*[57] Nietzsche counterposes the demand that one *"look at science in the perspective of the artist but at art in that of life."*[58]

For Vattimo too, the modern stands in a necessary relation to a remote, objectified past known as "history." He points out that the modern critic, in order to recover and appropriate the foundation-origins (which provides the basis for establishing the identity of the new with value), must have recourse to an objectified understanding of history. This necessity makes of modernity an "era of history," and the discourse of modernity "gives ontological weight to history and a determining sense to our position in it."[59] Modernity relies upon a realism that treats the past as providing a fundamentally univocal History, a History without ideological overdetermination, that constitutes the privileged criterion to validate or invalidate all posited histories.[60]

---

[56]Jürgen Habermas, summarizing in *The Philosophical Discourse of Modernity*, 94.

[57]"On the Uses and Disadvantages of History for Life," 77. Of course, here Nietzsche is attending particularly to history; it can easily be argued that modernity demands that *everything* be a science.

[58]"Attempt at a Self-Criticism," in *The Birth of Tragedy and the Case of Wagner*, trans. Walter Kaufmann, Vintage Books (New York: Random House, 1967) 19. Significantly, Nietzsche also notes—though only in passing—that "men of 'modern ideas' believe almost instinctively in 'progress' and 'the future'" (*Beyond Good and Evil*, trans. Walter Kaufmann, Vintage Books [New York: Random House, 1967] 206).

[59]*The End of Modernity*, 4.

[60]Andreas Huyssen also argues that modernism cannot long survive without some form of realism to support it ("Mapping the Postmodern," 29).

Such a privileged species of "History" has not always existed, of course; Michel Foucault points out the specificity of the modern interest in history by contrasting our culture with "prehistoric" cultures:

> [I]n our culture, at least for several centuries, discourse has been linked together through history as a mode: we receive things which have been spoken as if they come from a past where they succeeded one another, were opposed, influenced, replaced, engendered and accumulated. The cultures "without history" are obviously not those where there was neither event, nor evolution, nor revolution, but where the discourses were not added together according history as a mode; they are juxtaposed; they replace one another; they are forgotten; they are transformed.[61]

Modern critics construct the past from which they distinguish themselves; they graft onto this past the categories of event, evolution, and revolution, which they have learned to deploy; and they pronounce that, in knowing the past differently from the ways in which it has been known before, they are nearer to the truth of history (when in fact, the very notion of history with which they operate forbids the possibility that the past could have known itself adequately).

## • Modernity and Scientific Legitimation •

In my discussion of the role of time in modernity, I mentioned Sloterdijk's observation that the Enlightenment engendered a categorically different basis of legitimation; whereas before the modern era claims were legitimated by appeal to authority, or tradition, or some other material category, modern culture privileges legitimation on the basis of formal reason. My earlier reference stressed the chronological (ancient vs. modern, antitraditional) aspect of this characteristic. In the following section, I will foreground the formal

---

[61]"The Discourse of History," an interview collected into *Foucault Live*, trans. John Johnston, ed. Sylvère Lotringer, Foreign Agents Series (New York: Semiotext(e), 1989) 29.

aspect of modern legitimation. In such theorists as Weber, Habermas, and Lyotard, a pivotal question in the debate over modernity is the question of criteria: how does modernity judge?

Max Weber initiated the thoroughly modern *scientific* analysis of modernity. In traditional societies, Weber argued, a single cosmological/mythological value system dictated the structure of the whole. Modern societies, however, were no longer "enchanted" by this unitary perspective. Modernity is the "disenchantment" of the world; humanity no longer has recourse to magic (as would be appropriate to a mythological culture) to change its environment, but now resorts to technique.[62] In this sense, modernity is the condition of humankind realizing what has been true all along. Disenchantment affects not only the technical world, but also the social world. The unmasking by which modernity has revealed the subject to be the source of all social structures, all "natural" laws, marks a step from which there is no turning back.

Once having relocated the source of values from the cosmological to the social, Weber went on to endorse the divisions of rationality into separate spheres such as those indicated by Kant's *Critiques* (and supported by Hegel). Modern knowledge was thereafter knowledge of science, *or* morality, *or* art; one would not think of consulting the sciences for knowledge about God, or about art.[63] As Richard Wolin observes, "concretely, this means that each of these spheres is 'rationalized' in that they no longer need a priori invoke the authority of an antecedent and determinative cosmological standpoint to legitimate themselves, but instead become self-validating, i.e., they gain their right to exist in terms of a set of *internally developed criteria.*"[64] While he customarily presupposes

---

[62]In the lecture "Science as a Vocation," in *From Max Weber: Essays in Sociology*, trans. and ed. H. H. Gerth and C. Wright Mills (Oxford: Oxford University Press, 1946) 139, 155; "disenchantment" (*Entzauberung*) is also discussed in numerous other essays.

[63]"Science as a Vocation," 142. Much of the last half of this lecture suggests the gaps between these discourses without, unfortunately, defining the divisions of the "value spheres."

[64]"Modernism vs. Postmodernism," *Telos* 62 (1984/1985): 10.

these divisions rather than discussing them directly, Weber clearly assumes that rationality is field specific: "we are placed into different value-spheres, each of which is governed by different laws."[65] He gives the example of progress, which has different relations to science and to art. Scientists know that today's insight will be obsolete tomorrow, whereas the artist's form of progress does not entail this inevitable transience of achievement.[66] Likewise, in the essay "Religious Rejections of the World and Their Directions," Weber lists five different "spheres" that harbor tension between "religion" and "the world."[67] Though the spheres are presumably equally rational (each in its own way), they do not coexist peacefully: "The value spheres of the world stand in irreconcilable conflict with one another."[68] Weber himself privileges the sphere of scientific rationality as singularly appropriate to modernity; the rationality of art or morality might thrive under traditional circumstances, but it is the special genius of modernity that it permits the extraordinary development of scientific rationality in a way a traditional (enchanted) culture could not. In one sentence, Weber wraps up a parcel of modernity including progress, rationalization, and the autonomy of the spheres:

> The rationalization and the conscious sublimation of man's relation to the various spheres of values, internal and external, as well as religious and secular, have then pressed towards making conscious the *internal and lawful* autonomy of the individual spheres. . . . This develops quite generally from the development

---

[65]"Politics as a Vocation," *From Max Weber*, 123. Here he goes on to discuss religious ethics; but in this case, he seems to be referring to the material conditions of our lives (caste, status, national origin) as much as the differentiations between art, science, and religion.

[66]Weber notes that the discovery of the laws of perspective has not diminished the stature of paintings composed earlier ("Science as a Vocation," 137-38).

[67]"Religious Rejections of the World and Their Directions," *From Max Weber*, 331-57.

[68]"Science as a Vocation," *From Max Weber*, 147.

of inner- and otherworldly values towards rationality, towards conscious endeavor, and towards sublimation by *knowledge*.[69]

When the scientific/technical sphere is the field in which "progress" is most clearly exemplified, there exists a strong motivation for value-spheres which might otherwise insist on their autonomy to adopt or emulate the laws of scientific rationality; thus the dominance of scientific rationality becomes a defining category for the interpretation of modernity.

This relation of scientific rationality to modernity corresponds to the domination of what Weber called *formal* rationality (*Zweckrationalität*, reason that operates according to formal rules but without specific attention to content) over "*substantive* rationality" (*Wertrationalität*, reason limited by the invariant "natural" or "divine" norms characteristic of the traditional, cosmological foundation of a culture).

> In the case of substantive rationality there are values that are accepted as simply true and that fit with a picture of the world so accepted. Modernity is not just a weakening of such a tradition, but a reversal. . . . While all rationality connotes consistency and efficiency, formal rationality makes these the only norms, untrammeled by substantive restrictions.[70]

For example, in a case where a patient is dangerously ill, a doctor may choose to tell the patient of her condition (in the *wertrational* principle which makes truthfulness an overriding priority) or deceive the patient (in the *zweckrational* hope of avoiding a depression which might lead to death).[71] In the modern world, formal rationality has become dominant over substantive rationality,

---

[69]"Religious Rejections of the World and Their Directions," *From Max Weber*, 328.

[70]David A. Kolb, *The Critique of Pure Modernity* (Chicago: University of Chicago Press, 1986) 11.

[71]The example is taken from Rogers Brubaker, *The Limits of Rationality*, Controversies in Sociology 16 (London: George Allen & Unwin, 1984) 51-52.

to the point that the hegemonic dominance of formal rationality is a distinctive mark of modernity in Western culture. Formal rationality in authority takes the form of bureaucracy, and bureaucracy in turn reinforces the tendency of modernity to parcel up knowledge into specific manageable areas. Weber's modernity constitutes an intellectual postulate, but much more as well. The theories of rationalization, of bureaucratization, and of the modern divisions into spheres are themselves theories of the conditions of life (rather than æsthetic, epistemological, or metaphysical speculations), so that Weber's theory of modernity is intimately entwined with the material conditions of existence.[72]

Though Jean Baudrillard discusses the *querelle* as an aspect of modernity's history, he, like Weber emphasizes the social conditions that fostered the development of modern society. He is specifically interested in the effects of the industrial revolution. The industrial revolution of the late eighteenth century engendered the expectation of continual progress in science and technology and the division of labor; the 1789 Revolution enthroned the modern bourgeois state, which set in motion continual turnover in government leadership at the same time it established the dictatorship of the bureaucrat. These social and political circumstances "introduced into social life a dimension of permanent change, of destruction of traditional mores and culture. At the same time, the social division of labor introduced deep political breaches, a dimension of continual social battle and of conflicts which would have repercussions throughout the 19th and 20th centuries."[73]

Through the offices of these two major impulses—the political and the social—modernity exploded into "a social practice and way of life articulated on change, innovation, but also on anxiety, instability, continual mobility, moving subjectivity, tension, crisis. . . ."[74] And once society reflected upon its own modernity (Baudril-

---

[72]My reading of Weber here is strongly influenced by the sources through which I have read him: Kolb, Habermas, Wolin, and Surin.

[73]"Modernité," 140.

[74]"Modernité," 140.

lard suggests that this comes in the 1850s, with Gautier and Baudelaire, while Calinescu has already noted Stendhal as the earliest self-conscious modernist), "'modernity' becomes a transcendent value, a cultural model, a morality—a myth of universal presence, and thereby masking in part the structures and the historical contradictions which had given it birth."[75]

Baudrillard identifies four particular aspects of modernity. The technological-scientific aspect is modernity's maximizing of productivity (including the increasing commodification of time), and is a near relative to the increasing rationalization and dominance of the scientific value-sphere that Weber underlined. Modernity's political aspect is the development of the abstract State and the abstract private life of the individual. The psychological aspect of modernity is the simultaneous emphasis on the autonomous individual conscience and on the individual's loss of identity. Finally, Baudrillard specifies the peculiar relation of modernity and time. Modern time is precisely divided, exactly calculated, on a scale that abolishes the rhythmic time of day and night, of seasons and years, of festivals and labor. Modern time is laid out on a linear axis, and is especially oriented toward the future (while at the same time constructing a dead "past" of completed time, time which no longer affects the modern present). At the same time, modernity thinks of itself with relation to a historically concrete past rather than a mythical origin. Modernity is characteristically obsessed with being *up-to-date*, with attaining simultaneous universal presence.

Lyotard's modernity is likewise characterized by particular kinds of knowledge. He identifies modern knowledge with "scientific knowledge." Scientific knowledge makes no appeal to anything outside its own discursive location in a discourse of verification and performativity. It stands opposed to what Lyotard calls "narrative knowledge," knowledge that depends for its verification upon such extrinsic criteria as the character of the speaker, or the content of the message itself. "Nine out of ten

---

[75]"Modernité," 140.

Icelanders in a controlled experiment refused to lie, whatever inducements were offered them" is valid scientific knowledge whether it is taught by a saint or a reprobate; "The inhabitants of Iceland are honest under even the most trying circumstances" is a message that depends for its validity upon one's evaluation of the speaker. According to Lyotard, modernity encourages scientific knowledge, and discounts narrative knowledge (even though scientific knowledge is ultimately justified by appeal to warrants drawn from narrative knowledge). Scientific knowledge is more productive, less variable. The West's economies (and this must include not only capital industries, but also intellectual economies), in keeping with their commitment to their founding metanarratives of progress, have come to rely almost exclusively upon the criterion of performativity to the exclusion of the inefficient, ambiguous criteria characteristic of narrative knowledge. The modern metanarratives are peculiar—and derive their current resilience—in that they legitimate themselves not with reference to a founding event of the past (the nurture of Romulus and Remus, the seven-day creation of the world, Moses' transmission of the Law to Israel) but with reference to the future. Their legitimacy is therefore always deferred; and attempts to call this legitimacy into question are readily rebuffed by apologists of modernity as distractions which themselves constitute a threat to realizing the modern project. That is, in order to attain the telos of modernity, one must not be sidetracked by worrying over whether that telos is legitimate; and if one wastes time weighing the alternatives to the modern telos, one will surely never attain it.[76]

Whereas modernity in the sphere of knowledge takes the form of the dominance of the criterion of performativity and the orientation toward a future legitimation, Lyotard argues that modernity in æsthetics takes the form of pointing out that not everything can

---

[76]Of course, wasting time at all is a dire transgression, on modern terms. Nonetheless, behavior which seems like "wasting time" to modern people can seem much less clearly baneful to residents of nonmodern cultures.

be represented—the realization that the particulars which art had traditionally been occupied with depicting always escape representation. This unrepresentable, which Lyotard associates with "the sublime" as Kant defined it in *The Critique of Judgment*, is itself the subject of modern art. It is perhaps most easily recognized in abstract art, or in avant-garde art which undermines the sense that the painter is endeavoring to convey some expression of Reality. What is peculiarly modern in this effort to address the sublime is the accent that typically falls on the artist's muteness, on modern art as a *failure* to present the sublime: "The emphasis can be placed on the powerlessness of the faculty of presentation, on the nostalgia for presence felt by the human subject, on the obscure and futile will that inhabits him in spite of everything."[77] Lyotard submits that the distinctive emphasis upon the failure, the melancholy, is a fateful turn that marks æsthetic modernity, which therefore testifies to the heterogeneity of the life-world.

Yet in one of the contradictions that inheres to modernity, the emphatic æsthetic message of heterogeneity coexists with another aspect of the continuing reliance upon metanarratives of progress (or of emancipation, which is generally the "social" side of the same coin): their drive toward homogenization. Given the importance of performativity to modernity, this drive is easily understood. Heterogeneity is inefficient; it introduces extra variables into the equations of production, and requires duplication of effort. Lyotard spots this as the point at which modernity is most vulnerable to resistance. It is at this point that he directs his battle cry of postmodernity: "Let us wage war on totality; let us be witnesses to the unpresentable; let us activate the differences and save the honor of the name."[78] By "activating the differences," by inventing unforeseen moves in the practices in which modern criteria of

---

[77]"Answering the Question: What Is Postmodernism?" in *The Postmodern Condition*, 79.

[78]"Answering the Question: What Is Postmodernism?" 82.

performativity dominate, Lyotard hopes to accelerate the gradual crumbling of modernity's foundations.[79]

Lyotard's principal antagonist in the conflict over modernity is Jürgen Habermas.[80] Habermas argues that the problems which distress Lyotard are not the necessary outcome of modernity, but are instead the results of modernity *gone wrong*. The project of the Enlightenment ought not to be abandoned, but reformed and revived.

> The project of modernity formulated in the 18th century by the philosophers of the Enlightenment consisted in their efforts to develop objective science, universal morality and law, and autonomous art, according to their inner logic. At the same time, this project intended to release the cognitive potentials of each of these domains to set them free from their esoteric forms. The Enlightenment philosophers wanted to utilize this accumulation of specialized knowledge for the enrichment of everyday life, that is to say, for the rational organization of everyday social life.[81]

Habermas undertakes his recuperation of the Enlightenment by showing how modernity entails a wrongheaded interpretation of the Enlightenment's vices and virtues. To this extent, he too is a critic of modernity. Yet Habermas wants to hold on to several of the aspects of modernity that Lyotard suspects of fostering terror, intellectual authoritarianism, and philosophical ethnocentricity.

Habermas's diagnosis of modernity's problems goes back to the nineteenth-century roots of the philosophical discourse of modernity. He argues that the two pivotal theorists of modernity—Hegel and Marx—missed their opportunity to set modernity on the right path when each of them fell into a trap of their own devising. For

---

[79]Lyotard does not here account for the appearance that he is simply playing into modernity's hands by underwriting the autonomy of divergent value-spheres.

[80]In "Answering the Question," Lyotard coyly describes "a thinker of repute" who defends modernity, then identifies him as Habermas, adding "everyone had recognized him" (72).

[81]"Modernity versus Postmodernity," *New German Critique* 22 (1981): 9.

Hegel, the problem arises from the relation of the critique of ideology (the young Hegel's resistance to the "false positivities" of a culture) and the critique of subjectivity (the later Hegel vs. Kant and Fichte).[82] According to Habermas, Hegel came to devalue the first sort of critique and to approve the second because philosophy had already done its most important work toward removing the false idols in culture; the valid task left to philosophy was to criticize the "obscure abstractions shoved between subjective consciousness and an objective reason."[83] In so doing, Hegel moved away from a theory of communicative ethics, in which the unforced assent of a community constitutes a medium for adjudicating claims (this will be Habermas's ideal for modernity, which all his predecessors will have had an unsuccessful crack at elaborating). Instead, Hegel posited that philosophy had penetrated to an understanding of the absolute self-mediation of the spirit to the self-conscious subject, and thereby opted for a theory of the rational subject as Absolute Spirit in miniature, and disabled criticism by equating the rational and the real.[84]

Habermas goes on to show how Marx also fell into the trap of subject-centered rationality (as opposed to the intersubjective rationality which goes along with a theory of communicative reason). Marx got off to a good start by criticizing Hegel's *Philosophy of Right* (which enshrined subject-centered rationality); Marx argued that a citizen's power as a social force (connected with production) had become alienated from that citizen's political power. What was therefore required was a polity wherein that alienation would be overcome, wherein everyone was as much a politician as a producer.[85] Habermas points out with regret, how-

---

[82]*The Philosophical Discourse of Modernity*, 42.

[83]*The Philosophical Discourse of Modernity*, 43.

[84]*The Philosophical Discourse of Modernity*, 67.

[85]"The parallels between Hegel and Marx are striking. In their youth, both thinkers hold open the option of uncoerced will formation in a communication community existing under constraints of cooperation for the reconciliation of a divided bourgeois society. But later on, both forsake the use of this option, and they do so for similar reasons. Like

ever, that Marx gave up this insight in favor of a subjective rationality grounded not upon speculative philosophy but upon production; "[this] remains a variant of the philosophy of the subject that locates reason in the purposive rationality of the acting subject instead of in the reflection of the thinking subject."[86] The difficulty Habermas sees here is that on Marx's account (as was the case with Hegel before), there is no longer any ground from which to criticize existing structures, since the subject which might undertake that critique is always already inscribed within the dominant systems of purposive rationality. Once again, the real is rational.

Habermas clarifies his own positive view of modernity in the first and last chapters of *The Philosophical Discourse*. At the outset, he describes modernity's characteristic consciousness of its own novelty, and its anxious effort to locate its legitimacy. At the end, after he has illustrated the way all previous theoreticians of modernity have chosen the wrong path (of subject-centered rationality), he concludes with a chapter on "The Normative Content of Modernity,"[87] which stresses the path that offers hope for a positive outcome for the project of modernity. First and foremost, one must not shirk the task of modernity—that of providing a basis for the self-assurance of modernity. Without the criteria to which one or another tradition gave unquestioned authority, a nontraditional modernity has both to supply its own criteria *and* to legitimate them, which task is best fulfilled when "there appear the structures of cognitive instrumental, moral-practical, and aesthetic-expressive rationality, each of these under the control of specialists who seem more adept at being logical in these particular ways."[88] A corresponding necessity is the rigorous maintenance of the division of spheres of value, each with its particular rationality. "A knowledge specialized in only one validity claim, which, without sticking to its specific context, bounces across the whole spectrum of validity,

---

Hegel, Marx is weighted down by the basic conceptual necessities of the philosophy of the subject" (63).

[86]*The Philosophical Discourse of Modernity*, 65.

[87]*The Philosophical Discourse of Modernity*, 336-67.

[88]"Modernity versus Postmodernity," 8.

unsettles the equilibrium of the life-world's communicative infra-structure."[89] The diremptions Kant, Hegel, and Weber bequeathed to modernity must not be violated, lest the order of things be upset and we forfeit "the dignity specific to cultural modernity."[90]

Finally, the presupposition of Habermas's discourse on modernity is the necessity of a rational/theoretical court of appeals for adjudicating truth-claims. There must always be a principle, a sphere, a drive to unity that transcends the partiality of each particular truth-claim. There is a quality of communicative behavior that *implies* appeal to a criterion of rationality that goes beyond the particular claims the given communicative act advances; otherwise, Habermas argues, understanding itself would be impossible. "From the perspective of the participant, a moment of *uncondition-edness* is built into the *conditions* of action oriented toward under-standing,"[91] and that unconditioned moment refers to a pre-supposed norm of rationality that underwrites our life together.

## • Modernity versus the Masses •

There is a final aspect of modernity (usually mentioned only in passing) that will figure in the ensuing chapters: the relation of the modern to mass culture. As noted above, Baudelaire distinguished sharply between the mere current popularity of Hugo, and the genuine *modernity* of Guys. The diagnostic function of the modern prevents too close an association between the modern and mass culture.[92]

---

[89]*The Philosophical Discourse of Modernity,* 340.

[90]"The Entwinement of Myth and Enlightenment," trans. Thomas Y. Levin, *New German Critique* 26 (1982): 18. Cf. the corresponding passage in *The Philosophical Discourse of Modernity,* 112.

[91]"Questions and Counterquestions," trans. James Bohman, in *Habermas and Modernity,* ed. Richard J. Bernstein (Cambridge: MIT Press, 1985) 195.

[92]Likewise, the "Art for Art's sake" movement among French artists was not simply an excuse to avoid confronting social realities; it was as well an expression of the artists' revulsion at the commodification of

Modernity's "relentless hostility to mass culture"[93] is based not only upon its claim to the privilege to diagnose culture's short-comings, but also upon its claim to the privilege to prescribe remedies. Paradoxically, however, the hard work which justifies the modern scholar's claim to be able to help the masses tends also to divorce her from those she would help. As Habermas notes, under the conditions of modernity

> there appear the structures of cognitive-instrumental, moral-practical, and æsthetic-expressive rationality, each of these under the *control* of specialists who seem more adept at being logical in these particular ways than other people are. As a result, the distance has grown between the culture of the experts and that of the larger public.[94]

This gap between expert and public has the effect of setting the modern scholar over against an Other who doesn't possess the expertise necessary to judge the scholar's prescriptions. When Habermas asserts that the value-spheres are *controlled* by these modern experts, he points out an important and dangerous facet of modernity: those who are in control of a particular discourse are not subject to questioning from outside their (increasingly narrow) field of specialization.[95]

The modernity of expertise—which in the æsthetic value-sphere is typically known as "high modernism"—has characteristically defined itself in opposition to mass culture.[96] High-modern art is,

---

taste, the enthronement of bourgeois philistinism which had been effected by the middle class's buying power. "Art for Art's sake" repudiated the notion that popularity and financial success were in any way related to what an artist ought to do.

[93]Andreas Huyssen, "Mapping the Postmodern," 16.

[94]"Modernity versus Postmodernity," 8; my emphasis.

[95]The "expert" is not the only opponent of the masses in modernism; the cult of the genius, the stylistic innovator, is—as Jameson points out (see 23-24, above)—likewise a cardinal mark of modernism.

[96]Huyssen ("Mapping the Postmodern," 23) cites Clement Greenberg and Adorno as examples of theorists who understood the "adversarial

on one account, concerned to escape the transition to the status of exchange-value commodity; but the tactics high modernism typically deploys—self-referentiality, withdrawal from referentiality, denial of materiality—ironically render the high-modern work of art desirable as a fetishized commodity.[97] The unhappy dilemma leads on the one hand to elitist disdain for the masses, and on the other hand to the deliberately offensive character of some avant-gardes (from dandyism through Dada to contemporary performance art); Raymond Williams observes that "in remaining antibourgeois, [modernism's] representatives either choose the formerly aristocratic valuation of art as a sacred realm above money and commerce, or the revolutionary doctrines, promulgated since 1848, of art as the liberating vanguard of popular consciousness."[98] In both instances, modern art remains cut off from mass culture. In the first instance, the masses haven't the expertise to appreciate art; in the second, the autonomy of art's value-sphere must remain inviolate in order to maintain the emancipatory logic that is, ideally, immanent to modern art.

Modernity's dessicated abstraction from life—whether to preserve an immaculate emancipatory intent or an introspective autonomy—impressed Nietzsche as "decadent"; such a modernity leads people away from vitality and health, toward weakness and ineffectuality. In *The Case of Wagner*, Nietzsche equated decadence with Wagner, and Wagner with modernity—thus, by implication, of modernity with decadence.[99] Modernity's decadence is not bad in itself; it is bad, however, to the extent that it longs to extend its own weakness to the still-healthy aspects of life. Just as the modern historian hates life, and seeks to extinguish it with abstractions and minutiæ, so the partisans of decadence in modern life try to infect their culture's vital organs with the desire for weakness and ineffectuality. They mystify decadence, presenting

---

relationship between high art and mass culture" as "one of the pillars of modernist dogma."

[97]Cf. Eagleton, "Capitalism, Modernism, and Postmodernism," 67.
[98]"When Was Modernism?" *New Left Review* 175 (1989): 51.
[99]Quoted from Calinescu, 179.

its effects as its causes, setting a people the task of attaining weakness. Decadence is the natural soil of *ressentiment*, as in Nietzsche's definition of morality: "Morality—the idiosyncrasy of decadents, with the ulterior motive of revenging oneself upon life—successfully."[100] Its degenerative power thrives upon self-deception.[101] Modernity, understood as a haven of decadence, entails intellectual hypertrophy, self-deception, and the ambition to extend these conditions to those who are not already afflicted by them—typically, the masses.

## • Conclusion •

This, then, is the composite portrait that results from the preceding analysis: Modernity is (1) committed to novelty and progress and opposed to tradition; (2) particularly concerned with questions of chronology; (3) committed to a rationalized scholarly practice; and (4) intellectually elitist and antipopulist. It is time now to see how this portrait fits theorists of New Testament theology.

---

[100]*Ecce Homo*, trans. Walter Kaufmann (New York: Random House, 1967) 333.

[101]As in Calinescu's discussion, 181-94. It should be noted that Nietzsche saw that decadence's most powerful mask is vigor and health, just as madness and sickness might well be signs of well-being in a decadent milieu. "Are there perhaps—a question for psychiatrists—neuroses of *health*? of the youth and youthfulness of a people?" ("Attempt at a Self-Criticism," 21). Claims of progress in an enterprise are not proof against its decadence, especially in an intellectual endeavor.

# Chapter 2

# Modern
# New Testament Theology

*The name New Testament theology is wrong in both its terms.*
—William Wrede

The preceding chapter concluded with the question of whether
there might be any family of New Testament theology that fits the
given composite sketch of "the modern." In this chapter, I will
argue that indeed the dominant strand of New Testament theology
in the twentieth century—guided by the theoretical claims of
Johann Philipp Gabler (1753–1826), William Wrede (1859–1906),
and Krister Stendahl (1921–)—exemplifies the presuppositions of
modernity.[1] These theologians do not by any means exhaust the
examples of modern New Testament theology, but their work
includes three of the most influential essays on the topic: Gabler's
"On the Proper Distinction," Wrede's "The Task and Methods of
New Testament Theology," and Stendahl's article on "Contempo-

---

[1]For guidance in assaying the history of biblical theology, see Gerhard
Ebeling's "The Meaning of 'Biblical Theology'," in *Word and Faith*, trans.
J. W. Leitch (Philadelphia: Fortress Press, 1960) 79-97; and Ben C. Ollenburger's "Biblical Theology: Situating the Discipline," in *Understanding the
Word*, ed. J. T. Butler, E. W. Conrad, and B. C. Ollenburger, JSOT Supplement Series 37 (Sheffield: JSOT Press, 1982) 37-62, and "Biblical and Systematic Theology: Inventing a Relationship" (typescript, 1990) which useful-
ly illustrates biblical theology's role as oppositional strategy directed
against pietism on the one hand and dogmatic orthodoxy on the other.

rary Biblical Theology" in the original *Interpreter's Dictionary of the Bible*.[2] Their considerable influence—or, to be more exact, the considerable influence of Wrede's appropriation of Gabler, refigured through Stendahl—constitutes a definitive characteristic of a distinctively modern New Testament theology.

## • Gabler's "Proper Distinction" •

If the conventional narratives that describe the origins of biblical theology are to be believed, Johann Philipp Gabler's *Antrittsrede* on accepting the chair of theology in Altdorf changed the world. Robert Morgan describes the lecture as "epoch making,"[3] and helpfully goes on to declare it "the birth-hour of modern New Testament theology."[4] Otto Merk refers to the the period before this lecture as "the prehistory of 'biblical theology' as a discipline";[5] Wrede took the address as programmatic and normative for subsequent biblical theology;[6] Boers refers to it as "the decisive breakthrough in biblical theology";[7] and one could amass countless other testimonies to the influence of this relatively short lecture.[8]

---

[2]The claim that these three essays provide suitable points of orientation is supported directly by Gerhard Hasel's selection of just these three to outline the history of biblical theology ("The Relationship between Biblical Theology and Systematic Theology," *Trinity Journal* 5 [1984]: 113-27), and indirectly by the testimony of the sources cited hereinafter.

[3]*The Nature of New Testament Theology* (Naperville IL: Alec. R. Allenson, 1973) 2.

[4]"Gabler's Bicentenary," *Expository Times* 98 (1987): 164-68; my emphasis.

[5]From the name of the first chapter of his *Biblische Theologie des Neuen Testaments in ihrer Anfangszeit* (Marburg: N. G. Elwert Verlag, 1972): "Zur Vorgeschichte der 'Biblischen Theologie' als Disziplin" (5-28).

[6]"The Task and Methods of 'New Testament Theology'," trans. Robert Morgan, in *The Nature of New Testament Theology*, 68.

[7]*What Is New Testament Theology?* (Philadelphia: Fortress, 1979) 23.

[8]Heikki Räisänen refers to it as "the declaration of independence of 'biblical theology'," in *Beyond New Testament Theology* (Philadelphia: Trinity Press International, 1990) 3. Amos Wilder calls it "the decisive

Gabler introduced his lecture with the assumption that "the sacred books, especially of the New Testament, are the one clear source from which all true knowledge of the Christian religion is drawn," "the only secure sanctuary" of stability in knowledge.[9] Whence, then, come doctrinal arguments and differences of interpretation? Gabler points to the four factors. The first obstacle to attaining the secure sanctuary of Christian knowledge is the obscurity of the biblical texts. Gabler breaks this down into four further categories: first, the complexity of the subject matter; second, the unusual language scripture employs; third, the chronological gap that separates us from the biblical authors; and, finally, the depravity of interpreters who willfully "indulge their own ingenuity for its own sake"[10] (typically confusing metaphors with the universal notions in order to impose on the texts a meaning they themselves devise). A second problem arises from an exegete's predetermination to reach a given interpretation of a text. Third, Gabler deplores the frequent confusion of "religion" with "theology," a problem that constituted one of the major themes of Gabler's lecture. Finally, Gabler cites the problem of "an inappro-

---

landmark" in the evolution of biblical theology ("New Testament Theology in Transition," in *The Study of the Bible Today and Tomorrow*, ed. Harold R. Willoughby [Chicago: University of Chicago Press, 1947] 419). Rudolf Smend allows that we generally count Gabler as the father of biblical theology in the form familiar to us in "Johann Philipp Gablers Begründung der biblischen Theologie," *Evangelische Theologie* 22 (1962): 345. Ben Ollenburger notes that "the discipline of biblical theology has looked upon Gabler's 1787 Antrittsrede as its founding document," but later submits that Gabler can be regarded as the founder of biblical theology only to a limited degree ("Biblical Theology: Situating the Discipline," 39, 48).

[9]From the translation of his lecture, "On the Proper Distinction between Biblical and Dogmatic Theology and the Specific Objectives of Each," by John Sandys-Wunsch and Laurence Eldredge in "J. P. Gabler and the Distinction between Biblical and Dogmatic Theology: Translation, Commentary, and Discussion of his Originality," *Scottish Journal of Theology* 33 (1980): 134.

[10]"On the Proper Distinction," 135-36.

priate combination of the simplicity and ease of biblical theology with the subtlety and difficulty of dogmatic theology."[11] All of these problems of biblical interpretation cause uncertainty and confusion in theology. Gabler's goal in his lecture was to reestablish clarity and certainty in biblical and dogmatic theology.

In his lecture, Gabler did not address the problems of obscurity or interpretive depravity at any length. While such problems constitute grave threats to interpretation, Gabler evidently was satisfied with the expositions of hermeneutics in Ernesti and Morus (whom he cited favorably in the course of his lecture).[12] He did devote the remainder of the lecture to exploring the benefits of upholding a more rigorous separation of religion from theology, and of biblical from dogmatic theology.

"Religion" differs from "theology" principally in complexity. Gabler emphasizes the theme that "religion is everyday, transparently clear knowledge; but theology is subtle, learned knowledge."[13] Whereas theology is a sophisticated enterprise drawing on discriminating familiarity with scripture, history, and philosophy, religion is a matter for common people. Hendrikus Boers sees this distinction of religion and theology as the primary distinction in Gabler's work;[14] though it does little explicit work in the remainder of the lecture, it lies behind much of Gabler's argument. Religion,

---

[11]"On the Proper Distinction," 135.

[12]He describes Ernesti paradoxically as "the late immortal J. A. Ernesti" ("der selige Ernesti, ein unsterblicher Mann") and Morus as "the very distinguished," and later calls Morus "that excellent man" ("On the Proper Distinction," 136n.i [German translation from Merk, *Biblische Theologie*, 274n.2]; 140n.v).

[13]"On the Proper Distinction," 136.

[14]*What Is New Testament Theology?* 24-25. Since Boers is writing an introductory text, he omits documentation of his claims. Considering the paucity of scholarly English-language treatments of Gabler—the articles by Ollenburger, Morgan, and Sandys-Wunsch and Eldredge, together with the appropriate section of Boers are the principal resources—and the difficulty of obtaining any but the most common of his writings, this omission is especially frustrating.

for example, is the principal subject matter of the Bible; scripture contains "those things which holy men perceived about matters pertinent to religion."[15] It is important to note in this connection that religion is contrasted with theology not as behavior with cognition (or reflection), but as simple, unsophisticated ideas with refined concepts. The Bible is thus replete with simple ideas about God, ideas like uncut gems which thoughtful reflection can polish and set.

The polishing process involves the heart of Gabler's lecture. The roughness, the simplicity of the biblical texts is the obscurity to which Gabler alluded at the beginning of the lecture. This unrefined quality contributes to Gabler's *bête noir*: variety in interpretation and doctrine. The way to limit the baneful proliferation of dogmatic systems (Gabler lists thirteen sets of dogmatic teachings in late-eighteenth-century Lutheranism alone[16]) was to clarify the biblical basis for all theologizing. Just as polishing and cutting a gem requires removing some nonessential parts of the mineral, so this theological operation would entail discarding portions of scripture that did not contribute to the integrity of the finished dogmatics.

The process has been analyzed into varying numbers of steps. The exact number is irrelevant; at its heart, the process involves passing from the unsophisticated content of scripture ("biblical religion") to subtle reflections on universal divine truths ("dogmatic theology"). The beginning stage of biblical religion includes all the teachings of the Bible, and indeed those of the apocryphal books as well, as testimony to what the sacred authors may have thought about the divine. Biblical religion therefore includes a great proportion of limited, time-conditioned truths; Gabler specifies "the Mosaic rites" and "Paul's advice about women veiling themselves in church" among these.[17] The ideas of biblical religion should then be arranged carefully, historically, by author and time,

---

[15]"On the Proper Distinction," 144.
[16]"On the Proper Distinction," 142.
[17]"On the Proper Distinction," 142.

literary genre, and geographical location. The result of this pains-taking task is what Gabler sometimes calls "biblical theology in the broader sense," and sometimes calls "true biblical theology" (that is, true to the testimony of the biblical writers).[18] In either case, the application of the word "theology" is misleading, since on Gabler's terms the results of this first operation cannot yet be theology. Instead, it is simply a record of varieties of biblical religion.[19]

The next step on the path from biblical religion to dogmatic the-ology involves reordering the results of the initial survey in such a way as will form a single, unified system.[20] Gabler cites the example of Tiedemann's treatment of Stoic philosophy: one com-pares the various "opinions of the holy men," notes the patterns of agreement and disagreement, and compares the opinions to "universal ideas" (or "universal notions"). The result would pre-sumably be an orderly arrangement of the doctrinal concepts—still not theology, since the concepts themselves have not been weighed or refined, but no longer the mere catalogue that the first step provided.[21]

---

[18]Gabler does not himself employ the phrase "biblical theology in the broader sense" in his lecture; he does distinguish the result of this first step from the subsequent step, which he names "biblical theology in the stricter sense" ("On the Proper Distinction," 144). The label "true biblical theology" ("wahre biblische theologie") occurs in an article in the *Journal für theologische Literatur* 21:402 (as cited in Merk, *Biblische Theologie*, 50).

[19]Adolf Schlatter refers to theologies that stop at this step—as he thought Bernhard Weiss's *Biblical Theology of the New Testament* (2 vols., trans. David Eaton and James Duguid [Edinburgh: T.&T. Clark, n.d.; orig. 1868, [7]1903]) did—as mere "statistics" ("The Theology of the New Testa-ment and Dogmatics," trans. Robert Morgan in *The Nature of New Testament Theology*, 136).

[20]Here I am following Morgan's analysis of Gabler's proposed method; "Gabler's Bicentenary," 164-65.

[21]I say "presumably" since Gabler himself did not elaborate on this phase of the endeavor. In "Gabler's Bicentenary," 165, Morgan reasons from the character of Tiedemann's work to what Gabler seems to have had in mind.

Gabler next required that the biblical theologian determine which of the religious opinions that had so far been included in the synthesis were merely historical; that is, which had a significance limited (by God's intent[22]) to the specific time to which they were given. This entails separating "those things which in the sacred books refer most immediately to their own times and to the men of those times from the pure notions which divine providence wished to be characteristic of all times and places."[23] As mentioned above, Gabler reckoned the Mosaic ritual laws and Paul's instructions on veils as examples of the merely historical aspects of the Bible. Gabler offers as guidelines for making this judgment the testimony of Jesus and the apostles, reason, and comparison with "the great unchanging testament of Christian doctrine."[24] He takes pains to apply these criteria to the apostles, whose teachings were always to be compared with Jesus' doctrine. While they would not have erred on any point necessary to salvation, Gabler has no hesitation in supposing that some of their opinions were "merely human," since upon points not involved with salvation, the apostles "were left to their own ingenuity."[25]

Having situated the opinions of the biblical authors in proper geographic, chronological, and generic categories; having rearranged these testimonies so as to form a coherent religious system; and having pinpointed the opinions that lacked the divine imprimatur of eternal truth, the final step in Gabler's program was to discard all the historical material, leaving only the unchanging truths of Christian doctrine. This pure, atemporal theology constitutes "biblical theology in the stricter sense," or "pure biblical theology"—and only at this point may one begin to construct one's dogmatic theology, building carefully and exclusively upon the refined foundation this biblical theology provides. The dogmatic theology that springs from this will not be monolithic or unchang-

---

[22]"On the Proper Distinction," 142.
[23]"On the Proper Distinction," 138.
[24]"On the Proper Distinction," 142.
[25]"On the Proper Distinction," 143.

ing, since the priorities for building upon the eternal foundations will change from age to age, theologian to theologian; but that is appropriate, since these dogmatic systems are of merely human origin. They will not disagree, however, upon the fundamental Christian truths that comprise the eternal heart of biblical doctrine, and this will provide the stability Gabler sought.

Merk and Boers emphasize that while Gabler's inaugural lecture principally addresses this question of doctrinal stability, it simultaneously involves the important problem of the autonomous role of biblical criticism.[26] Merk counts it as a principal accomplishment of Gabler's that his influence effected "the release of biblical theology from the clutches of dogmatics."[27] By distinguishing biblical theology from the content of scripture ("biblical religion") on the one hand, and from dogmatics on the other, Gabler maintains an independent, critical role for biblical theology. He reserves some of his most pointed polemic for "that unfortunate fellow"—whom Sandys-Wunsch identifies as Carl Friedrich Bahrdt—"who heedlessly dared to attribute some of his own most insubstantial opinions to the sacred writers themselves—how he increased the unhappy fate of our religion!", and he regarded the custom of importing one's own judgments into the Bible as "depraved."[28] Gabler feared that manoeuvre by which contemporary authors claim the authority of scripture for their own dogmatic systems. The independence of biblical theology, and its derivation from biblical testimony alone, is intended to protect the public from willful theologians.

---

[26]Merk: *Biblische Theologie*, 39, 42, 51, 52-54, 207ff., and passim. See esp. the aphorism "Dogmatik muß von Exegese, und nicht umgekehrt Exegese von Dogmatik abhängen" ["Dogmatics must depend on exegesis, and not conversely exegesis on dogmatics"] (from Gabler's introduction to Eichhorn's *Urgeschichte*); Boers: "Biblical theology was freed from a *predetermination* by dogmatic theology but remained determined by it with regard to its purpose"; *What Is New Testament Theology?* 37 (his emphasis).

[27]*Biblische Theologie*, 271: "die . . . Herauslösung der biblischen Theologie aus der Umklammerung durch die Dogmatik."

[28]"On the Proper Distinction," 135.

Gabler expresses his resistance to (alleged) eisegesis not only in his writings devoted specifically to biblical theology, but also in an extended scholarly dispute with Immanuel Kant (and the Kantian writings of C. F. von Ammon).[29] Whereas Kant, in *Religion within the Limits of Reason Alone*, justifies theological interpretations that defy the literal sense of the text in the interest of promoting morality, Gabler is horrified at the prospect that any sense other than the literal be granted authority. Kant argues that scriptural interpretations must be judged by the extent to which they tend toward "the moral improvement of men."[30] Even if the interpreter is obliged to twist the literal sense, he or she must seek the guidance of the Spirit which instructs and edifies. Kant distinguishes this scriptural interpreter from the scriptural scholar, who adopts a philosophical stance with regard to scripture: it may or may not actually be God's revelation, but it has human roots and expressions that are subject to scholarly investigation.[31] Finally, Kant argues that the biblical theologian is principally a theologian, not a historian: "the biblical theologian is actually a scribe for the faith of the church."[32] The point of biblical theology, on Kant's account, is to produce a harmonious synthesis of biblical teachings on the topics that concern theologians.

---

[29]This conflict is discussed extensively in Smend, "Gablers Begrundung," 349-53, and Merk, *Biblische Theologie*, 82-90.

[30]*Religion within the Limits of Reason Alone*, trans. Theodore M. Greene and Hoyt H. Hudson (New York: Harper & Row, 1960) 102.

[31]*Religion within the Limits of Reason Alone*, 103 (and cf. 105, where he defines Scripture scholarship as that which "deals with the historical aspect of that religion"). Kant further discusses the claim of pietism to produce valid interpretations of scripture based on an "inner feeling," but dismisses the probative value of any kind of "inner feeling" (104-105).

[32]*The Conflict of the Faculties / Der Streit der Fakultäten*, trans. Mary J. Gregor (New York: Abaris Books, 1979) 60. The quoted passage is my own translation; Gregor renders *"Schriftgelehrte"* as "one versed in Scripture," which is certainly one aspect of the term but which misses the ironic pun of the Luther Bible's identification of the opponents of Jesus as *Schriftgelehrter*.

Of course, Gabler was deeply distressed by Kant's approach, especially as it was brought to bear within the theological faculty by Christoph Friedrich von Ammon's *Entwurf einer reinen biblischen Theologie.*[33] Gabler regarded von Ammon's work as no better than a collection of prooftexts, concluding that "it is by no means a genuine biblical theology."[34] The whole approach that Kant sponsored seemed no better to Gabler than the long-despised allegorical method of the church fathers. Gabler's commitment to the hermeneutic of Ernesti and Morus (based on the principle of understanding a text, as opposed to Kant's hermeneutic based on the idea that interpretation uses texts for different purposes in different contexts) impelled him to deride von Ammon and Kant as irresponsible and naive. "Let us not," he urged in his lecture, "by applying tropes forge new dogmas about which the authors themselves never thought."[35]

Another subtext to Gabler's distinction is the necessity of formulating a theology that is appropriate to his own time.[36] This need is the logical outcome of several of Gabler's starting assumptions. First, Gabler warned that there is a critical gap between the biblical writers' ideas and behavior and those of our times. (This is one aspect of the problem of obscurity alluded to above.) Second, Gabler saw the only possibility for theologically valid biblical theology in the discovery and isolation of the atemporally true divine teachings in the Bible. The merely human elaborations of this eternal divine truth are exclusively relevant to the times that produced them, whether these interpretations are by the biblical

---

[33](Erlangen, 1792).

[34]"[E]igentlich biblische Theologie ist es doch nicht"; *Journal für auserlesene theologische Literatur* 2 (1805/1806): 403-404; quoted in Smend, "Gablers Begrundung," 350.

[35]"On the Proper Distinction," 140. Here Gabler is restating (in a very different context!) the venerable rule of thumb that allegorical interpretations cannot be used to establish the truth of a doctrine, but only to illustrate or support it—a rule that was almost as widely ignored as it was widely cited.

[36]So Ollenburger, "Situating the Discipline," 39.

writers or by contemporary academic theologians. Gabler's time demanded a theology that harmonized the pure biblical theology with the dictates of reason, but he allowed for the possibility that others might develop dogmatics that answered other needs. In both cases, Gabler unequivocally makes a case for a gap between the contemporary interpreter and the text, which gap could be bridged only by a suitably rigorous and disinterested historical research.

## • Gabler's Modernity •

Gabler exemplifies the physiognomy of modernity in all four of the traits with which the first chapter concluded. The most obvious of these is Gabler's emphasis on the historicity of the biblical-theological enterprise, the chronological determination of true biblical theology. Gabler's understanding of biblical theology also reflects the rejection of tradition, the overcoming of the past typical of modernity. His hope for an indisputable foundation for biblical theology is likewise modern, and there are traces of the antipopulist, elitist strain of modernity in a number of asides in his lecture.

Gabler's emphasis on historicity is not unequivocally modern. The notion that there might be a core of truths in the Bible that were not chronologically overdetermined, and that might therefore provide an atemporally true basis for dogmatic theology, is clearly out of step with the modern inclination to see everything as inescapably enmeshed in historical processes. Yet Gabler envisions this atemporal center as the outcome of a historical investigation. The eternal divine truths emerge in comparison with merely temporal, human truths. The authority of the truths in scripture depends upon their origin: those truth-claims that can be attributed to the local interests of their authors must finally be discarded, whereas those truth-claims that evidently are independent of their historical context form the invariant divine kernel to which we must attend; as Sandys-Wunsch observes, for Gabler "what is historical is secondary to what is true."[37]

---

[37]"J. P. Gabler and the Distinction between Biblical and Dogmatic

Gabler's emphasis on the chronological situation of contemporary dogmatics likewise points to modern interests. Gabler notes that theology, like other disciplines, "experiences various changes along with other fields";[38] dogmatic theology teaches "what each theologian philosophizes rationally about divine things, according to the measure of his ability or of the times, age, place, sect, school, and other similar factors."[39] Dogmatic theology is animated by the principle of chronological (geographic, etc.) change: "history teaches that there is a chronology and a geography to theology itself."[40] The scholastics produced turgid, impenetrable dogmatics; the Fathers, austere and lucid dogmatics; and so on. A scholar who follows Gabler's guidelines carefully will thereby produce a dogmatic theology adapted to his or her own time.[41]

Modern biblical theology further insists on its novelty, on the difference it represents from previous inferior understandings of biblical theology. Gabler fulfils this requirement by derogating his predecessors both distant and recent. He dismissed von Ammon's *Entwurf einer reinen biblischen Theologie* (1792) as by no means a real biblical theology, and suggested that von Ammon was "a beginner in theology."[42] The Fathers (whose work was contrasted favorably with the gloomy, barbarous Scholastics in the lecture) indulged in the despised practice of allegorical interpretation. Gabler opposed both Orthodox dogmaticians who read the Scriptures in the light of their creeds and confessions, and pietistic biblicists who relied upon their own uninformed spiritual interpretations; both of these practiced the prooftexting, which, according to Gabler, "inflict[s] violence upon the sacred books" by tearing them from their context.[43] Gabler expected that his program for a pure biblical theology mediating the truth of Scripture could supply a means by

---

Theology," 147.

[38]"On the Proper Distinction," 136.
[39]"On the Proper Distinction," 137; my emphasis.
[40]"On the Proper Distinction," 137.
[41]"On the Proper Distinction," 144.
[42]Quoted in Smend, "Gablers Begrundung," 350, 352.
[43]"On the Proper Distinction," 135.

which all these misleading past alternatives could be taken up and surpassed in a newly coherent theological enterprise.

Exactly Gabler's hope for a new unanimity constitutes the third aspect of his modernity. Gabler firmly believed that once unbiased historical investigation had revealed which biblical truths were historical and thus dispensable, the unquestionable core of Christian truth would be revealed. This longing for eternal truths (which attentuates his historical modernity), and the confidence that general agreement could be reached on the basis of these eternal truths, stand firmly in the modern tradition which upholds the possibility and value of rational consensus. Similarly, his sense that the variety among dogmatic theologies was approaching dangerous proportions, which demanded the new, ahistorical, universal foundation, reflects Baudrillard's description of the modern proclivity for crisis,[44] a point Sandys-Wunsch underlines by noting that the drive to unanimity and scientific confirmation of Christian truth was common in Gabler's time.[45]

Finally, Gabler consistently maintains definitions of "theology" and "genuine biblical theology" that reserve these for the learned elite. "Religion," which is adequate for the salvation of souls, is simple and clear; it is suitable for anyone. "Theology," however, is "subtle, learned knowledge":

> [N]ot only does theology deal with things proper to the Christian religion, but it also explains carefully and fully all connected matters; and finally it makes a place for them with the subtlety and rigor of logic. But religion for the common man has nothing to do with this abundance of literature and history.[46]

---

[44]Baudrillard's article stresses modernity's continual flight from crisis to crisis; "[Modernité] fait de la crise une valeur": "Modernité", *Encyclopaedia Universalis* 11 (Paris: Encyclopaedia Universalis France, 1968) 139.

[45]He cites the example of J. G. Toellner's dream that exegesis could attain mathematical certainty and eliminate conflict among Christians; "J. P. Gabler and the Distinction between Biblical and Dogmatic Theology," 145.

[46]"On the Proper Distinction," 136; my emphasis.

Gabler's resistance to allegorical interpretation is likewise a modern antipopulist stance. Readers who have not already been taught that the historico-literary sense of Scripture is exclusively valid frequently adopt allegorical interpretations to rationalize apparent contradictions or to draw a connection between the biblical text and their own circumstances. Carlos Mesters has compared scholars who banish allegorical interpretations to curators who exclude peasants from a museum of their national heritage;[47] anyone, after all, can devise a valid allegorical interpretation, but only a learned historian can propound a valid hypothesis on, for example, the authenticity of a deutero-Pauline epistle.

All these aspects of Gabler's lecture do not add up to the conclusion that Gabler was himself a modern biblical theologian. His overriding interest in biblical theology's subservience to dogmatics and his allegiance to supposed "eternal divine truths" prevent categorizing Gabler as a thoroughly modern biblical theologian. At the same time, it is clear that Gabler set biblical theology on a course congenial to modernity; and, as the next sections will show, it was the particularly modern aspects of Gabler's essay that were remembered and developed into the dominant approach to biblical theology.

The reception of Gabler's lecture has been colored strongly by the fact that it was delivered in dense scholarly Latin and was not commonly available even in a full German translation until 1972, and was first published in English in 1980.[48] The voice of Gabler's

---

[47]Quoted in James Dawsey, "The Lost Front Door into Scripture: Carlos Mesters, Latin American Liberation Theology, and the Church Fathers," *Anglican Theological Review* 72 (1990): 292-305. Mesters's own *Defenseless Flower* has been translated into English by Francis McDonagh (Maryknoll NY: Orbis Books, 1983) and his essay on "The Use of the Bible in Christian Communities of the Common People" is available in *The Bible and Liberation*, ed. Norman K. Gottwald (Maryknoll NY: Orbis Books, 1983) 119-33.

[48]Cf. Clarence T. Craig, "Biblical Theology and the Rise of Historicism," *Journal of Biblical Literature* 62 (1943): 281. Amos Wilder refers to

interpreters was for a long time the principal vehicle by which his address influenced scholars. It is therefore not surprising to find that in mid-twentieth-century America, Gabler was perceived to have argued that biblical theology ought to be "the theology held by the biblical writers," the product of a strictly historical enterprise. C. T. Craig here represents the interpretation of Gabler's distinctions that William Wrede cultivated, and which has since become canonical for modern biblical theology.

### • Wrede's *sogenannte* New Testament Theology •

As numerous scholars observe, Gabler's program for biblical theology was never realized; in fact, it is not clear that his contemporaries even understood Gabler's claims. His inaugural lecture made no immediate impact, though it is now deemed a foundational document: "rightly or wrongly, it was not so seen by his contemporaries."[49] Rudolf Smend observes (with considerable justification) that "On the Proper Distinction. . . . is still known more for its name than its content."[50] The emphasis quickly shifted from biblical theology's role in mediating divine truths of Scripture to dogmatic theology, to biblical theology's independent status as a historical discipline—making what had been an incipiently "modern" enterprise in Gabler's lecture a thoroughly modern endeavor. Indeed, in the important essay "Die biblische Kritik innerhalb des

---

Gabler initiating biblical theology as "a strictly historical procedure" ("New Testament Theology in Transition," 423). Excerpts from Gabler were included in Kümmel's *The New Testament: The History of the Investigation of Its Problems*, trans. from 2nd German ed. (1970; [1]1958) by S. MacLean Gilmour and Howard Clark Kee (Nashville: Abingdon, 1972).

[49]Sandys-Wunsch, "J. P. Gabler and the Distinction between Biblical and Dogmatic Theology," 149. On the other hand, Boers marks it as "the next important step in the development of New Testament Theology" (*What Is New Testament Theology?* 39).

[50]"[I]st mehr dem Namen als dem Inhalt nach bekannt": "Gablers Begrundung," 345.

theologischen Studiums,"[51] Wrede explicitly emphasizes the character of his approach to interpretation as "modern." Once biblical theology had been practically redefined in this way, it attracted the interest of the history-of-religions school (A. Eichhorn, Gunkel, Bousset, Troeltsch, Wrede); Wrede's "Task and Methods of 'New Testament Theology' "[52] epitomizes the *religionsgeschichtlich* appropriation of Gabler's program.

Wrede nods to Gabler at the outset of his essay, but quickly proceeds to discuss the ways he believes that New Testament theology has refined Gabler's insights. He cites as examples the "natural" separation of Old Testament theology from New Testament theology, of the teaching of Jesus from that of the apostles, of the different apostolic teachings from one another. Likewise Wrede finds the necessity of discussing New Testament ideas in terms of their historical development, and with no attention to subsequent dogmatic interests, to be valuable refinements of Gabler's plan.[53] He then raises the fateful question of whether New Testament theology should be conceived as a strictly historical discipline, and—despite the absence of any examples of a strictly historical New Testament theology—claims that the principle has been conceded almost unanimously, and that henceforward he would presuppose "the strictly historical character of New Testament theology."[54]

---

[51]"Biblical Criticism within the Theological Course of Studies," in *Vorträge und Studien* (Tübingen: J. C. B. Mohr [Paul Siebeck], 1907) 40-63.

[52]Georg Strecker refers to this essay as "grundlegend für das Verständnis Wredes" ("William Wrede," *Zeitschrift für Theologie und Kirche* 57 [1960]: 67) and Ollenburger submits that this essay "best illustrates how a history-of-religions approach bears on the way biblical theology is conceived" ("Situating the Discipline," 40). Note that the German title of Wrede's essay modifies "New Testament Theology" not with scare quotes, but with the adjective *sogenannten;* Wrede resists the idea that either the N.T. or theology has a decisive relation to this enterprise.

[53]"Task and Methods," 68-69.

[54]"Task and Methods," 69. Though Adolf Deissmann had used almost identical language four years earlier in asserting that "über den rein his-

In a telling illustration of Wrede's distaste for anything doctrinal or dogmatic, he proceeds to denounce the "old" doctrine of inspiration. Inspiration is a purely dogmatic category; the New Testament theologian will have nothing to do with it, since New Testament theology has a strictly historical character, and "for logical thinking there can be no middle position between inspired writings and historical documents."[55] New Testament theology ignores such doctrinal issues as inspiration in order zealously to maintain its disciplinary autonomy. It is a science that sets its own goals, and is indifferent to the interests of collateral disciplines. Pure, objective, disinterested, scientific, New Testament theology leads to facts, and "facts need no legitimation."[56]

Here Wrede is driving toward one of the cardinal principles of his approach to New Testament theology. The enterprise of New Testament theology is not, for Wrede, theological at all. Since historical investigation can only be threatened by the interests of dog-

---

torischen Charakter der neutestamentlichen Theologie kaum noch ein Zweifel besteht" ["hardly any doubt remains concerning the purely historical character of New Testament theology"] (*Zur Methode der biblischer Theologie des Neuen Testaments* [1893] 67; cited in Erich Grässer, "Offene Fragen im Umkreis einer Biblischen Theologie," *Zeitschrift für Theologie und Kirche* 77 [1980]: 200) Wrede concedes that this represents the assumption of something yet unrealized, and concludes his essay with the exhortation "[Biblical theology] is not yet in the true and strict sense a historical discipline at all. May it become one!" (116).

Much of Wrede's criticism throughout the essay is directed against scholars who imagine that they are adopting an adequately historical approach, but who have failed in some respects. Long passages detail the errors of historical-critical colleagues who "overinterpret," who construct complex conjectural literary relationships between texts, who exercise poor judgment in describing the New Testament writers. This emphasis on the material failings of his contemporaries complicates Wrede's position in this formal study: Wrede can assume the common end of a truly historical interpretation of the New Testament, and so generally does not make explicit his position on the status of "history" for interpretation.

[55]"Task and Methods," 69.
[56]"Task and Methods," 70.

matic theology, Wrede insists on the uncompromising independence of the historical over against potential encroachment from theological restraints.

> One might say that this account of New Testament theology entirely surrenders its specifically theological character. It is no longer treated any differently from any other branch of history in general or the history of religion in particular. This is correct.[57]

Wrede's antipathy to dogmatic theology is likewise reflected in the observation I have used as the epigraph for this chapter, with which he concluded his essay:

> [T]he name New Testament theology is wrong in both its terms. . . . The appropriate name for the subject matter is: early Christian history of religion, or rather: the history of early Christian religion and theology. If anyone protests that this is no longer a New Testament theology, that is a strange objection. The name is obviously controlled by the subject matter, not vice versa.[58]

Thus Wrede clearly indicates that his exclusive interest is in the history that lies behind the literature of early Christianity, rather than in any theological conclusions that might be reached on the basis of the New Testament writings.

Part of the urgency for restricting New Testament theology to historical interests lies in the necessity Wrede posits for New Testament theology to be a scientific discipline. Granted this premise, Wrede sees his conclusions as self-evident; scientific inquiry must be autonomous, may not serve the interests of anything outside the subject matter itself. Practical needs only imperil the scientific character of the inquiry itself, and Wrede presupposes that investigation of the New Testament must above all remain scientific (though he does not argue his case explicitly in this essay).[59]

---

[57]"Task and Methods," 70.

[58]"Task and Methods," 116.

[59]Along with "Biblische Kritik und theologische Studium" see the essays "Der Prediger und sein Zuhörer" and "Das theologische Studium

Whereas "science" (or "history') is Wrede's preferred avenue to biblical theology, his nemesis is the method of "doctrinal concepts" (*Lehrbegriffe*). This method—the dominant mode of biblical theologizing at Wrede's time—does exactly what Wrede inveighs against by mixing theological interests (which dictate the selected doctrinal concepts) with the necessarily historical task of interpreting the New Testament. Moreover, the method of doctrinal concepts confuses the religion that is expressed in the New Testament writings with doctrine, of which the New Testament contains relatively little. "It is only justifiable to speak of doctrine when thoughts and ideas are developed for the sake of teaching. That happens only rarely in the New Testament."[60] The New Testament writers were typically not intellectually distinguished enough to produce theology; they address the everyday religious concerns of "believers and hopers."[61] Wrede even denies Paul the title "theologian," though he concedes that "his epistles do contain a strong theological element. He is a Christian thinker, and reflects like a theologian."[62] In this respect, Wrede contrasts Paul with the writers of Revelation and the Pastoral Epistles, who cannot be counted as theologians however great the theological content of their writings.

The method of doctrinal concepts is for Wrede little more than the old *dicta probantia* come back in another guise. Just as the earlier compilations of proof texts disregarded context and pounced upon any passage that might confirm a doctrine, so the method of doctrinal concepts overemphasizes the trivia of biblical interpretation. Wrede excoriates Bernhard Weiss for devoting three pages to the doctrine of election in James, when the verb

---

und die Religionsgeschichte," in *Vorträge und Studien* (Tübingen: J. C. B. Mohr [Paul Siebeck], 1907) 1-39, 64-83. In these essays Wrede stresses the essential need for scientific study of the Bible in the theological curriculum (cf., for but one example, 55-56 of "Die biblische Kritik innerhalb des theologischen Studiums").

[60]"Task and Methods," 75.

[61]"Task and Methods," 75.

[62]"Task and Methods," 76.

ἐκλέγεσθαι appears only once in the entire letter (and in that one occurrence, it is used in an indifferent, theologically neutral way).[63]

Wrede likewise denounces the manner in which scholars sought literary connections among the New Testament writings. He argues that the development of religious ideas depends much less on contact with other documents and much more on the laws of the history of religions.[64]

Once again, Wrede emphasizes the distinction between simple, unreflective religion (which follows natural developmental processes) and sophisticated, self-conscious theology (which is shaped by the thoughtful assimilation and rejection of previous theological ideas).

Finally, Wrede shows how the method of doctrinal concepts relies too heavily upon quite fragmentary sources. He claims that the extant literature of early Christianity is insufficient for the task of elaborating the doctrinal concepts of either the document's authors or nascent Christianity as a whole. The canon of the New Testament reflects "Christianity" no better than "two popular biographies of Lassalle, an academic treatise of Marx, a few letters of Lassalle, Engels, and one or two unknown workers active as agitators; then a few pamphlets two or three pages long and finally a socialist inflammatory writing describing the socialist picture of heaven on earth" would reflect the complex phenomenon of "social democracy."[65] According to Wrede, the information available in the New Testament sources do not provide enough information accurately to reconstruct the historical character of the doctrinal concepts that New Testament theologians pretended to find therein.

Wrede does not inveigh against his contemporaries only on the basis of their use of the method of doctrinal concepts. He criticizes

---

[63]"Task and Methods," 78. The passage comes in James 2:5: "Has not God *chosen* the poor in the world to be rich in faith and to be heirs of the kingdom that he has promised to those who love him?" (NRSV)

[64]"Task and Methods," 81.

[65]"Task and Methods," 82.

Beyschlag's *New Testament Theology* for "modernizing," for failing to recognize the problem of the relation of the past historical record to contemporary believers.[66] The task that Beyschlag sees as "set[ting] forth the results obtained from an investigation of the sources, not merely as a well-arranged collection of raw material, but to restore from that the living image itself, the fragmentary evidence of which lies before us in these results,"[67] Wrede sees eliding the hard problems of the gap between the ancient past and the modern present. He would agree with Beyschlag that the object of historical investigation is "objective and alien to us," that "the religious doctrines of the New Testament . . . are parted from us by eighteen centuries."[68] He balks, however, at the idea that a New Testament theologian has the responsibility of bridging that gap; for Wrede, the task might more precisely be defined as emphasizing the extent and dimensions of that gap.

The real goal of New Testament theology for Wrede is not the subjective appropriation of New Testament truth, but rather it is the most precise possible delineation of "what was believed, thought, taught, hoped, required, and striven for in the earliest period of Christianity."[69] "New Testament theology must show us the special character of early Christian ideas and perceptions, sharply profiled, and help us to understand them historically."[70] To this end, the important aspects of the documents will be those in which the operation of theological genius is distinguishable from "simply average Christianity."[71] Wrede is concerned only with

---

[66]"Task and Methods," 83.

[67]Willibald Beyschlag, *New Testament Theology*, vol. 1, trans. Neil Buchanan (Edinburgh: T.&T. Clark, 1899) 17. Beyschlag is distancing himself from Weiss's approach to the task of N.T. theology. Note that Wrede himself, in language reminiscent of Beyschlag's project, mourns the absence of "the living freshness" of the thought of the N.T. from the N.T. theologies based on doctrinal concepts ("Task and Methods," 78).

[68]Beyschlag, *New Testament Theology*, 17.

[69]"Task and Methods," 84.

[70]"Task and Methods," 83.

[71]"Task and Methods," 86. Wrede grudgingly commends the author

those writers who "have had an epoch-making influence on the church."[72] Those writers who only reproduced what we might expect them to say on the basis of standard history-of-religions assumptions are of no interest to the New Testament theologian.

## • Wrede's Modernity •

Wrede's prescription for New Testament theology fits the physiognomy of modernity in several pointed ways. Perhaps most striking is Wrede's repeated insistence on the autonomy of biblical interpretation. Over and over, Wrede takes pains to stress the necessity of divorcing biblical interpretation from any association with dogmatics; as Hans-Joachim Kraus observes,

> The autonomy of the historical is clearly and consistently proclaimed here. The theologian has to obey the historical object "as Master." A change of command has taken place with Wrede. Until now, doctrinal concepts were the masters; from now on, history should and must be the master.[73]

Consider the passage from "Biblische Kritik und theologische Studium"[74] wherein Wrede enumerates one of the marks of prog-

---

of Hebrews, allowing that "One can even call him a theologian. The average Christian could not have written an epistle like this" (86).

[72]"Task and Methods," 85.

[73]*Die Biblische Theologie* (Neukirch: Neukirchener Verlag, 1970) 164: "Klar und konsequent wird hier die Autonomie des Historischen proklamiert. Der Theologe hat dem historischen Objekt »als Herrn« zu gehorchen. Ein Herrschaftswechsel wird von Wrede kundgetan. Bisher »herrschten« die Lehrbegriffe: fortan soll und muss die Historie der Herr Sein." In "Biblische Kritik und theologische Studium," Wrede couches his discussion of biblical criticism's autonomy in terms of an assault ("Angriff") on dogmatics. Even the then-recent schools of dogmatics, which understood that historical investigation undermined the authority of creeds and orthodox formulae, were insufficiently appreciative of the radical challenge that historical criticism entails ("Biblische Kritik und theologische Studium," 44-45).

[74]"[Geschichtliche Bibelforschung] hat das alte Verhältnis zur Dog-

ress that distinguishes contemporary exegesis from past interpretation: "Historical biblical research has more and more separated itself from the former relation to dogmatics, and has become independent." This stress on the autonomy of New Testament theology coincides with strenuous emphasis on the scientific character of biblical interpretation. For Wrede, as for Habermas, it is necessary that the spheres of reason remain distinct lest they contaminate one another. Wrede believes scientific historical inquiry yields facts that are intimately connected with the historical realities to which they refer:

> he knew himself to be supported by the subject matter itself, which is only served when one so arranges it that it presents itself in its dependence on its specific historical situation, not however by veiling the state of affairs revealed by historical criticism for the sake of a dogmatic prejudice.[75]

Theological interests could only obscure the historical New Testament interpretation that is at the heart of New Testament theology.

The evidence suggests strongly that this is at the core of Wrede's interpretation of Gabler. When Wrede invokes the name of his predecessor at the beginning of his essay, he immediately proceeds to discuss the extent to which New Testament theology has been recognized as a strictly historical phenomenon (not—to allude to one of Gabler's expressed themes—the extent to which the work of true biblical theology has facilitated dogmatic theology). Alas, Wrede mourns, biblical theology is not yet strictly historical; until it is, "biblical theology will be pressed for an answer to dogmatic questions the biblical documents do not really give,

---

matik mehr und mehr gelöst, sie ist selbständig geworden," "Biblische Kritik und theologische Studium," 43.

[75]Georg Strecker, "William Wrede," *Zeitschrift für Theologie und Kirche* 57 (1960): 87: "wußte er sich durch die Sache selbst gestüzt, der nicht anders zu dienen sei, als daß man sie so darstellt, wie sie in der Gebundenheit an ihre spezifische historische Situation sich selbst gibt, nicht aber, indem man die durch die historische Kritik aufgedeckten Tatbestände einem dogmatischen Vorurteil zuliebe verschleiert."

and will endeavor to eliminate results that are troublesome for dogmatics."[76] Of course, this marks a distinct turn from the path Gabler projected. Whereas Gabler's essay commends a biblical theology that (though separate from dogmatics) always has theology as its aim, Wrede remains unconcerned about what the systematic theologian does with his truly historical biblical theology: "that is his own affair."[77]

Wrede's relation to modernity is marked just as much by his assumption that chronology determines existence and understanding. The rhetoric of "The Task and Methods" is heavy laden with assertions about the distance that separates the contemporary interpreter from the world of the New Testament texts. As noted above, he chastises Beyschlag for modernizing; instead, one must recognize that

> It [biblical research] has gotten used to the notion that these ideas and perceptions have their own character that they quite typically differ in many respects from today, and it demands that one not "modernize" or spiritualize the ancient ideas, that is, boil off their alien (to us) form, and emphasize only that which seems to be a sort of kernel acceptable to today's thought.[78]

---

[76]"Task and Methods," 69.

[77]"Task and Methods," 69. Interestingly, Wrede argues that though N.T. theology is autonomous with regard to dogmatics, dogmatics is thoroughly dependent on (modern, historical) N.T. theology. Since everything of theological relevance is historically mediated, historical research has a position superior to every other theological discipline ("Biblische Kritik und theologische Studium," passim; cf. 51: "Die Dogmatik ist also genötigt, auf die historische Forschung ihrerseits einzugehen; historischen Gründen kann sie nur mit besseren historischen Gründen begegnen" ["Therefore dogmatics is in turn obliged to enter into historical research; historical arguments can only be answered with better historical arguments"]).

[78]"Biblische Kritik und theologisches Studium," 44: "Sie [geschichtliche Bibelforschung] hat sich sodann an denn Gedanken gewöhnt, daß diese Gedanken und Empfindungen ihren eigenen Charakter haben, daß sie sich in vielen Beziehungen ganz charakteristisch unterscheiden von

What was not doctrine (in Wrede's strict sense[79]) when the early Christians wrote it, must not be developed into doctrine in a contemporary New Testament theology. The whole burden of Wrede's program concerns summarizing and evaluating the early Christian texts in their own context, with no interest whatever in relating the texts to contemporary readers. Though he bemoans the tendency among seminarians to demand what relevance the historically reconstructed Paul has for faith or for pastoral life, Wrede offers no answer—this despite the implicit assumption that the correct historical reconstruction is a necessary prerequisite for responsible appropriation of the Bible.[80] Wrede does discuss the conversion of students from dogmatic to purely historical interests, and commends the way in which historical research builds character (presumably through the intellectual hygiene of submitting cherished beliefs to disconfirmation), but finally can propose no other argument than that is is necessary for modern seminarians to study in this modern way.

Another aspect of Wrede's commitment to chronological determination is the stress he places on development.[81] He supposes that the only appropriate arrangement for a New Testament theology is a developmental scheme. Why? Because the true character of the writings is revealed only by such an arrangement. The

---

heutigen, und sie dringt darauf, daß man die antiken Gedanken nicht »modernisiere,« auch nicht spiritualisiere, d. h. ihre uns fremde Form verflüchtige und nur das, was etwa ein dem heutigen Denken annehmbar Kern zu sein scheint, hervorhebe." Wrede may well be referring here to Beyschlag, who uses the kernel/husk metaphor to describe his mediation of N.T. theology to a contemporary audience; Wrede comments on this sarcastically in "Task and Methods," 187n.30. Cf. "Über Aufgabe und Methode der sogenannten Neutestamentlichen Theologie" (Göttingen: Vandenhoeck und Ruprecht, 1897) 31n.1.

[79]"Task and Methods," 75.

[80]"Biblische Kritik und theologische Studium," 58ff.

[81]For one example, "A New Testament theology should try to make clear so far as is possible the development and developments," "Task and Methods," 91.

various differing testimonies are only understood correctly when they are set in a developmental order that clarifies the relations of one position to the others. This tendency—which Wrede inherits from Baur and the Hegelian tradition[82]—finally locates the importance of the New Testament in its role as testimony to the history of the early church, without making any connection to its possible significance for any other time.

Wrede's unabashed modernity is likewise manifest in his promotion of his program for New Testament theology as part of a movement that has brought something entirely new into the world. The Ancients, in Wrede's world, were those who imagined that there might be any significant continuity between what had been believed about the New Testament (or dogmatics) and what present scientific study revealed to be the truth about early Christian literature; the Moderns recognize that the historical-critical revolution has revealed countless contradictions and discontinuities which disrupt the Ancients' account. "The modern biblical critic, the historian of the Old as well as the New Testaments, is an *entirely new* figure in positions of pedagogical authority."[83] Indeed, the dividing line that separates modern from premodern biblical critics can be fixed at a very recent date: the modern biblical critic is entirely different from the biblical critic of even fifty years ago. So it is that although Wrede admits that no one yet has written an adequately historical New Testament theology, he can assume that that is the proper way for the task to be done.

A final correspondence of Wrede's program to the physiognomy of modernity involves the tendency to separate that which is valuable and true, which is accessible only to the few, from the errors and confusion of nonexperts. Wrede breezily claims that it is "self-evident" that the Old and New Testaments should be

---

[82]Wrede repudiates the specific developmental scheme that Baur proposed, but endorses Baur's insistence that the N.T. writings can be understood only in a developmental context. "Task and Methods," 92.

[83]"Der moderne Bibelkritiker, der Historiker des Alten wie des Neuen Testaments ist eine *ganz neue* Figur auf den theologischen Lehrstühlen"; "Biblische Kritik und theologisches Studium," 42; my emphasis.

treated separately, that the teaching of Jesus should be treated separately from those of the apostles, that distinctions must be drawn among the latter, that there must be a historical arrangement, and that the arrangement must not follow a pattern drawn from dogmatics, but one drawn from the material itself; yet the degree to which these were really "self-evident" must be questioned, since Wrede feels obliged to polemicize against interpreters who neglect these imperatives. He perpetuates the religion/theology distinction that associates "religion" with simple piety: "The step from religion to theology is always of fundamental importance. It is felt at first to be a descent, from what is simple, immediate, natural to something complicated, secondary, reflected."[84] Wrede consistently depreciates the value of the pedestrian New Testament writers' testimonies—despite his repeated insistence that it is exactly the general beliefs and theological understandings of earliest Christianity that the New Testament theologian seeks to uncover.

Robert Morgan points out that Wrede could easily discard the work of dogmatic theology because he stood in the liberal Protestant tradition which placed a low value on dogmatic theology in general. "There was no need for him as a Christian to take dogmatic theology seriously."[85] Yet even liberal Protestants have some stake in dogmatics; as Wrede noticed, the recognition that historical criticism had "arrived conquering" spawned a generation of theological camp followers who longed to incorporate the new insights of historical scholarship into a modern dogmatic setting.[86] For would-be New Testament theologians who accepted Wrede's historicism but longed to develop more specifically the relation of the history of early Christian religion to contemporary dogmatics, one step was missing: the step which might relate the disciplines Wrede had torn apart (in the name of autonomy). Krister Stendahl bridged this aporia: he proposed that the offhand dismissal of dog-

---

[84]*Paul*, trans. Edward Lummis (London: Philip Green, 1907) 177.
[85]*The Nature of New Testament Theology*, 22.
[86]"Biblische Kritik und theologisches Studium," 42 ("erobernd aufgetreten ist").

matics was a casual anticipation of a relation that could be formalized by clarifying the roles that pertained to each discipline.

## • Stendahl's "Meant"/"Means" Distinction •

It is difficult to overstate the extent to which Krister Stendahl's "Biblical Theology" contribution to the *Interpreter's Dictionary of the Bible*[87] has been accepted as standard by the discipline of biblical studies. Ben Ollenburger submits that "the distinctions for which Stendahl pleaded have come to be seen as virtually axiomatic, and self-evidently so";[88] no contribution to the discussion of biblical (or more specifically New Testament) theology can fail to address the guidelines Stendahl establishes therein. It is in this article that Stendahl sets up his enormously influential distinctions between "what the text meant" and "what it means," between the descriptive and normative tasks of theology, and between the role of the biblical theologian and the systematic theologian. Stendahl's program has been so widely acknowledged that he could reprint this essay (without consequential changes) twenty years later as the keystone of his book *Meanings*.[89]

Stendahl begins his definition of "Contemporary Biblical Theology" with a rapid survey of past explanations of biblical theology, which leads to the pivotal emergence of a "New Stage for Biblical

---

[87]Krister Stendahl, "Biblical Theology, Contemporary," *Interpreter's Dictionary of the Bible* (Nashville: Abingdon Press, 1962) A-D:418-32. Though Stendahl discusses some of the past theorists he sees as important precursors of his position, he mentions Wrede only in the concluding bibliography.

[88]"What Krister Stendahl 'Meant'—A Normative Critique of 'Descriptive Biblical Theology'," *Horizons in Biblical Theology* 8 (1986): 61-98.

[89](Philadelphia: Fortress Press, 1984). In the interim, he restated the necessity for his distinctions in—among other essays—"Method in the Study of Biblical Theology," in *The Bible in Modern Scholarship*, ed. J. P. Hyatt (Nashville: Abingdon Press, 1965) 196-216, and in "The Bible as a Classic and the Bible as Holy Scripture," *Journal of Biblical Literature* 103 (1984): 3-10.

Theology," "a new phenomenon in biblical studies," that of the "descriptive study of biblical thought."[90] The new phase, descriptive New Testament theology, sees the importance of the *religionsgeschichtliche Schule*, which emphasized the particular, time-conditioned character of the New Testament texts. Therefore descriptive New Testament theology locates the texts in their own time, for fear of "modernizing."

> The distance between biblical times and modern times was stressed, and the difference between biblical thought and systematic theology became much more than that of diversification over against systematization or of concrete exemplification over against abstract propositions.[91]

Stendahl specifies three ways in which descriptive New Testament theology differs from its antecedents. First, such developmental schemes as are applied to the New Testament writings are less axiologically charged; "progress" and "degeneration" are not necessary aspects of development. Instead, the various texts are treated in their own terms. Second, the question of factual reference recedes in importance as the *Sitz im Leben* becomes increasingly important. The privileged question is not "whether it happened," but "why it would be reported to have happened." Finally, "the question about relevance for present-day religion and

---

[90]"Contemporary Biblical Theology," 418, col. 2; "Biblical Theology: A Program," 12, 13 (hereafter page numbers for the latter essay will simply be enclosed in brackets after the reference to the *IDB* definition). Though Stendahl's essay is entitled with reference to biblical theology, and though he does devote some space to questions of O.T. interpretation, he concentrates on N.T. theology throughout his work. Since the emphasis of this book is upon N.T. theology, and since Stendahl himself concedes that in his work the relation of biblical theology to N.T. and O.T. theology is one of formal identity ("Method in the Study," 198), I refer throughout this section to "New Testament theology" and "theologians" even where Stendahl use the more general "biblical theology/theologians."

[91]"Contemporary Biblical Theology," 418, col. 2 [13].

faith was waived, or consciously kept out of sight." These distinguishing characteristics—summed up in the divergence between what a text meant and what it means—set the stage upon which a "radically new," modern New Testament theology might appear.[92]

Stendahl divides the interpretive backdrop against which descriptive biblical theology shines so brightly into the errors of conservatism and of liberalism. The conservative, or orthodox, interpreters undertook expositions of New Testament theology which assumed that the entire biblical witness was available for harmonization and systematization into dogmatic characters; the liberals recognized that there were time-conditioned strands of biblical tradition, and sought to edit them out. For orthodox interpreters, the whole was relevant; for liberals, only the residuum. In both cases, however, the criteria for determining relevance elided the hard questions posed by the *religionsgeschichtliche Schule*. Descriptive New Testament theology welcomes "the experience of the distance and strangeness of biblical thought as a creative asset, rather than as a destructive and burdensome liability."[93] Others had recognized the gap; only descriptive New Testament theology celebrates it.

Stendahl follows his initial characterization of descriptive biblical theology with an analysis of three approaches to New Testament theology: Barth's, Bultmann's, and Cullmann's. Stendahl finds Barth's interpretation of Romans inadequate to the extent that it self-consciously denies the problem of the chronological-hermeneutical gap. Barth dissolves the tension between "meant" and "means," which descriptive biblical theology had worked so hard to hammer out. "What is intended as a commentary turns out to be a theological tractate,"[94] and, like shellfish or pork, must be avoided. From Stendahl's point of view, Barth simply forfeits the insights of modern New Testament theology.

---

[92]"Contemporary Biblical Theology," 418-19 [13-14].
[93]"Contemporary Biblical Theology," 420, col. 1 [16].
[94]"Contemporary Biblical Theology," 420, col. 2 [17].

Rudolf Bultmann's New Testament theology, on the other hand, fails Stendahl's standards because it minimizes the element of particularity that the *religionsgeschichtliche Schule* stressed. Bultmann interprets the New Testament kerygma in a way that de-emphasizes the time-bound aspects of the ancient text, but Stendahl objects that this illegitimately dehistoricizes the message that Bultmann presents. Stendahl argues that it is incorrect for Bultmann to assume from the outset that the New Testament texts are relevant to the present; it is precisely this relevance that descriptive biblical theology has to ignore in favor of presenting the text on its own terms.[95]

Cullmann, according to Stendahl, has the proper emphasis on the texts' own understanding of their historical character, but he does not develop the relation of this "religious philosophy of history" to the present. The descriptive quality of Cullmann's work is beyond criticism, but he implicitly supposes that this itself constitutes the whole of the task of biblical theology. Stendahl, however, objects that Cullmann ought explicitly to disown the possibility that his reconstruction of the texts' original intent may be transferred directly to the twentieth century. All three scholars fail to maintain the tension between "meant" and "means" on which the legitimacy of descriptive New Testament theology hangs.

Does the failure of these critics imply that descriptive New Testament theology will remain nothing but an unattainable ideal instance? Stendahl thinks not. While no one is purely objective, scholars can attain a sufficient degree of critical objectivity to find out what the authors and speakers whose words are recorded in the New Testament meant. So, for example, agnostic, Christian, and Jew all can cooperate in the task of descriptive biblical theology, because their faith commitments affect only the task of developing "what the text meant" into a systematic-theological presentation. The only legitimate approach to a descriptive Old Testament theology is based not on categories drawn from New Testa-

---

[95]It is not to be assumed that Bultmann would agree that he wasn't presenting an accurate explanation of the text's own terms.

ment or later Christian or Jewish interpretation but from "the very life situations out of which the OT material emerges as meaningful to the life of the people."[96] Such an approach systematically prescinds from addressing the question of whether the Christian (or rabbinic) interpretation of the Old Testament might be right; that, according to Stendahl, is not a question for historians to answer.

The descriptive study of biblical theology can, however, provide a correct basis for construing the Old and New Testaments as a unity. Since the New Testament—like the Old Testament—sees its addressees as participants in the history of a chosen people, descriptive biblical theology can formulate an accurate theology oriented toward this theme. Since it is descriptive study that underlines this common theological viewpoint, Stendahl feels justified in reporting that his analysis "yields the original in its own terms," and that therefore he has outlined "*that unity that actually holds the material together in the Bible itself.*"[97]

This sort of descriptive work is necessary for the New Testament theologian who recognizes the full extent of the hermeneutical problem of relating an ancient text to the contemporary world. The present has seen an unparalleled emphasis on the difference of the first-century context of the biblical texts from their contemporary situation, along with a tremendous increase in the sophistication of the tools for examining the ancient context, according to Stendahl. Moreover, the theological tradition has tended toward metaphysical speculation as to the nature of God, of Christ, and so on, in a way which is alien to the way that the Bible itself concentrates on particular historical descriptions of things God did, or what Jesus said. Therefore, Stendahl claims, we need a new hermeneutical approach that accounts for these developments; and he presents his two-stage hermeneutic as this desired new approach.

An alleged advantage of Stendahl's isolation of the descriptive task from the subsequent dogmatic enterprise is that a thorough

---

[96]"Contemporary Biblical Theology," 423, col . 2 [25].

[97]"Contemporary Biblical Theology," 425, col . 1 [29]; the emphasis in the second quotation is Stendahl's.

descriptive New Testament theology would provide a criterion for judging prior attempts of systematic theologians to express the truth of Scripture "for the present day."[98] Liberal theology's interpretation of the Bible in terms of "an evermore-refined religious insight with a higher level of ethics" would be possible, provided it were recognized that "its categories of meaning were utterly alien to biblical thought."[99] Likewise the romantic primitivism that found in everything Semitic an ideal from which the Hellenic represented a fatal decline errs by trying to shoehorn a "biblical" point of view onto a modern consciousness to which it is utterly alien. And the theologies of Paul Tillich and Rudolf Bultmann— juxtaposed because Stendahl finds that both tend toward the "antihistorical"—can be judged by the extent to which they reflect the Bible's intention (as discovered by descriptive biblical theology).[100]

Stendahl also sees the existence of the canon as an impetus to his two-stage hermeneutics. He argues that the decision to set certain writings apart as canonical implies the necessity of interpreting them on their own terms before applying them to other circumstances. The scriptural texts are valuable to the church in whatever age precisely to the extent that they stand over against whatever the church has made of them in the interim. They are the "original," of which all theologies (whether "biblical" or "systematic") are translations, and they exercise their function as a check on wayward theological trends only when they are first understood on the terms of descriptive biblical theology.

Just as the Reformation showed an interest in the critical function of the New Testament over against the contemporary church's

---

[98]"Or," as Stendahl notes, "for all times, if that is their conscious aim." "Contemporary Biblical Theology," 427, col. 1 [34]. This, despite Stendahl's disingenuous claim in "Method in the Study" that "the descriptive task has no claim or intention toward the normative" (199).

[99]"Contemporary Biblical Theology," 427, col. 2 [34-35].

[100]Tillich receives Stendahl's imprimatur because his analysis of Being "is capable of communicating a wider range of biblical intention than does Bultmann with his highly anthropological concentration" ("Contemporary Biblical Theology," 428, col. 1 [36]).

theology, Stendahl reckons that the current fascination with the circumstances of the church's origins may be vitally therapeutic for current dogmatics. Stendahl urges that New Testament theologians immerse themselves in the original texts, rather than perpetuate the chain of interpreters, whereby Augustine interpreted the Fathers, Aquinas interpreted Augustine, Luther interpreted Aquinas, Schleiermacher Luther, Barth and Tillich each refurbishing Schleiermacher, and so on. As an illustration, Stendahl suggests that the adoptionist Christology that many New Testament writings express might be deemed "most orthodox" at a time when the church had outgrown the ontological speculations that are congealed into the creeds.

Stendahl's essay concludes with the observation that his argument for descriptive New Testament theology is particularly important to preachers, who are especially responsible to mediate the ancient testimony to contemporary auditors. It is therefore all the more important that preachers attend to Stendahl's distinction, lest they propound "a strange—sometimes even beautiful—mixed tongue, a homiletical Yiddish which cannot be really understood outside the walls of the Christian ghetto."[101] Stendahl submits that since the task of New Testament theology entails bringing the original meaning of the Bible into relation with twentieth-century reality, "we cannot pursue the study of biblical theology adequately if the two tenses ["meant" and "means"] are not kept apart."[102]

## • Stendahl's Modernity •

Stendahl seems actively to seek out modernity; his essay, after all, comes with a built-in chronological modifier (*"Contemporary* Biblical Theology") that distinguishes it from the countless earlier attempts to define biblical theology. One ought not push this circumstance too hard; it is not clear that Stendahl was in any way responsible for the organization of the *Interpreter's Dictionary of the Bible* entries on biblical theology ("Contemporary" and "History

---

[101]"Contemporary Biblical Theology," 430, col. 2 [42].
[102]"Contemporary Biblical Theology," 431, col. 1 [44].

of"). Stendahl did change the title (to "Biblical Theology: A Program") when he incorporated the essay into *Meanings*; at the same time, the new title implies the essay's status as a revolutionary manifesto, a very modern phenomenon. He likewise refers to a biblical theology consonant with his program as "modern biblical theology,"[103] and the first section of his essay bears the heading, "A New Stage Set for Biblical Theology."[104] His proposed radical emphasis on the original context of the biblical writings marks his descriptive biblical theology as decisively new. At every turn, he distinguishes his new descriptive approach sharply from past approaches which did not adequately come to terms with the differences between the two tasks Stendahl assigns to New Testament theology.[105] Previous interpreters, though they receive some positive attention, must be put aside in descriptive New Testament theology. Their theological interpretation amounts to nothing but "heavy layers of interpretation" from which the modern scholar must "liberate" the Scriptures.[106] The golden chain of "precritical" interpreters must be broken; they were not sufficiently attuned to "what it meant," so that their estimates of "what it means" (dubious from the beginning, since it is no longer the time to which they addressed their interpretations) are necessarily misleading.[107]

---

[103]"Contemporary Biblical Theology," 419, col. 1 [14]. Brevard Childs summarizes this portion of the essay as saying, "the fundamental element which differentiates *modern* biblical theology from all earlier theological endeavors is its recognition of the descriptive task" ("Interpretation in Faith," *Interpretation* 18 [1964]: 434; my emphasis).

[104]"Contemporary Biblical Theology," 418 [12]. On 419, col. 1 [14], this stage has become radically new (his emphasis).

[105]Consider "Contemporary Biblical Theology," 425, col. 2 [29-30]: "No period of Christian theology has been as radically exposed to a consistent attempt to relive the theology of its first adherents. The ideal of an empathetic understanding of the first century without borrowing categories from later times has never been an ideal before. . . . But never before was there a frontal, nonapologetic attempt to describe OT or NT faith."

[106]"Method in the Study," 205.

[107]Cf. "Contemporary Biblical Theology," 430, col. 1 [40-41].

Exactly the strict division of labor into "descriptive" and "normative" tasks once again recalls the modern concern for scientific autonomy. Just as Wrede was content to shrug that the dogmatic import of his New Testament theology was not his business, so Stendahl insists strenuously that the complement to descriptive New Testament theology—"normative biblical theology"—is the task of the systematician. He marks the gesture with which the New Testament theologian distances herself from "the question of relevance for present-day religion and faith" as a sign of the emergence of modern biblical theology.[108] "We are anxious," he observes, "to leave the assessment of these matters to the systematic theologian."[109] Most New Testament scholars, he points out, are unqualified to speculate on theological matters. Modern New Testament theology is most clearly seen, according to Stendahl, by the respect it shows for the separation of these two tasks. He likewise warns, frequently, of the baneful effects of methodological miscegenation, of the "wide variety of hybrids where biblical and systematic categories were hopelessly intermingled."[110] If we do not distinguish the two disciplines rigorously, how will we tell one from the other? The New Testament theologian who minimizes the "meant"/"means" distinction runs the risk of slipping into the "mixed tongue" which, Stendahl suggests, threatens to degenerate into "an inarticulate language."[111]

Modernity's chronological determinism runs through Stendahl's essay as well. Indeed, the "meant"/"means" distinction that lies at the heart of Stendahl's program is a perfect instance of this modern trait. It trades upon the axiom of the chronological gulf that separates the contemporary interpreter from the text (though Stendahl's case requires a slightly different metaphor: here, a fog of intervening ages conceals the original meaning of the text from

---

[108]The quoted passage is from "Contemporary Biblical Theology," 419, col. 1 [13].

[109]"Method in the Study," 205.

[110]"Contemporary Biblical Theology," 427, col. 1 [34].

[111]"Contemporary Biblical Theology," 422, col. 1 [21].

the interpreter).[112] He can simply assume a tension between "past and present meaning"; the *religionsgeschichtliche Schule* freed New Testament scholars from "anachronistic interpretation" and forced them "to accept the hiatus between the ideas and ideals in the biblical materials" and the ideas of the twentieth century.[113] There is a barrier of "distance" and "strangeness" which some New Testament scholars may find "a creative asset," while others find it "a destructive and burdensome liability," but which Stendahl assumes all must recognize.[114]

This distance separating reader from text justifies Stendahl's subsequent insistence on the necessity of a descriptive account of what the text meant in the first place, of what the naked text might look like if it were not obscured by the clouds of witnesses. So Stendahl stresses that the descriptive task of determining what the text meant is necessary to understand the texts "in [their] own terms," "in [their] original setting," "when uttered or written," "within the presupposition of their respective centuries," and so on.[115]

Stendahl diverges from the physiognomy of modernity at one point: he does not explicitly express the characteristic elitism of modernity, which Gabler and Wrede expressed by emphasizing the sophistication required for theological reflection (as opposed to the simplicity of the average person's religion). But even here, Stendahl shows tendencies to make of New Testament theologians an academic caste. Despite such disclaimers as the assurance that "we

---

[112]Stendahl does use the "gap" metaphor (cf. "Contemporary Biblical Theology," 428, col. 2 [37]), though he uses it to disarm the implication that there is no way from here to there; the "chasm" is bridged by history itself. This point fits his overall argument poorly, since he is obliged elsewhere to claim that the interpretive history which connects "then" to "now" is unreliable—thus necessitating the descriptive task of recovering "what it meant."

[113]"Contemporary Biblical Theology," 419, col. 2 [15].

[114]"Contemporary Biblical Theology," 420, col. 1 [16].

[115]"Contemporary Biblical Theology," 422, col. 1; 430, col. 2; 422, col. 1; 426, col. 2 [21, 42, 22, 33].

would have to make very clear that the descriptive task has no claim or intention to the normative," Stendahl goes on to envision for New Testament theologians the role of "the 'public health' task of theology."[116] The exercise of this sort of "public health" function requires a special sort of knowledge, and implies the normative authority which Stendahl elsewhere specifically disclaims. At this point Stendahl is evidently inclining toward a modern construction of elite specialization and authority.

The family resemblance that unites the positions Gabler, Wrede, and Stendahl developed for New Testament theology is unmistakable, and it points strongly to the physiognomy of modernity outlined in the first chapter. All three see themselves overturning the misleading interpretive policies of the past (Gabler rejecting prooftexting, Wrede "doctrinal concepts," Stendahl the confusion of "meant" with "means"). For all three, the radically new step involves recognition of the time-conditioned character of the ancient text; whereas their opponents overlook or deny the distance that separates the modern reader from the New Testament text, these scholars stress that distance (and, at the same time, propose that the "other" of New Testament theology, the dogmatician/systematician, is determined by relation to the present). They argue that the proper way to deal with the chronological gap involves the separation of the historical, descriptive task of deciding what the New Testament writings meant from the dogmatic, constructive task of construing the relation of these ancient meanings to Christian life today. And Gabler and Wrede (and Stendahl too, to an extent) present this as the task of a highly trained, sophisticated cadre of reflective scholars who will refine crude religion into complex theology, for the health of simple believers.

---

[116]"Method in the Study," 199; "Meanings," in *Meanings*, 4.

# Chapter 3

# The Modern Consensus in New Testament Theology

*Modern exegesis of the Bible is rooted in Deism and Enlightenment.*
—Heikki Räisänen

The modern consensus in New Testament theology surfaces not only in the foundational texts of Gabler, Wrede, and Stendahl, but also in the work of the preponderance of contemporary New Testament theologians. The claims Gabler and his heirs struggled to establish have become dogmas for a distinctly modern period of New Testament theology. Though an increasing number of writers express dissatisfaction with the shape of contemporary New Testament theology, the assumptions that undergird the modern form of the enterprise remain intact.

The modern definition of New Testament theology has become so commonly accepted that it seems natural or necessary. Might it be the case, then, that Gabler et al. do not so much sponsor a "modern New Testament theology" as they enunciate the actual ruling sentiment of New Testament theologians? In other words, is there anything *but* modern New Testament theology? The answer is ambivalent.

On one hand, current New Testament theologies almost all bow to the prevailing standards enshrined by modern scholars. At this point, it is important to remember that New Testament theology has come by its modernity not by a process of self-conscious decisions—"The various fields of art, architecture, dance, physics, and so on all have distinctively modern forms; perhaps we New

Testament theologians ought to as well"—but under specific conditions that promote the expansion and reproduction of "modern" enterprises and hinder the reproduction of "traditional" or "outdated" ideas. It is perhaps this unselfconscious quality that warrants Joseph O'Leary's argument that theology as a whole has not yet attained modernity.[1]

On the other hand, the continuing existence of nonmodern New Testament theologies is attested very simply by the polemic modern New Testament theologians direct against their opponents. If there were no other approaches to New Testament theology, there would be no others to denigrate.

In fact, however, modern New Testament theology has been visibly different from various other options all along. Amos Wilder submits that biblical theology of the modern period shares the rationalism and historicism he finds characteristic of modernity in general. He notes that the New Testament theologies to which he is referring show no interest in their relevance to contemporary life, focusing instead on an interest in the ancient context itself.[2] Likewise, Clarence T. Craig argued for a "modern revival" of biblical theology, based on the insights of the *religionsgeschichtliche Schule* and following the general strictures set out by Wrede.[3] Craig

---

[1]"Theology on the Brink of Modernism," *Boundary* 2 13 (1985): 145-56.

[2]"New Testament Theology in Transition," 420. Though Wilder (writing in 1947) identifies modern biblical theology with the path from Gabler through Wrede, at the same time he believes this period has come to an end. He notes that historical method is coming under increased self-criticism and that "modern man" is less interested in history (420-21). From a perspective nearly a half-century later than Wilder's essay, it is hard to see that interest in "the historical" has diminished; on the contrary, it has deepened, taking more varied routes (sociological, structural, literary, rhetorical, and so on). Similarly, the self-criticism in historical inquiry that Wilder saw was quickly overwhelmed by a backlash of historical confidence epitomized by such sophisticated works as Van Harvey's *The Historian and the Believer* (Philadelphia: Westminster Press, 1966) to which I will devote more consideration below.

[3]"Biblical Theology and the Rise of Historicism," 289ff.

decries "modernizing" the ancient text, and insists that historical analysis is the only way to understand the Bible; he warns that the danger represented by calls for a more satisfactorily theological exegesis of the New Testament "can be met only as men of sound historical training accept the challenge to interpret the meaning of Christian faith."[4]

Although virtually all prominent New Testament theologies of the twentieth century are more-or-less modern, there appears to be one modern New Testament theology par excellence: Rudolf Bultmann's *Theology of the New Testament*.[5] Bultmann is well known as a brilliant historical critic; he wrote the best-known form-critical study of the gospels, his *History of the Synoptic Tradition*[6] (to which he refers in his *Theology*). Bultmann's *Theology* is manifestly informed throughout by his historical-critical judgments—from the relative inaccessibility of Jesus to historical research, to the critical explication of the Pauline kerygma, to the reconstruction of the earliest stratum of the theology of John's Gospel. He is well known for emphasizing the epistemological consequences of the temporal gap that separates modern readers from a message cloaked in obsolescent mythological terms. The methodological reflections with which he closes his *Theology* show that he explicitly eschews an interest in systematic or dogmatic theology; he prefers to elucidate the individual theological positions of the various writings of the New Testament.[7] He argues for a difference between "religion" (which is "an existential attitude") and "theology" (which is "the explication of believing comprehension"),[8] and he clearly stands in the *Wredestrasse*'s evaluation of Paul and John as the only *real* theologians in the New Testament. In short, there is prima facie evidence that the outstanding New Testament theology of the twenti-

---

[4]"Biblical Theology and the Rise of Historicism," 294.

[5]*Theology of the New Testament*, 2 vols., trans. Kendrick Grobel (New York: Charles Scribner's Sons, 1951, 1955).

[6]*History of the Synoptic Tradition*, trans. John Marsh (Oxford: Basil Blackwell; New York: Harper & Row, 1963).

[7]*Theology of the New Testament*, 2:239.

[8]*Theology of the New Testament*, 2:247, 238.

eth century is a distinctively *modern* New Testament theology, and Bultmann's work has been read as such by polemical opponents such as Alan Richardson and Karl Barth—even though his use of the ideas of "history" is much more subtle than is common among *modern* interpreters, and his whole project is nuanced in ways that belie the complaints of most of Bultmann's critics.[9]

Alan Richardson likewise makes methodological statements that explicitly align him with modern New Testament theologians. In such articles as "Biblical Theology and the Modern Mind," "Historical Theology and Biblical Theology," "Present Issues in New Testament Theology," and "What Is New Testament Theology?" Richardson has recognized that history is the make-or-break problem for twentieth-century interpreters;[10] he claims that no one can see through the eyes of first-century Christians, nor can we any longer even see through the eyes of our theological predecessors.[11] The question of history is for Richardson the cardinal point of New Testament theology, which he defines as "the attempt to reconstruct by means of critical historical research from the evidence of the New Testament and of its total environment the

---

[9]Cf. Gareth Jones's *Bultmann: Towards a Critical Theology* (London: Polity Press, 1991) and Schubert Ogden's pointed response in *Modern Theology* 8 (1992) that together shed considerable light on Bultmann's subtle appreciation of problems that many of his colleagues elide. In chap. 6, below, I will propose a reading of Bultmann's *Theology of the New Testament* that—while it abandons certain positions to which Bultmann would surely hold fast—illustrates some ways Bultmann goes beyond the limitations of modern New Testament theology.

[10]"Biblical Theology and the Modern Mind," *Theology* 39 (1939): 244-52; "Historical Theology and Biblical Theology," *Canadian Journal of Theology* 1 (1955): 157-67; "Second Thoughts. III. Present Issues in New Testament Theology," *Expository Times* 75 (1963/1964): 109-13; "What Is New Testament Theology?" *Studia Evangelica* 6, ed. Elizabeth A. Livingstone (Berlin: Akademie-Verlag, 1973) 455-65.

[11]"Second Thoughts," 109. He is referring here to Bultmann, and it is patently an open question whether seeing through Bultmann's eyes—at least, approximately—is as hard for all interpreters as it is for Richardson.

origin and significance of Christian faith."[12] In harmony with this commitment to the role of historical explanation in New Testament theology, Richardson accepts Stendahl's formulation of the "meant"/"means" distinction.

Richardson, however, is not finally a *modern* New Testament theologian. His *Introduction to the Theology of the New Testament* is, for example, the object of a vehemently negative review by Leander Keck, whose criticisms of Richardson provide a pertinent illustration of modern New Testament theology with which we may begin a survey of the extent to which modern criteria define contemporary reflection on New Testament theology.[13]

The scope of Keck's critique is remarkable; no doubt because his argument with Richardson has a methodological basis, Keck concentrates especially on Richardson's preface and table of contents. Keck notes that although Richardson pays lip service to historical criticism, he undermines that commitment by positing that the traditional Christian faith provides "a more coherent and rationally satisfying 'history'" than any alternative.[14] Richardson admits that "no pretense is made of remaining within the limits of purely descriptive science," an admission which itself clearly places Richardson outside the limits defined by the modern New Testament theologians. This admission is diametrically opposed to Stendahl's insistence that New Testament theology be restricted to the descriptive task. Keck points this out, suggesting that Richardson blurs the necessary distinction of past and present meaning. Keck likewise wonders whether Richardson's insistence that New Testament theology be formulated with an eye to the concerns of the least sophisticated Christians ("the Sunday sermon, the Bible class, the catechism, and indeed the whole life of the local

---

[12]"What Is New Testament Theology?" 455.

[13]Alan Richardson, *An Introduction to the Theology of the New Testament* (London: SCM Press, 1958); Leander Keck, "Problems of New Testament Theology," *Novum Testamentum* 7 (1964/1965): 217-41.

[14]"Problems of New Testament Theology," 218, quoting Richardson's *Introduction*, 13.

church"[15]) does not indicate that Richardson is unaware of how complicated the hermeneutical problem of New Testament theology really is.

Keck's final criticism of Richardson's *Introduction* subjects the book's topical arrangement to the complaint that an order that is topical—rather than developmental and individualized by author—obscures the pivotal scheme of development by which earlier New Testament writers influenced their later colleagues. In all these points, Keck finds that (Richardson's programmatic assertions to the contrary notwithstanding[16]) Richardson shows no sensitivity to the necessity of historical foundations for New Testament theology.

Keck's concluding summary points exactly to the characteristics of modern New Testament theology as it is reflected in the work of Gabler, Wrede, and Stendahl. First, Richardson opts for continuity with the Ancients of the interpretive tradition: Augustine stands in the index next to Aulén, Cranfield with Cranmer, Jülicher with Justin Martyr. Second, Richardson neglects the inestimable chronological gap that separates the alien worldview of the New Testament from contemporary readers. Keck finds it "painful" that Richardson so calmly assumes that we can understand "ideas and concepts from which our estrangement is clear and far advanced."[17] Third, Richardson contaminates the disciplinary purity of his work by mixing historical with theological warrants. Finally, Keck condemns Richardson's commitment to the catechetical task of New Testament theology: on Keck's account,

---

[15]*Introduction*, 14.

[16]I do not want to suggest that Richardson ever sees the historical task in the same way as Keck. In fact, it is precisely Richardson's understanding of history which Van Harvey assails in *The Historian and the Believer*; Richardson argues for the propriety of a Christian construal of history (comparable to a Marxist, or feminist, or Hegelian construal). Richardson sees *this* historical background as justifiable and necessary; Keck (with Harvey) responds that this is not proper *history* at all.

[17]"Problems of New Testament Theology," 239.

"to most men biblical jargon sounds like jibberish."[18] The trouble with Richardson's New Testament theology, in a nutshell, is that it is not *modern* enough.[19]

What is particularly interesting about the obituary Keck offers for Richardson's book[20] is that Keck and Richardson are in agreement regarding many of the basic formal criteria in question. They agree about the importance of history, but disagree about the extent to which the New Testament theology is continuous with the dogmatic tradition of the church. They agree that there is a chronological gap (the "meant"/"means" gap) that separates the modern interpreter from the ancient text. They agree that New Testament theology entails a historical investigation into the origins of Christian faith (although Keck insists that Richardson fails to present a truly *historical* survey). Evidently, neither Keck nor Richardson doubts that a New Testament theology depends on particular historical warrants, that there is a significant chronological gap separating the contemporary interpreter from the ancient text, or that this interpretive work lies in the domain of experts.[21]

These interpretive assumptions continue to hold firm in the field of New Testament theology. Though the stream of articles on the theory and method of New Testament theology continues unabated, the principal advice these articles have to offer is, in effect, to pursue the goals of modern New Testament theology

---

[18]"Problems of New Testament Theology," 240.

[19]In view of the fact that in subsequent chapters I will call into question the necessity of modern New Testament theology's criteria, it is important to stress here that I am not doing so in order to rehabilitate Richardson. There are other serious problems with his theological construal of the New Testament; Keck notes some of these, and others linger even if specifically *modern* criteria are discounted.

[20]Keck refers to the book's "fatal flaw" (234) and his "fatal" misunderstanding of *dogmengeschichte* (235); Richardson's inadequacies "seal the doom of this way of writing the theology of the New Testament" (238).

[21]Once again, Richardson *handles* these assumptions in ways very different from Keck's ways; this is surely one source of the friction between these two interpretive stances.

*better*, or *more thoroughly*, or *without being distracted by peripheral concerns* (or even "more in keeping with what this author thinks is right"). Thus contemporary essays on New Testament theology argue from a set of axioms that depend on the prior validity of what I have described as modern assumptions. Scholars do not allude to their assumptions explicitly—they are assumptions, not premises—but certain typical patterns of argument in New Testament theology reveal these scholars' common allegiance to these modern assumptions.

## • The Moral Necessity of Modern New Testament Theology •

These assumptions come to the fore most clearly when scholars argue that New Testament theology should be conducted on the basis of the norms for inquiry into any other field. This was the demand Van Harvey set before biblical interpreters in *The Historian and the Believer*.[22] Harvey argued that "a certain morality of knowledge"[23] obliges biblical interpreters to adopt the same procedures and criteria as historians in other fields. Though Harvey credited Troeltsch with the fundamental insights on this point, Harvey himself elaborated them more clearly and more forcefully than anyone before or since.

Harvey assailed biblical interpreters whose theological interests cloud their capacity to make sound historical judgments—a group which at the time the book was written included virtually every interpreter who had picked up the Bible.[24] Harvey, like Keck, singled out Alan Richardson for particular derision; like Keck, Harvey was particularly irritated by the fact that Richardson did not repudiate the rules of historical inquiry, but *blurred* and *bent* them.

---

[22]See 106n., above. Though *The Historian and the Believer* is not an essay on New Testament theology itself, Harvey is immediately concerned with theological interpretation of the New Testament, and deals with just the methodological questions which concern this essay.

[23]*Historian and Believer*, xi and passim.

[24]Harvey seems sympathetic only to Schubert Ogden and Fritz Buri.

What does Harvey require of interpreters? His overriding concern is that biblical interpreters not indulge in special pleading when they make their claims. It seems a simple enough desideratum, yet Harvey finds that interpreters typically deploy fallacious arguments to justify historical judgments (at least, *ostensibly* historical judgments, since Harvey argues that these decisions are not strictly historical enough). Interpreters sometimes claim that the standards Harvey presses are secular, rationalist standards, and are therefore intrinsically incapable of generating sufficient justification for Christian interpretive truth-claims. They go on to suggest that inasmuch as there is no such thing as an uninterpreted "fact," that the very "facts" the historical perspective adduces are always already saturated with rationalist presuppositions.[25] Harvey calls this "Hard Perspectivism," and responds that if there are truth-claims whose justification rests upon warrants that are unavailable to secular rational deliberation, then the very notion of "truth" has dissolved; a "truth," according to Harvey, *must* be amenable to rational assessment, or it degrades to a perspective. "[This] argument fails to dispel a feeling of dissatisfaction, a feeling that the word 'fact' cannot be telescoped into the word 'interpretation' without a certain loss, a feeling that the word 'truth' cannot be defined simply in terms of the coherence of a perspective."[26] Harvey finds this argument deficient because it asks that interlocutors commit themselves to the truth of a perspective before they could possibly assess the truth-claims that perspective makes. Moreover, most such arguments contradict themselves by asserting that the Christian perspective is correct—an evaluation they could not know, inasmuch as (on their own account) they cannot adequately judge their interlocutors' arguments.[27]

Some other interpreters suggest that the distinction between perspectives is not so stark as the previous argument implies;

---

[25]Harvey cites Alan Richardson as a paradigm case of this argument: *Historian and Believer*, 205ff.

[26]*Historian and Believer*, 208.

[27]*Historian and Believer*, 204-30.

instead, the divergence of Christian and secular interpreters comes in the interpretation of facts concerning which both camps can agree. Thus the theological interpreter of the Bible and the secular historian share reference to a narrative of the actual events and their relations to one another; what separates the two is the biblical interpreter's conviction that the truth about these events goes beyond the events themselves to a posited relation of these events to God.[28] Harvey calls this "Soft Perspectivism," and grants that this is probably the approach that best reconciles theological interests and historical rigor, so long as theological interpreters do not slip into "Hard Perspectivism," and so long as interpreters avoid the mistaken supposition that there might be exactly *one* Christian perspective. Harvey grants that Christians will interpret the facts that historical science uncovers in a way different from secular interpreters; the catch is that Harvey doubts that the facts historical inquiry can establish will satisfy most interpreters (and he can cite a long list of scholars who have felt an obligation to explain why one or another "event" must be counted a fact despite its failure to satisfy Troeltsch's criteria). Moreover, Harvey points out that Christian theology typically treats at least some of the events narrated in the Bible as having intrinsic, once-for-all importance—but the concession that secular historians have equal access to the facts of history precludes precisely this possibility (otherwise, historians would necessarily miss a vitally important fact about the event in question).

Harvey suggests that the concept "historical method" embraces not only methodological issues, but also the autonomy of historical inquiry and the historian's obligation to provide criteria by which one might assess his or her claims rationally. This complex of principles is the specifically historical branch of a more general "morality of knowledge," a term Harvey uses to describe the con-

---

[28]Though Harvey points out that Richardson uses this argument as well as the preceding one, the leading exemplar of this approach is H. Richard Niebuhr, in *The Meaning of Revelation* (New York: Macmillan, 1947).

victions about knowledge and scholarship that "[have] seized the imagination of the scholar in the Western world."[29] Harvey argues that this intellectual ethic obliges all who would speak about historical knowledge to verify their claims with respect to the complex "historical method." Since Harvey points out that all knowledge has some or another historical component, the force of his argument is that before theological interpreters may make truth-claims, they must obtain *nihil obstats* from historians who adhere to the new morality of knowledge. Theological knowledge depends upon historical knowledge (very stringently defined historical knowledge, at that).[30] By the same token, no historical assertion about Jesus can ground Christian faith, inasmuch as the historical facts about Jesus can be significant only if faith is already present.

---

[29]*Historian and Believer*, 38.

[30]Harvey uses a more ruthless historical scalpel in operating upon his colleagues than in formulating his own judgments concerning Jesus (a criticism he obliquely acknowledges in the preface to the paperback edition of *Historian and Believer* when, on p. xvi, he reminds his reader that he claims only the status of "the sketch of the outlines of a model" [alluding to p. 253] for his own proposal). He posits that we can safely grant that "we have every reason to believe that the image of his teachings and deeds [conveyed by the gospels] is a trustworthy one, despite the additions and interpolations and the lack of chronology and significant detail" (269), a claim which would raise considerable resistance in today's New Testament guild. Harvey may now be less salubrious about the general trustworthiness of the gospels than he was in 1965, or he may argue that those contemporary New Testament historians who propose that the gospels are systematic distortions of Jesus' teachings and deeds (cf. the works of Burton Mack, to name but one) are poor historians. Of course, Harvey's argument for the morality of knowledge doesn't depend on his being an exemplary New Testament interpreter, but the extent to which his own interpretive assertions appear to fall short of historical rigor illustrates some of the ambiguity which inheres in this "new morality." Would he be as satisfied with his "paradigmatic event" approach to New Testament theology if card-carrying New Testament historians gave credible reasons for doubting that Harvey's chosen paradigmatic events ever happened?

"No remote historical event—especially if assertions about it can solicit only a tentative assent—can, as such, be the basis for a religious confidence about the present. Even if it were historically probable, say, that Jesus was a man who was completely open to transcendence, this belief in no way makes it any easier for someone two thousand years later to be so open—unless, of course, the silent presupposition is present that the object of faith is the same and can be trusted."[31] Finally, since theological truth-claims must be checked against historical criteria, and since historical criteria do not permit claims to uniqueness or exclusivity,[32] theologians cannot legitimately claim that any particular event of Jesus' life was unique, or that Jesus was of exclusively decisive importance to humankind. A theologian who transgresses these guidelines violates the morality of knowledge—treating "knowledge about Jesus" as categorically different from other kinds of knowledge in order to assert truth-claims which, if they were proposed in any other intellectual arena, we would quickly recognize as special pleading. The morality of knowledge obliges New Testament theologians to be, first and foremost, New Testament historians.

Harvey argued that interpreters should adopt a strictly historical posture for the sake of intellectual integrity. More recently, Heikki Räisänen has suggested that New Testament theologians should pursue their inquiries with more historical concerns for the sake of the whole world.[33] Räisänen points out that the present social and political circumstances are so perilous and so important

---

[31]*Historian and Believer*, 282.

[32]Troeltsch's principles of analogy and correlation militate against there being any historical events which are "unique" in a nontrivial sense; Harvey makes a theme of the groundlessness of claims to uniqueness.

[33]*Beyond New Testament Theology: A Story and a Programme* (Philadelphia: Trinity Press International, 1990). Though Räisänen does not offer an argument for this claim, we may most reasonably guess that he thinks the perils of the contemporary world situation are so urgent that they exercise a preemptive claim upon the exegete's attention.

that it is the New Testament interpreter's duty to humanity to concentrate upon historical interpretation.[34]

Räisänen writes from his concern that world peace may rest upon our capacity to attain a kind of international understanding that would ultimately rest upon interreligious understanding. To that end, he claims that "the truly appropriate horizon today for biblical study (or any other discipline, for that matter) is humankind as a whole. Theology and exegesis need a global perspective, an 'ecumenical' horizon, in the original sense of the word."[35] If New Testament interpreters want so to serve humankind, they must concentrate on the historical interpretation of the early Christian literature, inasmuch as historical interpretation provides information that makes it possible for colleagues from other religious traditions to understand Christian origins. Indeed, Räisänen embraces Wrede's redefinition of New Testament theology as "the history of early Christian thought," but goes him one better by proposing that an even more appropriate task would be "the *phenomenology* of early Christian religious thought."[36] Scholars should produce such a historical phenomenology rather than a New Testament theology because the former would smooth interreligious relations, thus perhaps furthering the cause of world

---

[34]Räisänen does concede that some interpreters may choose to restrict their efforts to canonical texts or to ecclesiastically defined theological issues, but he regularly undermines this concession by stressing the global importance of historical inquiry; one must come away with the impression that Räisänen thinks that ecclesiastically interested New Testament theologians are fiddling while the rain forests burn. "Exegesis orientated on a world society cannot aim at a kerygmatic goal," and Räisänen has little use for any other orientation. Räisänen acknowledges Gerd Petzke's article "Exegese und Praxis. Die Funktion der neutestamentlichen Exegese in einer christlichen oder nachchristlichen Gesellschaft," *ThPr* 10 (1975): 2-19, as another powerful expression of this perspective.

[35]*Beyond New Testament Theology*, 96.

[36]*Beyond New Testament Theology*, 118.

peace; the latter merely serves the parochial interests of an anachronistic institution.[37]

Räisänen proposes first that scholars who are inclined to study the New Testament broaden the focus to all the literature of the early Christian movement. He can think of no justification for a scholar oriented towards social or political interests to confine one's study to the New Testament. Second, he submits that the importance of interreligious understanding (as well as the scholar's intellectual autonomy) demand that this literature be interpreted on a strictly historical basis. If scholars wish to go beyond this frontier, they must make sure their historical conclusions are rightly formed before venturing on to what Räisänen calls "actualizing interpretation."[38] "A phenomenology of early Christian thought does not answer questions about the present significance of that thought, but it must provide materials and clues to assist the reader who asks such questions."[39] Third, the interpreter will strive to keep personal commitments at a distance in order more fairly to represent the possibly alien views expressed in the early Christian literature. Finally, the emphasis of this phenomenological inquiry should be thematic, because a thematic approach permits the most lucid exposition of the development of the tradition and the ways in which social conditions influenced that development. Räisänen expects his proposals, if followed faithfully, will undermine Christian claims to exclusivity and uniqueness: "The absolutizing interpretation given by early Christians to the 'Christ-

---

[37]Räisänen thinks that we are obviously situated in a post-Christian period, so that interpretation which attends to the needs and interests of the church is "a survival from the good old days" (*Beyond New Testament Theology*, 98; cf. 95).

[38]Räisänen, like Wrede, celebrates the dilemma of the theological inquirer who is dismayed that historical criticism calls cherished beliefs into question: "This crisis should be assessed positively: it opens up the possibility that a person finds her or his way to an independent stance or to personal freedom in relation to a tradition with massive claims on him or her" (*Beyond New Testament Theology*, 112).

[39]*Beyond New Testament Theology*, 121.

event' would seem to be somewhat exaggerated—now, at the latest, from the perspective of two millenia of frustrated hope for the Kingdom of God."[40]

Both Räisänen and Harvey stress the extent to which the New Testament interpreter is accountable to public standards of "tolerance," "dialogue," "global community," and "the morality of knowledge."[41] One should not be surprised, then, to find that the standards to which their analyses appeal share the modern assumptions that mark the programmatic works of Gabler, Wrede, and Stendahl. Both Harvey's and Räisänen's books trade on the modern fixation on chronology, both stress the disciplinary divisions that distinguish historical interpretation from theological interpretation (and grant the former epistemological priority). Though neither makes a theme of the gap between interpretive experts and the untrained readers, the distinction operates in the background in both books. In other words, the way these theorists define their argument for the "public accountability" of New Testament theology is thoroughly modern.[42]

Both Harvey and Räisänen, for example, place principal emphasis on the historian's role in mediating legitimate interpretations of the literary evidence for theological reflection in ways that underline the distinction between ancient and modern, and the gap between past and present. Räisänen concentrates so exclusively on theological interpretation after Gabler (more to the point, "after Wrede") that he hardly even refers to the premodern history of interpretation; he is so committed to his particular interpretive vision that premodern interpreters do not appear even as negative illustrations (contemporary interpreters suffice for this). On the other hand, Räisänen makes passing allusions to our fall from the "pre-Gablerian state of innocence" (in a criticism of Ethelbert Stauffer's work) and to the importance of breaking with the ten-

---

[40]*Beyond New Testament Theology*, 136.

[41]*Beyond New Testament Theology*, 108, 107; *Historian and Believer*, passim.

[42]The first sentence of Räisänen's book reads: "*Modern* exegesis of the Bible is rooted in Deism and Enlightenment" (1; my emphasis).

dency from "down the ages" to treat fairly those branches of early Christianity that were later judged heretical.[43] Räisänen approves Stendahl's meant/means distinction, and evidently supports Stendahl's emphasis on "the gulf which separates the question about the historical meaning of a text from that concerning its actual significance."[44] He insists that the interpreter maintain a strict separation of the past—the textual-interpretive aspect of New Testament scholarship—from the critic's own worldview and interests in the present: "the understanding of a text takes place between two foci, the pastness of the text and the presentness of the reader."[45] Though Räisänen concedes that the interpreter cannot maintain this strict separation in practice, he submits that interpreters should preserve the separation to the extent possible, and should present the results of their work in conformity to the past/present distinction.

Harvey takes the issue of chronological determination as the *point d'appui* for his book; he refers to a "revolution in consciousness" that separates interpretation before the advent of historical consciousness from earlier interpretation; he is eager to associate his project with the adjective "modern."[46] He assents to Troeltsch's

---

[43]*Beyond New Testament Theology*, 44, 99. Though Räisänen does not discuss premodern theological interpreters, he does stress the need for *new* interpretive practices, and he apparently shares John Bowden's belief that "the problem [of constructing a synthetic New Testament theology] lies 'in the tension between the precritical understanding of the Bible so deeply embedded in the Christian tradition and the demands of truth in the modern academic world'" (ibid., 188n.16; the embedded quotation is from Bowden's *Jesus: The Unanswered Questions*, 3; cf. also Räisänen's reference to "simply . . . fall[ing] back on *precritical* modes" of interpretation (137; my emphasis).

[44]*Beyond New Testament Theology*, 75.

[45]*Beyond New Testament Theology*, 106.

[46]"Modern" clearly bears a positive valence in *The Historian and the Believer*; Harvey consistently applies it to disciplines and endeavors of which he approves: "the modern critical spirit," "modern historiography," "modern logic," and so on. By the same token, the word "traditional"

conviction that the historical-critical method marks a radical break from previous interpretations; when Troeltsch claims that "Once the historical method is applied to biblical science and church history, it is a leaven that alters everything and, finally, bursts apart the entire structure of theological methods until the present," Harvey quotes him with enthusiasm.[47] He consigns Augustine, Clement, Bernard, Francis, and Thomas Aquinas to an "age of authority, before the recovery [sic] of the historical Jesus," before "the advent of biblical criticism."[48] He contrasts "traditional" and "naïve" beliefs with the historical conclusions that are contemporary commonplaces. At every turn, Harvey contrasts present with past; the modern has supplanted the traditional, the present must provide the criterion by which one ascertains the truth about a distant and murky past.

The weight of both scholars' arguments, however, falls on the disciplinary status of historical investigation. Harvey's new intellectual morality entails the claim that "orthodox belief corrodes the delicate machinery of sound historical judgment."[49] He defends this delicate machinery by insisting on the historian's radical disciplinary autonomy; the historian must accept no judgment on the authority of its source lest "he abdicate his role as a critical

---

flags a position that Harvey will disparage.

[47]*Historian and Believer*, 5, translating Troeltsch's *Gesammelte Schriften* (Tübingen: J. C. B. Mohr, 1913) 2:730. Harvey adds that "Christianity must, therefore, build its religious thought upon it or be consigned to the limbo of antiquated forms of religious belief" (5-6). He posits a similar watershed—for historical Jesus research—with the publication of Strauss's *Life of Jesus* (9).

[48]*Historian and Believer*, 280-81. It should be noted that Harvey is defending these theologians against the charge of having an impoverished faith; but his defense pales considerably when it is read in the context of his charges against naïve interpreters.

[49]*Historian and Believer*, 119. The passage continues: "The accusation is not that the traditionalist lacks learning or does not possess the tools of scholarship but that he lacks a certain quality of mind." Harvey contrasts the *traditionalists'* failure with *historians'* probity.

historian. He is no longer a seeker of knowledge but a mediator of past belief; not a thinker but a transmitter of tradition."[50] Harvey's New Testament theologians are first of all, ascetic historians who weigh evidence without attachment to any particular possible conclusion; only when they have attained a degree of historical confidence they deem satisfactory do they consider a theological account that incorporates these critically approved facts. This is not, of course, a job for just anyone (indeed, Harvey gives few—if any—New Testament theologians credit for adequately having grasped his argument), but Harvey shows no concern for the his theory's ramifications outside the ranks of academic theologians.[51] It is not clear whether Harvey's morality of knowledge permits nonexperts to take the historians' authority for truth-claims, or how those who aren't historians might judge whom to believe.

Räisänen's argument also rests on the assumption that the historian holds a privileged role in determining what the New Testament texts mean. Just as Harvey feared the corrupting influence of "orthodox belief," so Räisänen advises that "only when the biblical scholar gives up theological pretensions will sufficient space be left for considerations arising from other perspectives."[52] He warns scholars who opt to focus their interest on theological interpretation that this amounts to capitulating to an arbitrarily instituted authority, and entails a dangerous *sacrificium intellectus*. Peter Stuhlmacher provides Räisänen with the example of a scholar engaged in a "desperate struggle," in the "hopelessly narrow" task of correlating exegesis with homiletics, "kicking against the goads of historical criticism."[53] Räisänen urges that the primary task—that of constructing a phenomenology of early Christian religious

---

[50]*Historian and Believer*, 42.

[51]At one point Harvey calls up a hypothetical traditionalist's possible objection to this thorough emphasis on historical interpretation: "Would the Holy Spirit dictate a document that could only be understood by a trained historian?" (20). He does not, however, follow up the interesting implications of the question.

[52]*Beyond New Testament Theology*, 108.

[53]*Beyond New Testament Theology*, 97.

thought—be undertaken without theological actualization; as in the dictum quoted above, the historical phenomenologist simply passes on clues to the present theological significance of early Christian thought.[54] When the exegete does turn to actualizing interpretation, the exegete should not—indeed, *cannot*—produce a theology *of* the New Testament, but may theologize *about* the writings he or she has interpreted. Räisänen sees his new-model New Testament scholars as historical phenomenologists with a strong area of expertise circumscribed by a less well-defined area of "interests"; they exercise "the historical conscience of theology," but they cannot be expected to offer reliable guidance outside this area of expertise.[55] "Truly founded statements can only be reached, if the different disciplines cooperate," and each interpretive or theological cobbler sticks to his or her last where truth is concerned.[56]

In short, Räisänen and Harvey argue that, whereas in the past readers undertook theological interpretations on the assumption that their own interests were adequately shared with the New Testament texts, *now* scholars must turn their back on this tradition of biblical theology, must recognize the temporal abyss that separates the contemporary interpreter from the ancient text, and must respect the specialization of knowledge that authorizes one scholar legitimately to speak about early Christian religious thought and another to speak about the ways contemporary people can appropriate such insights as can be salvaged from early Christianity.[57] This argument is not incidentally modern, but is intrinsically modern; each of these principles provides necessary support for the whole project. If there were no temporal gap, for instance, there would be less need for specialized scholars, and no particular

---

[54]*Beyond New Testament Theology*, 121; cf. above, 115-16n.

[55]Räisänen refers to K. Rudolph's phrase, "the historical conscience" on *Beyond New Testament Theology*, 137.

[56]*Beyond New Testament Theology*, 140.

[57]And nonexperts who have an interest in these issues, at least in their traditional forms, should presumably acquire enough familiarity with contemporary scholarship to understand why the traditional modes of interpretation and proclamation are no longer valid.

reason to abandon traditional theological interpretation, and so on. These careful, discerning scholars have not overlooked a fatal flaw to their program; they have refined the imperatives in favor of modern New Testament theology, and have presented strong, persuasive cases for this particular way of envisioning the task of theological interpretation. But both scholars have an overriding commitment to specifically modern angles on interpretation and scholarship, so that their proposals will convince their audience only to the extent that their audience shares this commitment to modern presuppositions.

## • The Practical Necessity of Modern New Testament Theology •

Another group of critics defend modern criteria for New Testament theology on the basis that only the criteria that have been drawn from the sorts of methodological reflection considered so far can ensure that theological interpretation proceeds in an orderly, reasoned way. One typical essay from among such recent articles is Robin Scroggs's "Can New Testament Theology Be Saved?"[58] Scroggs writes from his uncertainty that New Testament theology—defined as "the description in coherent and structured form of the faith claims of the authors as revealed in their texts"—can endure when the proliferation of alternative approaches to New Testament interpretation tends to eclipse the quest for what the biblical authors meant, and how that ancient meaning might pertain to contemporary life.[59]

Scroggs fears that the various contexts within which New Testament texts have recently been read—socioeconomic, political, sociological, psychological, gender-based, literary, and rhetorical, to name a few—obstruct the pure theological interpretation of the texts. None of the methods associated with these contexts will return to the interpreter enough of a text on which to base a theological interpretation, especially not if that interpreter dutifully

---

[58]*Union Seminary Quarterly Review* 42 (1988): 17-31.
[59]"Can New Testament Theology Be Saved?" 17.

recognizes that the text should be considered in more than one of these contexts. We may imagine Scroggs lamenting with Joel, "What the economic context left, the sociological context has consumed; what the sociological context left, the gender-critical context has consumed; what the gender-critical context left, the literary context has consumed," and so on. There is no material left on which to base a reconstruction of Paul's theology, or John's Christology. "It should be clear that [these approaches] work against such reconstructions, that is, against any sort of systematic statement of a theological position."[60]

Scroggs poses two paths out of the dilemma he describes. First, one could follow Peter Stuhlmacher and adopt a "hermeneutics of consent" which makes room for dogmatic theology in the interpretive process. Scroggs abhors this alternative; he suspects it entails capitulating to the dogmaticians rather than entering into a truly consensual conversation with the New Testament authors. The second alternative is simply to discard all interest in the theological dimension of the New Testament and treat it as any other ancient document.

Scroggs argues that the desirable alternative to these misguided approaches requires interpreters to take the text itself seriously. The theological interpreter will use the standard repertoire of historical-critical devices to elicit a text's intentionality (that is, what the text actually expresses—not necessarily the author's self-conscious intention). If interpreters *were* so to read the New Testament, "the New Testament texts would be made secure for theological exegesis."[61] The text would control the conversation, limiting the variety of possible interpretations to those that are "based on careful scholarly preparation."[62]

Scroggs is less systematically modern than Harvey or Räisänen, but he too presupposes modern interpretive paradigms. He repeatedly drops references to methods and efforts that are no

---

[60]"Can New Testament Theology Be Saved?" 22.
[61]"Can New Testament Theology Be Saved?" 29.
[62]"Can New Testament Theology Be Saved?" 29.

longer pursued: Paul is no longer regarded as a systematic theologian; historical-Jesus research is no longer at the forefront of gospel interpretation; current scholars no longer treat the category of inspiration as ahistorically as did older scholars. He posits a fundamental gap that separates the past from the present (though he defends Gadamerian hermeneutics as a means of bridging the posited gap),[63] and he defends the historian's disciplinary autonomy both by restricting the New Testament theologian's work to the descriptive task of reconstructing a text's intentionality and by excluding foreign "contextualisms." Only those approaches that *"legitimately* elicit the tradition expressed in the text" may be added to the historian's repertoire.[64] While Scroggs does not claim that his excluded contextualisms are inherently invalid—indeed, he asserts that "we [mainline biblical scholars] take the validity of these contextualizations as self-evident"—they do pose threats to the existence of New Testament theology which historical inquiry (*pace* the fulminations of Harvey and Räisänen) does not.[65] In order to preserve the possibility of New Testament theology, historians must be given the upper hand in any interpretive inquiries.

Most analyses of New Testament theology adopt one or both of these lines of argument. Either intellectual integrity (or some unstated compulsion) obliges interpreters to hew close to the historical line, or the possible proliferation of undisciplined interpreters makes a solid defense of historical interpretation necessary.[66] Both lines of argument make strong cases to audiences who

---

[63]"Can New Testament Theology Be Saved?" 30.

[64]"Can New Testament Theology Be Saved?" 27; my emphasis. Of course, "legitimacy" will be defined by those who pursue unquestionably legitimate lines of inquiry—that is, by historians. Scroggs does allow that certain psychological and sociological methods may prove useful in excavating what an author unconsciously expressed, and that Bultmannian existentialism is likewise a legitimate tool for determining unconscious intentions.

[65]"Can New Testament Theology Be Saved?" 18.

[66]James Barr's criticisms, e.g., tend toward stressing the morality-of-knowledge side of the discussion (though he is a slippery rhetorician, and

share a commitment to the assumptions I have described as "modern." At the same time, these arguments involve little that is not already argued in the leading programmatic essays; with good reason, Räisänen treats twentieth-century New Testament theology as a series of footnotes to Wrede. The arguments have been refined, and they have been pressed more vigorously; but the basics of modern New Testament theology have been set out for almost a century.

The particular guidelines I have illustrated above constitute formal criteria that are tacitly held in common by a vast preponderance of New Testament theologians—of whatever allegiance—in the late twentieth century. With such consensus, it is odd that even a casual survey reveals a widespread sense of dissatisfaction with the state of New Testament theology. Nonetheless, books and articles that express this discontent proliferate. Since this discontent emerges against the background of a more general critique of modernity, to the extent that ours is now commonly called a "postmodern" era, I will discuss the unease of modern New Testament theology in the context of this interrogation of the project of modernity. To this end, the following chapter will elaborate upon the theological complaints against New Testament theology, and its sequel will undertake an examination of the philosophical case against modernity.

---

his arguments are often extremely difficult to pin down); Robert Morgan, when he disagrees with the general line of the argument advanced here, tends to stress the pragmatic necessity of modern criteria.

# Chapter 4

# Modern
# New Testament Theology
# under Interrogation

*It is better to confess the inadequacy of our accounts than to put too much stock in them.*                                    —John Caputo

In the first three chapters I have shown the affiliations between the dominant school of New Testament theology and the cultural conditions of modernity. Just as modernity typically emphasizes its superiority to its past, the distance that separates that past from the present, the necessity of disciplinary autonomy, and the distinction of disciplinary experts from lay interpreters, so modern New Testament theology credits itself with having surpassed previous efforts at theological interpretation, stresses the difference between what the New Testament texts *meant* and what they *mean*, requires that historical investigation (uncontaminated by dogmatic interests) found any New Testament theology, and preserves the separation of the sophisticated from the simple (as in the opposition of "theology" and "faith"). To the extent to which modern New Testament theology actually is dominant, these characteristics seem right and proper, indeed, almost natural. Modern New Testament theologians have underwritten this appearance of necessity by claiming exclusive legitimacy for their methods and assumptions (as in the articles described in the previous chapter). In this chapter, I will consider the demands and justifications for efforts to undertake New Testament theology on a *different* basis.

That there is much demand for *something* different from modern New Testament theology can hardly be denied. From Paul Minear's 1944 essay, "Wanted: A Biblical Theology," through Brevard Childs's *Biblical Theology in Crisis*, to more recent articles, scholars have expressed misgivings concerning the value—and, increasingly, the legitimacy—of the criteria and methods I have characterized as "modern New Testament theology."[1] Works with titles such as *The End of the Historical-Critical Method*[2] are typically provoked by the inadequacy or inappropriateness of historical criticism for theological edification. Their rejection of particular aspects of the modern project are often confused, however, by their unwitting assimilation of certain other modern assumptions.[3] More sophisticated critiques submit that modern New Testament theology both proceeds from misleading postulates and founders on internal incoherencies.[4] In sum, general assent to the principles of modern New Testament theology is counterbalanced by wide-

---

[1]Minear, *Theology Today* 1 (1944): 47-58; Childs, *Biblical Theology in Crisis* (Philadelphia: Westminster Press, 1970). For more recent work, see Childs, "Some Reflections on the Search for a Biblical Theology," *Horizons in Biblical Theology* 4 (1982): 1-12); Ben Ollenburger, "Biblical Theology: Situating the Discipline," in *Understanding the Word*, ed. J. T. Butler, E. W. Conrad, and B. C. Ollenburger, JSOT Supplement Series 37 (Sheffield: JSOT Press, 1982) 37-62, and "What Krister Stendahl 'Meant': A Normative Critique of 'Descriptive Biblical Theology'," *Horizons in Biblical Theology* 8 (1986): 61-98,; B. S. Wagner, "'Biblische Theologien' und 'Biblische Theologie,'" *Theologische Literaturzeitung* 103 (1978): 785-98, inter alia. Minear and Childs have long been critics of the interpretive status quo; as my argument develops it will become clear that my sympathy for their resistance to modern New Testament theology does not entail acceptance of their arguments.

[2]Gerhard Maier, *The End of the Historical-Critical Method*, trans. Edwin W. Leverenz and Rudolph F. Norden (St. Louis: Concordia Publishing House, 1977).

[3]Though Brevard Childs has been particularly sensitive to this phenomenon, I will argue below that he suffers from the same affliction.

[4]I am here anticipating my discussion of the work of Gordon Michalson and Ben Ollenburger (see below).

spread dissatisfaction with the results that come of compliance with those principles.

The problems with modern New Testament theology run even deeper, however, than the familiar complaints suggest. The premises of modernity itself have been subjected to a searching critique, particularly from the fields of philosophy and literary theory. Modernity can no longer simply assume that its progress from antiquity is unequivocally positive. Nonmodern readers understand texts and ideas as historically determined not in the sense that one must only interpret them in the light of their contexts of origin, but in the sense that no interpretation escapes determination by material/ideological conditions—not even ostensibly objective historical explanations. Disciplinary autonomy gives way to transgression and "travelling theory." And modern intellectuals' efforts to reserve a secure privileged place for their values must reckon with the resistance of groups whose values are being excluded.

The demand for alternatives to modern New Testament theology comes principally from theologians and biblical interpreters; they provide the impetus for questioning the status quo in New Testament theology. Since they are usually still operating within the network of assumptions that has legitimated modern approaches, however, their protests and counterproposals do not get to the root of the problems they sense. In chapter 5, I will try to show that these problems have been diagnosed more profoundly by the philosophers of (post)modernity, though they have not addressed their arguments to the uneasy biblical theologians. The philosophers' diagnoses will complete my radical interrogation of modern New Testament theology, after having cleared the ground for planting the seeds of other species of New Testament theology. First, however, we will consider biblical interpreters' theological discontentment.

Twenty years ago, Brevard Childs submitted that biblical theology was in a state of crisis. His news flash arrived on the scene somewhat belatedly: by the time his book was published, the crisis had been going on for more than a decade. Nevertheless, he aptly expressed what many had been feeling, and he has become one of the exemplary figures in the struggle to formulate an alternative to modern theological interpretation of scripture. Childs stands among the critics who seek to redress a perceived imbalance in the historical-critical method—whether it be in the context of interpretation, in the capacity of the method adequately to treat theological topics, or in the method's ideological determination.

A second category of scholars sees structural problems in the modern interpretive project itself: where modern New Testament theologians posit a chronological gap, these critics see continuity, and where the moderns see a fruitful (even "necessary") distinction, their critics see an unworkable confusion. In virtually every case, however, the critics seek to remain within the overall framework of modern interpretation by deploying patches and jury-rigged remedies to overcome the perceived deficiencies in the modern project.

## • Historical Context or Canonical Context? •

Brevard Childs indicts modern theological interpretation for falling into the same trap as medieval allegorism: reliance upon concepts beyond the text as the authoritative referents of the texts. Just as allegorical interpretations often gravitated away from the text, generating increasingly fanciful theories of anagogical reference, so also has historical criticism sought to find speculative historical referents farther and farther from the text.[5] Since the process of historical interpretation admits no impediment to its research, the increasingly tenuous relation between the text and the events and ideas (which are the "real" authority for the modern interpreter) poses no problem for historical interpretation; but since the Church recognizes the *text*—not the events—as canonical, historical interpretation is less and less useful at the same time it is more and more dominant. When the text is defined in advance as a source for extracting historical truth, Childs notes, "the possibility

---

[5]"The Sensus Literalis of Scripture: An Ancient and Modern Problem," in *Beiträge zur Alttestamentlichen Theologie*, ed. H. Donner, R. Hanhart, and R. Smend (Göttingen: Vandenhoeck & Ruprecht, 1977) 90-91.

of a genuine theological exegesis has been destroyed at the outset."[6]

Childs breaks with modern biblical theology's criteria at several crucial points. First, he accords interpretive priority to the canonical form of the text, so that the determinative context for interpretation is *not* the situation of the text's origin, but rather is the contingent destination at which the text arrived. This defies the modern insistence on chronological determination; while the historical study of the New Testament finds more and more pre-Pauline fragments, or isolates Matthew's redactional treatment of Q, Childs argues that the theologically authoritative text is the canonical whole (of Matthew, or 2 Corinthians), interpreted as part of the whole canon.[7] Second, the chronological determination of the New Testament is undercut by Childs's frequent reference to the chain of interpreters between the first and twentieth centuries. Here, the ancients are not opposed to the moderns, but are their hermeneutical guides. Third, Childs denies the autonomy of the historical aspect of modern interpretation. He proposes that theological interpretation must maintain a circular motion from disinterested historical investigation to interested theological application.[8]

Childs proposes that the church reclaim hermeneutical control over the text by interpreting the Bible in the theological context of the canon; yet he finally acknowledges the authority of modern criteria for interpretation. He emphasizes the essential importance of beginning from detailed historical investigation: "The central role is to be the historical study of the text."[9] Paradoxically, this

---

[6]"Interpretation in Faith: The Theological Responsibility of an Old Testament Commentary," *Interpretation* 18 (1964): 437.

[7]This is by no means a simple claim, as "the canonical text" is itself subject to revision on the basis of historical-textual criticism. The cases of Mark 16:9-20, John 7:53–8:11, and the Western "noninterpolations" in Luke-Acts underline the complexity of "the canonical text." Cf. 94-95 and "Excursus I" (518-30) of *The New Testament as Canon* (Philadelphia: Fortress Press, 1985).

[8]"Interpretation in Faith," 443.

[9]"Interpretation in Faith," 442.

inevitable reliance upon historical inquiry is both autonomous (nothing must "restrict the full freedom of the exegesis and [thus] destroy the grounds of precise textual description"[10]) and thoroughly theological ("The descriptive task lies at the heart of the theological task and is never something prior to or outside of the theological endeavor"[11]). Childs affirms the thorough theological determination of the interpretation at the same time he insists that no notions of "the sacred text" interfere with the freedom of the historical interpreter. Modernity, like a tar baby, traps the hand that moves to push it away.

## • Fine-Tuning the Historical Project •

Whereas Childs's complaints against modern biblical theology concern the context and application of historical criticism, the recent work of Peter Stuhlmacher, Gerhard Maier, and Ferdinand Hahn focuses on the method itself. Stuhlmacher's essays in aid of a hermeneutics of consent—which he sees as a recapitulation and development of Adolf Schlatter's hermeneutical program[12]—have their programmatic expression in *Historical Criticism and the Theological Interpretation of Scripture*, and their systematic elaboration in *Vom Verstehen des Neuen Testaments*.[13] Stuhlmacher recognizes the

---

[10]"Interpretation in Faith," 439.

[11]"Interpretation in Faith," 438.

[12]Stuhlmacher discusses Schlatter on pp. 46-48 of *Historical Criticism and the Theological Interpretation of Scripture*, trans. Roy A. Harrisville (Philadelphia: Fortress Press, 1977); on pp. 169-75 of *Vom Verstehen des Neuen Testament: Eine Hermeneutik*, 2nd ed., Grundrisse zum Neuen Testament 6 (Göttingen: Vandenhoeck and Ruprecht, 1986); and esp. in "Adolf Schlatter's Interpretation of Scripture," *New Testament Studies* 24 (1977/1978): 433-46. Stuhlmacher's description of Schlatter on p. 48 of *Historical Criticism* serves as an apt summary of Stuhlmacher's own work: "Schlatter is thus concerned for a critical theology with a biblical basis. He sets historical criticism in the service of this theological concern and requires of the theologian a capacity for dealing critically with his own method. But Schlatter does not require a special, spiritual hermeneutic."

[13]See particularly *Historical Criticism* and *Vom Verstehen*. "Consent" is

discontinuity between the searches for historical facts on the one hand and theological truths on the other. Historical research rightly respects Troeltsch's principles of criticism, analogy, and correlation (which demand methodological skepticism, the necessity of fundamental resemblance among events alleged to be historical, and explicable causal connections among historical events). Theological reflection, however, is entangled with truth-claims concerning faith in a God who transcends the causal order, who is capable of bringing about unique events. In order to bring the historical and theological pursuits into coordination (without sacrificing the integrity of either), Stuhlmacher first proposed a disciplined, scientific approach to interpretation that diverges from Troeltsch's historiography by adopting a fourth interpretive principle, the principle of "perception" ("*Vernehmen*"): "the readiness to take up and work through the claim of the tradition, its posited truth and its effective-history."[14] The principle of perception would entail an openness to transcendence, and a willingness to consider

---

perhaps not the most illuminating translation of Stuhlmacher's "Einverständnis": the Stuhlmacherian interpreter is not consenting to a particular proposition, but is striving for agreement with the text (Edgar McKnight proposes "empathy," which seems a good pointer to what Stuhlmacher desires: *Postmodern Use of the Bible* [Nashville: Abingdon, 1988] 80).

[14]The definition quoted is from "Neue Testament und Hermeneutik–Versuch einer Bestandaufnahme," *Zeitschrift für Theologie und Kirche* 68 (1971): 121-61; and "Zur Methoden- und Sachproblematik einer interkonfessionellen Auslegung des Neuen Testaments," in *Evangelisch-Katholischer Kommentar zum Neuen Testament*, as cited in translation by Edgar Krentz in *The Historical-Critical Method* (Philadelphia: Fortress Press, 1975) 84. Cf. *Vom Verstehen*, 244ff. Stuhlmacher actually counts this as a fifth principle, since he includes as the fourth principle Troeltsch's "principle of religious subjectivity" ("alle menschliche Religion wurzelt in religiöser Intuition oder göttlicher Offenbarung, die in spezifisch religiösen Persönlichkeiten gemeinschaftsbildende Kraft gewinnt und von den Gläubigen mit geringerer Originalität nacherlebt wird": from "Über historische und dogmatische Methode in der Theologie," cited in *Vom Verstehen*, 24). Anglo-American scholarship has conventionally concentrated on the first three of these principles, with which convention I am complying here.

the possibility that the texts studied make claims that the histori-cal-critical method is systematically unsuited to consider. (This would, in effect, entail a suspension or limitation of Troeltsch's principle of criticism; interpreters would be required at some points to be credulous, at others skeptical.)

In *Vom Verstehen*, however, Stuhlmacher acknowledges that historical research is treated more fairly as a complex of various different methods, all of which are affected by the cognitive and emotional relation of the interpreter to the text. He therefore suggests not simply an additional step to the historical-critical process, but a broader (but still quite disciplined) method for theological interpretation. Theological interpretation begins with a preunderstanding of the Gospel as preached from scripture in the present, and proceeds through a historical *analysis* of the effective-history of the New Testament text and thence through the historical character of the events narrated, leading to Christ Jesus (as he was proclaimed and promised in the Old Testament). In a reciprocal motion, the interpretation continues in a first step through the historically reconstituted apostolic witness to Christ. The second step critically considers the particular text in the entire canonical context. Finally, the interpreter considers the relation of the text to the present day, in the light of the church's interpretive and dogmatic tradition.[15]

Stuhlmacher obviously breaks away from the interpretive tradi-tion of modern New Testament theology,[16] but only to the extent that he emphasizes the importance of further aspects of the inter-pretive task. His stress on ascertaining the historical referents of a biblical account as the privileged context for the text accords per-fectly with the modern approach. When he writes, "The Bible is a book of history. Every single book is written in a definite historical

---

[15]Stuhlmacher illustrates this process with a very complex diagram in *Vom Verstehen*, 241; my summary explanation of the diagram here is a paraphrase from 241-42.

[16]For further discussion of the ways Stuhlmacher falls short of modern-ity's standards, cf. Erich Grässer's "Offene Fragen im Umkreis einer Biblischen Theologie," *Zeitschrift für Theologie und Kirche* 77 (1980): 200-21.

situation by people for people,"[17] he could be quoting a tenet of modern New Testament theology. Though Stuhlmacher is unwilling to take the results of historical-critical analysis as an end in themselves, he segregates the interpretive steps of historical analysis (step 1) and theological interpretation (steps 2 and 3) to preserve the autonomy of each; Stendahl could hardly ask more. Stuhlmacher remains deeply concerned to maintain the properly scientific character of his proposed path to New Testament theology.[18] The reason his proposed hermeneutics is so thoroughly diagrammed and parsed is that he insists that there be an explicable methodological justification for any interpretive decision. In sum, Stuhlmacher wants at the same time to have the methodological rigor and chronological determination that modernity posits, and also the theological truths the church has learned—often without historical-critical justification—from the scriptures as interpreted by the saints.

Stuhlmacher's critique of modern theological interpretation has been taken even further by Gerhard Maier, who argues that any "critical" interpretation of scripture has already missed the essential theological point: that it is inappropriate for humans *critically* to evaluate the inspired Word of God. Maier singles out Troeltsch's principle of analogy as the particular difference between "historical-critical" and "historical-biblical" interpretation.[19] A God who intervenes freely in human activity will never be subject to positive criticism on the principle of analogy; but this, Maier argues, is exactly the God we meet in the Bible. Instead of adopting the secular prejudice in favor of law-like generality, theological interpreters of the New Testament must adopt a prejudice in favor of theology when considering the events described in their text.

Maier's outright rejection of critical methods comes not only in the name of a transcendent God, but also in the name of the con-

---

[17]*Vom Verstehen*, 223.
[18]*Historical Criticism*, 86. Cf. also *Vom Verstehen*, §14, passim.
[19]*The End*, 51.

gregation of believers.[20] He acknowledges that churches may err, and have erred, but insists that the faithful have a voice in evaluating the adequacy of theological interpretation. The life of the believing community provides Maier important clues to the meaning of the New Testament.

Stuhlmacher abjures Maier's historical-biblical method as self-contradictory, biblicistic, and unintelligible;[21] yet their conflict is to a great extent a reflection of their hermeneutical proximity. In the end, Stuhlmacher is simply more *modern* than Maier. The men have similar aims, and their methods are roughly similar, but Stuhlmacher differentiates himself from Maier by stressing the necessity that theological interpretation be methodologically rigorous, that it not require a special hermeneutic (distinct from any other sort of interpretation), and that legitimate interpretation requires exactly the historical interpretation that posits the chronological determination of meaning, the priority of the original context for interpretation.[22]

The situation has most helpfully and temperately been summed up in Ferdinand Hahn's essay "Problems of Historical Criticism."[23] Hahn's essay is particularly illuminating because he concentrates on the difficulties attendant upon the effort to use historical-critical methods to produce theological interpretations that satisfy contemporary audiences. Hahn's principal emphasis falls on the way historical-critical interpretation "distances" the text from the interpreter: "the historical-critical analysis of texts has a decidedly alienating effect."[24] He cites as an example Schweitzer's reflection on the quest for the historical Jesus:

---

[20]*The End*, 56ff.

[21]*Historical Criticism*, 66-71.

[22]*Historical Criticism*, 66-71; *Vom Verstehen*, 238-40. Stuhlmacher also argues against the possibility—to which Maier holds firm—of biblical interpretation without criticism; see below.

[23]In *Historical Investigation and New Testament Faith*, trans. Robert Maddox (Philadelphia: Fortress Press, 1983) 13-33.

[24]"Problems," 27.

A curious thing has happened to research into the life of Jesus. It set out in quest of the historical Jesus, believing that when it had found him it could bring him straight into our time as Teacher and Saviour. It loosed the bands by which for centuries he had been chained to the rocks of ecclesiastical doctrine, and rejoiced when life and movement came into the figure once more, and it could see the historical Jesus coming to meet it. But he did not stay: he passed by our time and returned to his own.[25]

Historical analysis separates the text from any tradition of interpretation.[26] As a hermeneutic of suspicion, it must estrange the familiar; it is precisely where we are most confident that we already know the import of an expression that historical criticism digs in to show how unfamiliar the text really is.

Still, Hahn (like Stuhlmacher and even Maier) has no hesitancy about asserting that the historical-critical method is "indispensable," and he harbors no doubt that the original meaning of the biblical text is the appropriate basis for theological interpretation.[27]

The attempt to overcome the deficiencies of historical criticism from within the very (Lutheran Reformation) tradition that gave the distinctive impetus to the modern movement in theological in-

---

[25]"Problems," 27, paraphrasing Albert Schweitzer, *The Quest of the Historical Jesus*, trans. William Montgomery (Repr.: New York: Macmillan, 1968; orig. ET 1910) 399. The translation is also emended to correct Montgomery's use of present-tense verbs in the last sentence.

[26]"Problems," 20. Hahn here mistakenly covers up the fact that modern historical analysis itself constitutes a tradition (within the broader tradition of modernity). Cf. Joseph Prabhu, "The Tradition of Modernity," in *Religious Pluralism*, ed. Leroy S. Rouner, Boston University Studies in Philosophy and Religion 5 (Notre Dame IN: University of Notre Dame Press, 1984) 77-92. Alasdair MacIntyre conducts an arduous investigation of the role of tradition in constituting discourse (with special attention to the "tradition that is not a tradition," i.e., liberalism) in *Whose Justice? Which Rationality?* (Notre Dame IN: University of Notre Dame Press, 1988).

[27]"Problems," 14, 17, 19, 20, 30.

terpretation thus typically concedes the necessity of historical analysis as a starting point; it is willing to concede the modern points
that the text is chronologically determined on the one hand and,
on the other hand, that a great gulf separates twentieth-century
interpreters from the text. This is true not only of the German biblical theologians considered here, but also of their American
colleagues: the Frederick Neumann seminars at Princeton Theological Seminary, whose papers have been published in *Ex Auditu*. The
*Ex Auditu* scholars express almost unanimous admiration for Stuhlmacher's hermeneutics (volumes 2 and 3 begin with essays by
Stuhlmacher), and, like Stuhlmacher, they finally stress the
necessity of historical analysis as a prior condition for legitimate
theological interpretation.[28] For these interpreters, the problem with
modern New Testament theology lies in one-sided or heavy-
handed application of the historical method—but the modern
criteria that require historical foundations for New Testament
theology remain unquestioned.

### • A Transformative Paradigm for Interpretation •

"Historical biblical criticism is bankrupt."[29] Walter Wink begins
his haunting tract with the pointed metaphorical claim that,
although the machinery and labor force of historical criticism
remain intact, the industry is no longer able to deliver the goods.
"The goods" the industry can no longer produce are expositions
that "so . . . interpret the Scriptures that the past becomes alive

---

[28]Cf. inter alia Karlfried Froehlich, "Biblical Hermeneutics on the
Move"; Graham N. Stanton, "Interpreting the New Testament Today";
and Ben F. Meyer, "Conversion and the Hermeneutics of Consent," all
from *Ex Auditu* 1 (1985); Stuhlmacher, "*Ex Auditu* and the Theological Interpretation of Holy Scripture"; and Meyer, "The Primacy of Consent and
the Uses of Suspicion," from *Ex Auditu* 2; and Stuhlmacher, "The
Ecological Crisis as a Challenge for Biblical Theology," *Ex Auditu* 3.

[29]Walter Wink, *The Bible in Human Transformation* (Philadelphia:
Fortress Press, 1973) 1.

and illumines our present with new possibilities for personal and social transformation."[30]

Wink attributes this failure in large part to the industry's capitulation to a modern worldview that is functionally at odds with the goal he posits for the interpretive enterprise.

> In [the academic] context biblical study is rendered innocuous from the start. . . . The outcome of biblical studies in the academy is a trained incapacity to deal with the real problems of actual living persons in their daily lives. . . . The historical method as practiced has not been adequately commensurate with the biblical texts. In this case the carrying over of methods from the natural sciences has led to a situation where we no longer ask what we would like to know and what will be of decisive significance for the next step in personal or social development. Rather, we attempt to deal only with those complexes of facts which are amenable to the historical method. We ask only those questions which the method can answer.[31]

This problem arises from the academy's demand that biblical studies be disinterested, free from interests that have in the past limited the bounds of scholarly inquiry. "The descriptive approach became the magic key to academic respectability."[32] But Wink points out that the descriptive approach is not neutral; on the contrary, he argues that this attitude involves a radical subordination of theological, ethical, and explicitly political interests in favor of an interest in disciplinary self-perpetuation.[33] The historical-critical method served as a useful rhetorical tool in struggles against particular theological uses of power (Wink cites Richard Simon's effort to undermine the Protestant doctrine of *sola scriptura* and Reimarus's assault on Christianity as a whole);[34] but Wink argues—like the Tübingen theologians—that the historical-critical method de-

---

[30]*Human Transformation*, 2.
[31]*Human Transformation*, 6, 9.
[32]*Human Transformation*, 8.
[33]*Human Transformation*, 4, 6-7.
[34]*Human Transformation*, 11.

pends on fundamentally antireligious presuppositions, and is therefore incapable of supporting the goal of edifying the church.

Wink follows up his indictment of the autonomous investigation of the New Testament text—through the pursuit of historical criticism—with the charge that modern biblical interpretation has taken the Bible out of the hands of the believing community, and sequestered interpretive authority in the highly trained guild of professional interpreters. "Now, not dogmatic Christendom, but the biblical guild functions as a harsh superego in the self of many exegetes,"[35] that is, where theological dogma was, historical dogma now is. This charge, if justified, adds force to Wink's earlier complaint about the ideological overdetermination of the supposedly neutral descriptive method.

Since the historical-critical method is inadequate, Wink advocates a psychoanalytic avenue to appropriate interpretation. This turn was foreshadowed when he set as the goal of his interpretation "that the past becomes alive and illumines our present with new possibilities for personal and social transformation."[36] As Wink lays out his approach to personal psychological interpretation, he constantly relies on modern interpretive procedures as a tool to defamiliarize the text, though he emphasizes that these are "under new management,"[37] that they are not the final source of authority about the text but are tools to be used (to an end modern interpretation might well reject as "psychologizing"). Still, Wink does not successfully avoid the pitfalls of modernity. On the one hand, he subscribes to the modern chronological determination of meaning. In a section on preparation for Bible study, he instructs his readers to acquaint themselves with historical-critical sourcebooks in order better to know the period under study; the better

---

[35]*Human Transformation*, 29; also cf. 35: "If anonymous scribes, not Moses, wrote the Pentateuch, and Jesus never spoke the Sermon on the Mount as we now have it, who is to be believed?—the scholars, of course!"

[36]*Human Transformation*, 2.

[37]*Human Transformation*, 62; and cf. *Transforming Bible Study* (Nashville: Abingdon Press, 1980) chap. 7.

acquainted the leader is with these resources, the richer the group process may be.[38] On the other hand, he justifies the particular questions he poses with the imperative that one let the text speak for itself—a law that is problematic at least in part because it is so commonly cited by modern interpreters as the basis for their hermeneutics.[39]

## • Politics and the Modern Theological Interpreter •

Modern New Testament theology has been challenged not only on the grounds that it deviates from its presumed subject, that it methodologically excludes crucial theological aspects of the text, and that it falls short of addressing people's need for personal transformation; a number of scholars have also claimed that modern interpretation is complicit with political and institutional structures of oppression. Elisabeth Schüssler Fiorenza is perhaps the most visible among these political critics. Schüssler Fiorenza's 1987 presidential address to the Society of Biblical Literature[40] posed an

---

[38]*Transforming Bible Study*, 88-89. It is quite significant that, although Wink is concerned that those who emulate him are well prepared to help their study groups' personal development, he cites only standard historical-critical interpretations as preparatory sources—utterly ignoring the rich traditions of biblical interpretation in the practice of spiritual direction and theological interpretation. This may be due to the fact that the psychological approach he advocates is itself the child of the *modern* discovery/invention of the "self" as an object of study.

[39]I will argue below that the rule of "letting the text speak for itself" is dubious also on philosophical grounds: see chap. 6, pp. 171-72.

[40]Published as "The Ethics of Interpretation: De-Centering Biblical Scholarship," in the *Journal of Biblical Literature* 107 (1988): 3-17. Schüssler Fiorenza does not identify her work as "New Testament theology" per se, but she often includes her exegetical work as contributions to a feminst theology. I am not alone in taking her as an example of a countercurrent in N.T. theology; Heikki Räisänen treats her work as I do (though to a different end) in *Beyond New Testament Theology* (Philadelphia: Trinity Press International, 1990) 85-86.

explicit challenge to the interpretive establishment that it recognize an *"ethics of accountability* . . . not only for the choice of theoretical interpretive models but also for the ethical consequences of the biblical text and its meanings."[41] This lecture merely summarizes and spells out the conclusions of her prior works,[42] which show how the interpretive assumptions I have stressed in modern New Testament theology are inextricably entwined with questionable political consequences.

Schüssler Fiorenza deploys her strongest arguments against the notion of scholarly autonomy. Though the theoreticians of modernity who have most stressed this ideal—Weber and Habermas, for example—are often highly politicized intellectuals, in the biblical academy "autonomy" has underwritten efforts to exclude all interest in the political status of interpretations. The biblical interpreter's commitment to historical inquiry, and *only*

---

Though I concentrate on the work of Schüssler Fiorenza in these pages, the number of scholars willing to question the ostensible political neutrality of biblical scholarship has been growing steadily: cf. Stephen Fowl, "The Ethics of Interpretation or What's Left Over after the Elimination of Meaning," *Society of Biblical Literature Seminar Papers* (1988): 69-81, who addresses Schüssler Fiorenza directly. Schüssler Fiorenza does not always posit historical criticism as a necessity for feminist interpretation—her essay "Emerging Issues in Feminist Biblical Interpretation" (in *Christian Feminism: Visions of a New Humanity*, ed. Judith L. Weidman [New York: Harper & Row, 1984] 33-54) and the recent essays in *But She Said* (Boston: Beacon Press, 1992) and *Searching the Scriptures* (New York: Crossroads, 1993) open the door, tentatively, for interpreters to transgress the historical hard line—but the preponderance of her work expresses a consistent commitment to the necessity of historical-critical foundations for feminist theological criticism: "In my opinion such a process of theological-critical reading must include a historical-critical reading but is not identical to it" (in "Lk 13:10-17: Interpretation for Liberation and Transformation," *Theology Digest* 36 [1989]: 316n.4).

[41]"Ethics of Interpretation," 15.

[42]Cf. *In Memory of Her* (New York: Crossroad, 1983), and *Bread Not Stone* (Boston: Beacon Press, 1984).

historical inquiry, is a function of development of biblical studies as an autonomous discipline:

> The "scientist" ethos of biblical studies was shaped by the struggle of biblical scholarship to free itself from dogmatic and ecclesiastical controls. It corresponded to the professionalization of academic life and the rise of the university. Just as history as an academic discipline sought in the last quarter of the nineteenth century to prove itself as an objective science in analogy to the natural sciences, so also did biblical studies. . . . Since the ethos of objective scientism and theoretical value-neutrality was articulated in the political context of several heresy trials at the turn of the twentieth century, its rhetoric continues to reject all overt theological and religious institutional engagement as unscientific, *while at the same time claiming a name and space marked by the traditional biblical canon.*[43]

The autonomous historical critic, according to Schüssler Fiorenza, is not only defending his or her discipline from the possible encroachments of a marauding dogmatic authoritarianism, but is also denying responsibility for, and complicity in, the uses made of his or her biblical interpretations.

Schüssler Fiorenza deplores such a stance for at least two reasons. First, it masks the interpreter's own circumstances and motivations; this leads to a situation where feminist interpretation is seen as supplementary or secondary to conventional scholarship (as though feminists were ideologically biased, but historical critics are not).[44] The claim that the nonfeminist tradition of historical criticism transcends the partisan interests of feminists is itself an argument on behalf of perpetuating androcentric structures of legitimacy (and, *mutatis mutandis*, the same is true for hermeneutics that address the special situations of other oppressed groups). Second, it evades engagement in the aftereffects of interpretation,

---

[43]"Ethics of Interpretation," 11; my emphasis.

[44]Cf. *Bread Not Stone*, 106–108, and 138: "It is obvious in this context how damaging it is that almost all biblical scholars are middle-class, white males who are highly educated and belong to the clergy."

which effects are generally felt differently by those millions outside the interpretive profession. A historical critic could consistently accept promotion, tenure, and professional eminence for interpretations that have, for example, a malignant impact on women's lives.

Schüssler Fiorenza further notices that the modern presupposition that meaning is determined by chronology, by the time and context of origin, contributes to the problems that criticism's supposed autonomy creates. The meaning of a text includes just the consequences conventional historical criticism seeks to deny.

Finally, Schüssler Fiorenza points out another negative aspect of modern critical interpretation: it removes the Bible from the community of believers, reserving interpretive authority for the credentialled elite.[45] She argues forcefully that legitimacy must not be reserved for interpretations propounded by privileged scholars, but must recognize the various perspectives of concerned interpreters from outside the academy. "Insofar as 'ordinary' members of the community can read [and I would here add, "or hear"], they can understand and interpret the text."[46]

Though Schüssler Fiorenza is highly critical of modern interpretive conventions, she insists on the necessity of historical criticism as the basis for the feminist critical hermeneutics she advocates.[47] In one symptomatic case, she tells of having been asked why a feminist interpreter needs to pay attention to the work of "German men in the last century."[48] The question troubles Schüssler Fiorenza, and in her *apologia* she consistently fails to answer the

---

[45]Cf. chap. 2 of *Bread Not Stone*, "For the Sake of Our Salvation . . . , " 23-42, and her comments on Sandra Schneiders's hermeneutics on 133-35.

[46]*Bread Not Stone*, 134.

[47]In *In Memory of Her*, this takes the form of a rigorous investigation of Christian origins with an eye to recovering the repressed evidence of women's leadership in the early communities. In order so to do, she has frequent recourse to the argument from silence (41ff.; and cf. *Bread Not Stone*, 112). This is justified exactly to the extent that one sympathizes with her goal, and many unsympathetic exegetes found this alone reason enough to dismiss her work.

[48]*Bread Not Stone*, 93.

student's question. At best, she argues that historical criticism can be useful to feminist interpreters; but this falls considerably short of her claim that "we *need* to use the methods and means of historical inquiry developed by historical-critical scholarship."[49] Likewise, her presidential address concludes with a plea that biblical scholarship "continue its descriptive-analytic work utilizing all the critical methods available for illuminating our understanding of ancient texts and their historical location."[50] Schüssler Fiorenza wants to bring in a feminist critical reformation of biblical scholarship, but she wants it on the conditions established by modernity.

## • "What Krister Stendahl Meant" •

Whereas the preceding scholars have attacked the historical-critical grounds of modern New Testament theology, Ben Ollenburger questions the very possibility of realizing modern New Testament theology's goals.[51] In a detailed analysis of Stendahl's distinctions between "meant" and "means," and between a "descriptive" and a "normative" theological task, Ollenburger finds no logical coherence to this proposed foundation of New Testament theology.

Ollenburger's critique first examines the distinction Stendahl drew between "descriptive" and "normative" theological tasks.

---

[49]*Bread Not Stone*, 106; my emphasis.

[50]"Ethics of Interpretation," 16.

[51]"What Krister Stendahl 'Meant'—A Normative Critique of 'Descriptive Biblical Theology'," *Horizons of Biblical Theology* 8 (1986): 61-98.

Dan O. Via, Jr. questioned the legitimacy of Stendahl's distinction as early as 1967, in *The Parables* (Philadelphia: Fortress Press). Via found that Stendahl's analysis "leaves biblical theology unnaturally restricted and its relationship to systematic theology nonexistent or unclarified" (29). Moreover, the proposed division of interpretive labor posits a hermeneutical aporia; neither systematicians nor biblical scholars can judge the adequacy of any transmutations of "what it meant" into "what it means," since neither group can reach well-formed judgments about the other's specialty (ibid.).

Recall that Stendahl deployed this distinction to protect the autonomy of biblical theology over against systematic theology (and vice versa);[52] biblical scholars should do "descriptive" work, and systematicians' work should be "normative." But Ollenburger points out that, since the biblical theologian's work provides the material from which the pure theologian should work, it is fair to assume that the biblical theologian's work is normative as well as descriptive. This is especially plausible since, according to Stendahl, the Bible itself has a "normative nature."[53] Stendahl aggravates this problem inasmuch as he discusses the actual work of systematic theology in only the vaguest terms; the only aspect that seems clear is that this work concludes in normative theology.[54]

The difficulties inherent in Stendahl's "descriptive"/"normative" distinction are compounded by ambiguities in the "meant"/"means" distinction. Just what does "what it meant" mean? Stendahl is inconsistent in his response to this question. In his programmatic article, he simply says "our only concern is to find out what these words meant when uttered or written by the prophet, the

---

[52]In "Method in the Study of Biblical Theology," in *The Bible in Modern Scholarship*, ed. J. P. Hyatt (Nashville: Abingdon, 1965) 203, he points out that this distinction ought to benefit theologians, since "everything called 'biblical' easily becomes adorned with the authority of the Scriptures"; cf. also 205, and Krister Stendahl, "Biblical Theology, Contemporary," *Interpreter's Dictionary of the Bible*, ed. George Buttrick et al. (Nashville: Abingdon Press, 1962) A-D:419, col. 1 (= *Meanings* [Philadelphia: Fortress Press, 1984] 34).

[53]"The Bible as a Classic and the Bible as Holy Scripture." *Journal of Biblical Literature* 103 (1984): 8.

[54]"What Stendahl Meant," 65-68. Langdon Gilkey has discussed—and repudiated—the "descriptive"/"normative" distinction from the side of systematic theology, in "The Roles of the 'Descriptive' or 'Historical' and of the 'Normative' in Our Work," *Criterion* 20 (1981): 10-17. Systematic theologians are certainly involved in "descriptive" as well as "normative" theorizing; Ollenburger points to Barth's intent in the Dogmatics to describe "the distinctive utterance of the Church" ("What Krister Stendahl Meant," 73).

priest, the evangelist, or the apostle."[55] At one point, Stendahl submits that he is seeking "what Paul thought he meant."[56] In the next sentence, however, he begins an ambiguous transition from "meant a long time ago" to "meant very recently," by counting as "meanings," "what the Corinthians thought Paul meant," and subsequently adds all other interpreters' impressions of what Paul meant. In a different article, Stendahl treats "what it meant" as "its import relative to other possible utterances on the same topic"; the *lex talionis* "meant" that Torah was more humane than other laws on retaliation.[57] Stendahl recognizes that "what it meant" needs amplification ("to whom? when?"),[58] but then abstains from offering just the amplification the distinction needs. Stendahl offers no criterion for determining "what a text meant"— even though this is precisely what he is urging New Testament theologians to seek.

Ollenburger concludes his argument against the "meant"/ "means" distinction by demonstrating that the interpretive mechanics of Stendahl's proposal are unworkable. On Stendahl's account, the biblical theologian has the task of finding out what a New Testament text meant when the apostle wrote it. The systematic theologian then has the task of explaining what the same text means today; however, this explanation may not rest on the text, but rather on the biblical theologian's prior account of what the text meant. (If the systematician worked from the text, there would be no need for a biblical theologian. By the same token, if the biblical theologian were capable of explaining what the text means today, there would be no need for a systematician.) Therefore, both the "meant" and the "means" are temporally relative properties of the text, which are mutually exclusive: when the text meant its past meaning, it did not mean its present meaning, and vice versa. Yet the "means" is dependent upon the "meant," for the systematician can't know what it means without recourse to

---

[55]"Contemporary Biblical Theology," 422, cols. 1-2 (22)].
[56]"Method," 199.
[57]"The Bible as a Classic," 9.
[58]"Method," 200.

the "meant." The "means" is not a property of the text itself, in other words, but a property of the "meant." Moreover, how is the biblical theologian to find out what the text meant if the "meant" doesn't somehow reach out over the "meant"/"means" gap to make contact with the biblical theologian (who, after all, lives in the "means" time)?[59]

Nicholas Lash suggests thinking of Stendahl's proposal with the metaphor of industrial processing.[60] The text is raw material. From it, the biblical theologian refines the original meaning. This refined product is then shipped to the systematic theologian, who dresses it up suitably for the contemporary consumer. The problem is that texts are *not* materials, and interpretations do *not* refine pure meaning from texts. "[A] text, any text, becomes an expression of meaning only insofar as it becomes an element in the human activity that is its production, use or interpretation."[61] Lash expands on this suggestion by submitting that "the fundamental form of the *Christian* interpretation of Scripture is the life, activity, and organization of the believing community."[62] In other words, Stendahl's vision for modern New Testament theology—the production-and-consumption model—should give way to a more hermeneutically sophisticated vision, which treats the theological interpretation of Scripture as *performance*.

---

[59]"What Krister Stendahl Meant," 86ff.

[60]"What Might Martyrdom Mean?" in *Theology on the Way to Emmaus* (London: SCM Press, 1986) 85-86, working from a suggestion by Raymond Williams.

[61]"Martyrdom," 85. Fowl and Jones likewise point out some problems with treating the text as though it were simply unproblematically *there*: *Reading in Communion: Scripture & Ethics in Christian Life* (Grand Rapids: Eerdmans, 1991) 4-28.

[62]"Performing the Scriptures," in *Theology on the Way to Emmaus*, 42 (Lash's emphasis). Fowl and Jones explore this suggestion at length, in exemplary fashion, in *Reading in Communion*.

## • On Not Needing to Bridge the Ugly, Broad Ditch •

Another dogma of modern New Testament theology is that a great chronological chasm intervenes to separate twentieth-century interpreters from their first-century texts. Gordon Michalson has undertaken a thorough analysis of the many dimensions of this argument, and has shown that this argument (like the "meant"/ "means" distinction) has less philosophical than rhetorical weight.[63]

Michalson has published a number of studies on the relation of faith to history.[64] This question has many distinct aspects (and distinguishing clearly among them is one of the virtues of Michalson's work), but Michalson devotes considerable attention to the chronological gap that haunts modern New Testament theology. The temporal problem with which he tangles grows out of Lessing's famous essay "On the Proof of the Spirit and of Power," wherein Lessing argues that the passage of time distances him from the possibility of accepting the testimonies recorded in Scripture. Since Lessing himself had not experienced the miracles and resurrection of Jesus, he is dubious about accepting the religious truths to which those alleged events point:

> [H]ow is it to be expected of me that the same inconceivable truths which sixteen to eighteen hundred years ago people

---

[63]John Howard Yoder has mounted a very different, but quite compelling, argument against taking Lessing's ditch as an insurmountable obstacle to interpretation; see "'But We Do See Jesus': The Particularity of Jesus and the Universality of Truth," in *The Priestly Kingdom* (Notre Dame IN: University of Notre Dame Press, 1984).

[64]"Theology, Historical Knowledge, and the Contingency-Necessity Distinction," *International Journal for Philosophy of Religion* 14 (1983): 87-98; "Pannenberg on the Resurrection and Historical Method," *Scottish Journal of Theology* 33 (1980): 345-59; "Faith and History: The Shape of the Problem," *Modern Theology* 1 (1985): 277-90; *Lessing's "Ugly Ditch": A Study of Theology and History* (Philadelphia: Pennsylvania State University Press, 1985).

> believed on the strongest inducement should be believed by me
> on an infinitely lesser inducement?[65]

(This is not exactly the same chronological gap as that which separates modern New Testament theologians from the texts they interpret, but the principle is closely related, and if I can close Lessing's gap, I will be much nearer to closing the textual temporal gap.)

Michalson attacks Lessing's gap in two ways. First, he shows that Lessing operates with an unjustified empiricist presupposition: that being a firsthand observer of miracles and resurrection would provide an advantage in credibility. ("If I had lived at the time of Christ, then of course the prophecies fulfilled in his person would have made me pay great attention to him. If I had actually seen him do miracles. . . . I would have gained so much confidence that I would willingly have submitted my intellect to his."[66]) Michalson points out that Lessing still qualifies the certainty of the immediate experience for which he hopes; if it were possible to offer an alternative account of the supposed miracle, then Lessing would be off the epistemological hook. The only firm basis for believing in the first miracles would be additional, confirming miracles; thus, this argument simply restates—or, in this case, *pre*-states—Troeltsch's principle of analogy. The issue is not one of *chronology*, but of the character of the event (or nonevent) in question.[67]

The second facet of Lessing's gap concerns the general uncertainty concerning past events (once again anticipating Troeltsch). Michalson acknowledges that there is no way around this point, but suggests that this does not radically undermine any traditional

---

[65]"On the Proof of the Spirit and of Power," in *Lessing's Theological Writings*, trans. and ed. Henry Chadwick (Stanford: Stanford University Press, 1956), 53.

[66]"On the Proof," 51-52.

[67]The transmutation of this part of the chronological gap into a different sort of gap (Michalson points to metaphysical and existential aspects of this gap) does not banish problems of Jesus' identity or our understanding thereof. It does, however, show that N.T. theology is not responsible for addressing this problem as a question of historiography.

Christian assertions about the events surrounding Jesus. The force of the principle of criticism is that all claims about the past, whatever the evidence for them, can only be probable. The contingency of historical knowledge can pose a problem only to the extent that "certainty" is an available alternative. Absent *any* historical certainty, the claim that the events narrated about Jesus are at best only probable is no bad news.

The chronological gap is subject to question from another direction as well. The Orthodox church (preserving to some extent the view of the premodern Western churches) traditionally does not recognize the kind of discontinuity that necessitates a recuperative hermeneutic.[68] Instead, Orthodox theologians affirm the "principle of legacy," the conviction that the meaning of scripture has faithfully been handed down by the Fathers and the saints. Thomas Hopko casts this argument as a claim that "the Bible is under-

---

[68]Anton Ugolnick, "An Orthodox Hermeneutic in the West," *St. Vladimir's Theological Quarterly* 27 (1983): 94: "We envision ourselves as a people free of radical discontinuities, from one generation to the next, with the theology of the past." As Ugolnick points out, this is in part due to the fact that the Greek Orthodox church has always spoken the language of the New Testament.

Lest I be accused of oversimplifying and romanticizing, I should stress that the Orthodox tradition is by no means univocal on this point: cf. the testimony of Theodore Stylianopolis, "Historical Studies and Orthodox Theology, or the Problem of History for Orthodoxy," *Greek Orthodox Theological Review* 12 (1967): 394-419, esp. 395. Stylianopolis, who studied under Krister Stendahl at Harvard Divinity School, argues in favor of Stendahl's distinctions for the sake of safeguarding the autonomy of biblical studies: "Biblical Studies in Orthodox Theology: A Reply," *The Greek Orthodox Theological Review* 17 (1972): 79, as cited in Michael Cartwright, "Politics, Practices, and Performance" (Ph.D. diss., Duke University, 1988) 220. Cartwright devotes several pages to Stylianopolis's career, noting that Stylianopolis has in more recent works diminished the importance he attributes to historical-critical exegesis: cf. "Politics, Practices, and Performance," 219-27. (My awareness and understanding of the whole matter of Orthodox hermeneutics has been greatly enriched by Cartwright's work.)

standable and interpretable solely within the integrity of the Church, in which all aspects of reality are brought in to organic and vital synthetic unity."[69] Such Orthodox interpretation does not adopt wholesale the results of traditional exegesis, but reads scripture through traditional lenses; the exegete learns how to interpret not from technical manuals but from immersion in the interpretive tradition.[70]

Anton Ugolnick suggests a fundamentally synchronic interpretation of Scripture—not "synchronic" in the sense that recent structuralist/literary-critical studies have made current, but "synchronic" in the sense that it presupposes the contemporaniety of the community of interpreters (which community is temporally inclusive). Ugolnick advocates a social approach to the question of "meaning," which entails "a dynamic, dramatically defined relationship between a community of interrelated 'selves' and a text."[71] The Fathers provide guidance to the interpreters who undertake a "performance" of the scriptural text.[72]

For such an Orthodox hermeneutic, the chronological gap presents not an "ugly, broad ditch," but only a *difference* among interpretations no more disturbing than the difference between those interpreters of Matthew who find a five-part structure to the gospel and those who find a three-part structure. The gap only becomes a problem when an interpreter seeks to break the chain

---

[69]"The Bible in the Orthodox Church," in *All the Fulness of God* (Crestwood NY: St. Vladimir's Seminary Press, 1982) 90. The Orthodox interpreter might well claim that the Western insistence on discontinuity is not unrelated to the apparently insurmountable tendency to schism and denominationalism in Western Christendom.

[70]Cf. Savas Agourides: "Orthodox hermeneutics are not a repetition of the exegete Fathers, but the initiation into their entire interpretative thought" ("Biblical Studies in Orthodox Theology," *The Greek Orthodox Theological Review* 17 [1972]: 62, as quoted in Cartwright, "Practices, Politics, and Performance," 218).

[71]"Orthodox Hermeneutic," 110.

[72]Ugolnick refers to "performance" on 112; cf. Nicholas Lash's essay, "Performing the Scriptures" (cited above).

of interpretations; then most of the (very helpful) members of the community are silenced.[73]

### • Contra Modern New Testament Theology •

This chapter has shown a parade of witnesses who argue that there is something crucial lacking in modern New Testament theology. Childs regrets the absence of the New Testament itself; reconstructed *ur*-texts and *ipsissima voces* are not the same as the New Testament text. Stuhlmacher misses the possibility that God might actually be involved in these affairs in nontrivial ways, the theological sensitivity that ought to characterize *theological* interpretation. He resists the methodological skittishness that inheres in modern New Testament theology, or which has no room for anyone to say, "I am not ashamed of the gospel; it is the power of God for salvation." Interpreters with particular political concerns are suspicious of a method developed by nineteenth-century middle-class European men, especially when that method itself limits the amount of support self-consciously political interpreters can derive from the New Testament. Ollenburger and Michalson miss conceptual clarity. The Orthodox are reluctant to exchange the authority of the Fathers for the authority of the most recent article in *New Testament Studies*.[74]

---

[73]As, e.g., when Stendahl discusses the chain of interpreters in an effort to banish it ("Contemporary Biblical Theology," 430 col. 1 [41]). Though Stendahl is probably claiming no more than that earlier generations of interpreters have not sought "what it meant" as an authority for interpretation, he implies in this passage that each generation of theological interpreters was correcting its predecessors without regard for the biblical text. The former claim simply reinscribes the history of interpretation into the presuppositions of modernity; the latter is patently false.

[74]Ugolnick actually points out that the entire issue of "authority" reflects the knots Western Christianity has tied itself into. He claims that, since the Orthodox church did not experience the polarizing (distorting?) opposition of the authority of the biblical text versus the authority of the magisterium (emblematized in an infallible Pope), only in the Orthodox church is there a possibility of true shared authority of the community.

Yet in most of these cases, the reservation is expressed that, whatever the eventual alternative to modern New Testament theology, it must begin with the historical evaluation of the text.[75] The reason for this is simple: though many have criticized aspects of modern New Testament theology before, no one has yet criticized it *for its modernity.* Critics want to amend or reform modern interpretation, but do not want to leave the familiar rules and criteria that define modern interpretation. All concerned accept claims that the familiar modern rules enable us to allow the text to speak for itself; that they have freed us to hear once again the original meaning of the text; that submission to these rules ensures that we do justice to the text. It is argued (on the basis of a philosophical tradition that runs from Schleiermacher through Dilthey and Bultmann) that nothing else can help us to *understand* the text. This is all the more paradoxical since, if one were to sum up the various criticisms that have been made, they amount to nothing less than a thoroughgoing critique of the modern project of New Testament theology as a whole.

One can hardly blame these critics for hesitating to take the step of criticizing the basis of modern New Testament theology. The modern approach to New Testament theology—which rejects the testimony of "precritical" (frankly confessional) interpreters, locates the primary meaning of the text in a remote past, claims autonomy from ecclesiastical or dogmatic interests, and establishes its expertise at the cost of losing intimate contact with uncredentialled interpreters—has made it intellectually acceptable to show some interest in the subject of New Testament theology in the *modern* academy. A reader who prescinds from such insulation faces considerable professional and social risk. There have arisen, however, some cogent criticisms of modernity *outside* the field of biblical interpretation. Some of these philosophical and theoretical

---

[75]The obvious exception, of course, is the Orthodox church's communal hermeneutic discussed by Ugolnick and Cartwright; it is not coincidental that the Orthodox churches have been geographically, linguistically, and, to some extent, economically insulated from the strongest currents of modernity.

claims question the legitimacy of the characteristics I cited as the physiognomy of modernity; others strike at the heart of concepts that underlie New Testament theology's residual modernity: "meaning" as a property of a text, "understanding" as the goal of interpretation, and "history" as a discourse suitable for verifying claims relevant to theological interpretation. While these hard questions for modernity do not reveal that modern interests are bad or incoherent, they do show that modernity cannot be *required* of intellectual inquiry—except with reference to norms modernity itself posits.[76]

---

[76]This point is familiar in another guise from the hermeneutical debates of the mid-twentieth century, where it conventionally took the form of claiming that "since everyone has to have presuppositions, I'll have my presuppositions and you have yours." Van Harvey has criticized this stance from a modern point of view; I agree with him that a simple avowal of presuppositions solves no problems, but I disagree with his subsequent insistence that a "morality of knowledge" privileges modern interests.

# Chapter 5

# The Philosophical Erosion of Modernity

## • Toward a Radical Critique of New Testament Theology's Modernity •

The parties to the theological critique of modern New Testament theology agree on this much: something has to change. Yet each wants to change only the aspect, the rule or assumption, that obstructs the interest he or she advocates. Each suggests only a patch for the system, one that works around the critic's particular problem, rather than seeing the panorama of criticism as a signal that the enterprise is radically inadequate for the needs of these interpreters. It is possible, in other words, that for some interpreters, the insights modern New Testament theology offers are not worth its blindnesses.[1] In this chapter, I will argue that these blindnesses are directly related to the *modernity* of New Testament theology, and that interpreters who are committed to different insights (perhaps, into the gospel's power and promise of liberation to the oppressed) may find that reconceiving New Testament theology apart from modern priorities may help them realize their interpretive aims.

---

[1]I here adopt Paul de Man's metaphor for the inevitable dilemma of criticism, in which no insight can be bought except at the price of a blindness (*Blindness and Insight*, 2nd ed. [New Haven CT: Yale University Press, 1983] 106-10, 139-41).

By their continuing loyalty to the modern project, theological critics of modern New Testament theology show that that project offers many benefits. Our awareness of the historical and social circumstances of the first-century Mediterranean world has increased by orders of magnitude. Elisabeth Schüssler Fiorenza specifically notes that her reliance on the "19th-century German men" whom her student interlocutor deplores grows out of her own experience of historical criticism's liberating possibilities;[2] the application of historical-critical methods to claims about the events narrated in the New Testament has greatly clarified, if not utterly banished, conflicts involving the authority of ecclesiastical bodies to control interpretation. I would not wish away these benefits of historical criticism.

On the other hand, the particular benefits historical criticism procures are not necessarily the desiderata of theological interpretation. At this point, my argument is the reverse side of the coin minted by Van Harvey. In *The Historian and the Believer*, Harvey argued that Christian faith necessarily corrodes the delicate judgments of probability and analogy required by the historian;[3] here, I argue that both methodological skepticism and Harvey's (justified) insistence that chronological location determines correct interpretation may well corrode the delicate theological judgments we seek in a New Testament theologian. Likewise, the extensive training in historical method that separates legitimate interpreters from amateurs may not provide a reliable basis for legitimating the work of New Testament theologians. And though the concentration of New Testament interpretation on the discipline of history has clarified the character of the times, events, and attitudes that lie behind the New Testament, it is not clear that these times, events, and attitudes are the necessary building blocks of New Testament theology.

---

[2]*Bread Not Stone*, 94.
[3]*The Historian and the Believer* (New York: Macmillan, 1966) 119 and passim.

The defenders of modern New Testament theology pose several critical challenges to any proposed alternative. First, is it not *necessary* to address the problem of the chronological gap with properly historical methods? Are not New Testament theologians absolutely obliged to use the tools of historical inquiry in order even to *read* the New Testament? Second, does not the mingling of this required historical inquiry with concerns not proper to history itself engender the intellectual misalliance that Stendahl so fears? Third, would not this proposed nonmodern New Testament theology involve a regression to the darker days of precritical interpretation? These rhetorical questions, questions to which few in the interpretive guild would dare answer negatively, have haunted attempts to formulate more flexible approaches to biblical interpretation.

Such questions have analogues in the philosophical debates over modernity that have occupied increasing attention over the past twenty years. In this section, I will draw upon the writings of philosophical and literary theorists in responding to the preceding questions concerning the legitimacy of alternatives to modern New Testament theology.

It is important at this point to stress that I am not arguing that there is anything illegitimate about the project of modern New Testament theology, which then needs to be remedied by a new, improved New Testament theology. This very gesture—all too typical of casual "postmodern" claims—reinscribes the proposed project in the self-consuming modern enterprise, in which a new generation of Moderns ousts today's Ancients (who in turn were *yesterday's* Moderns ousting their own predecessors, and so on). Instead (as I will argue below), I propose only that modern New Testament theology acknowledge that it is not the only legitimate avenue to New Testament theology, but one interpretive path among many. Given differing circumstances—different interpretive interests and priorities—there exist other ways to construe the task of New Testament theology.

## • The Necessity of History •

One would have a hard time finding assent to the proposition that the New Testament can be read without recourse to any historical scholarship (as, for example, one reads this morning's grocery list). At the very least, historical philology is necessary for the task of translating the text into familiar languages, and textual criticism (which involves liberal portions of historical judgment) is necessary for determining which Greek text to translate. On the other hand, it is not at all clear just *how much* history—or, indeed, *what kind* of history—is necessary.

It is an indisputable fact that a great many people believe they need no help whatsoever from historical scholarship. Students entering introductory courses in New Testament at their college or seminary often need to be *taught* to recognize the importance of historical scholarship to New Testament interpretation. If these unschooled interpreters sense no chronological gap separating them from the text, how are modern New Testament theologians to justify their claim that recognizing such a gap is a necessary mark of the requisite hermeneutical sophistication?[4]

The claim is justified principally on the grounds that would-be New Testament theologians enter the domain of *wissenschaftlich* historiography when they claim, for example, that Jesus of Nazareth prophesied his own future return in heavenly majesty. Their interpretations have caught them up in the arena in which truth-claims are adjudicated according to the familiar rules of academic historiography, and historians of early Christianity will respond that there is insufficient evidence that Jesus said anything of the kind.

This hypothetical dispute concerning the legitimacy of nonhistorical interpretations involves all of the aspects of modernity that were described in the first chapter. Modernity defines itself posi-

---

[4]We may recall in this context Keck's derogation of Richardson for his "naïve" failure to recognize the gap ("Problems of New Testament Theology," *Novum Testamentum* 7 [1964/1965]: 238-40).

tively in contrast to (depreciated) antiquity; and in this case, literal interpretations of the New Testament are rejected as "antiquated." A more *modern* approach declines to treat the gospels as reliable reports about Jesus' acts and deeds. Likewise, modernity concerns itself with time, and particularly with chronological distance; so, too, part of the modern reluctance to place confidence in the gospels' historical value comes from our chronological distance from the events narrated therein; in the lines by Louis MacNeice that W. D. Davies has often quoted, "It was all so unimaginably different, / and all so long ago."

Modernity also reserves to autonomous disciplines the right to make authoritative decisions within their areas of competence, so it is the historian who alone has authority to judge truth-claims concerning what Jesus of Nazareth said. Finally, modernity resists populism; the autonomous discipline of historiography credentials only a few historians, whose point of view is thereafter valued over that of uncredentialled readers.

What makes this conflict revealing for my purposes is that all of the modern arguments against the literalist's interpretation are self-evidently convincing only to one who is already committed to the principles characteristic of modernity. But not all interpreters are so convinced, and not all of these dubious interpreters are anti-intellectual, reactionary, or perverse.[5] There are powerful philosophical arguments against each of these modern postulates.

### • Noncanonical Interpreters •

The first reaction of a trained interpreter to an interpretation offered by an interpreter who lacks advanced training is likely to be a keen awareness of their difference in disciplinary standing. The process of education in a discipline not only entails acquiring

---

[5]In this connection, David Steinmetz's essay "The Superiority of Pre-Critical Exegesis" (*Theology Today* 37 [1980]: 27-38) and his ten theses on theology and exegesis (in *Histoire de l'exégèse au XVIe Siècle*, ed. Olivier Fatio and Pierre Fraenkel [Geneva: Librairie Droz, 1978]) are exemplary of thoughtful rejections of modern theological interpretation.

a grasp of the facts and methods the discipline recognizes, but also involves a more subtle process of instilling in the student a reliable sense of what may and may not be said. W. K. Wimsatt cites the example of a student who argued that

> a couplet by Alexander Pope, "no Prelate's Lawn with Hair-shirt lin'd, / Is half so incoherent as my Mind," ought to be read in the light of a couplet in another poem by Pope: "Whose ample Lawns are not asham'd to feed / The milky heifer and deserving steed." Since I believe in the force of puns and all sorts of other resemblances in poetry, I do not know quite how to formulate the rule of context by which I confidently reject that connection.[6]

Frank Kermode observes in this connection that "the real difference between outside [the discipline of English literature] and inside is marked by the insistence of the outsider that he can say what he likes about Shakespeare and the tacit knowledge of the institution, which he therefore hates, that nothing he says is worth attending to."[7] The same may be said, *mutatis mutandis*, with regard to New Testament theology; there is a binary opposition between the discourse of New Testament theology as it is institutionally authorized and as it is practiced outside that discourse, and the privileged term of that opposition belongs to the institutional discipline—my Aunt Isabel's interpretations are simply excluded.

Barbara Herrnstein Smith has called interpretation's "Aunt Isabels" *noncanonical audiences*, that is, readers whose opinions we may safely ignore.[8] She ruthlessly exposes the ways in which the institutional and disciplinary constitution of acceptable audiences has excluded the interpretive interests of women, blacks, and

---

[6]W. K. Wimsatt, "Battering the Object," in *Contemporary Criticism*, Stratford-upon-Avon Studies 12, ed. Malcolm Bradbury and David Palmer (London: Arnold, 1970) 75-76; cited by Frank Kermode, "Can We Say Absolutely Anything We Like?" in *The Art of Telling* (Cambridge MA: Harvard University Press, 1983) 156.

[7]"Can We Say?" 160.

[8]*Contingencies of Value* (Cambridge MA: Harvard University Press, 1988) 24-27.

countless others who may not participate in the discourse of interpretation—except on the institution's terms. She speaks on behalf
of the student who questioned Schüssler Fiorenza on the necessity
of historical-critical studies: Why *should* interpreters whose interests differ from those of the established authorities have to assimilate the authorities' rules and criteria? If an interpretive framework
constructed by middle-class white Euro-American heterosexual
men is perceived to exclude interpretations that are necessary for
interpreters who are committed to the liberation of marginalized
peoples, why should the exclusive framework be privileged?

Kermode stresses the extent to which this exclusion cannot be
explained simply as the experts' superior knowledge and better
judgment. Within his own field, he cites the example of an
untimely interpretation of Caliban as Wild Man; it was published
too early, and with "incorrect" theoretical backing, and the *homo
sylvestris* interpretation of Caliban had subsequently to be reinvent-
ed. Kermode cites a similar testimony, with a more powerful
punch line, from Michael Polanyi's tract, *The Tacit Dimension*.
Polanyi notes an article (published as a joke in the journal *Nature*)
that showed that the females of various higher mammals carried
their unborn young for durations that were evenly divisible by $\pi$.
Despite ample evidence and reliable statistical agreement, *"no
amount of evidence* could convince a modern biologist that gestation
periods are equal to integer multiples of the number $\pi$."[9]

Modern New Testament theologians are, like the doctors
Michel Foucault discussed in *The Archaeology of Knowledge*, posses-
sors of an exclusive right to make true statements about their field.
They are "individuals who—alone—have the right, sanctioned by
law or tradition, juridically defined or spontaneously accepted, to
proffer such a discourse."[10] As Foucault points out, the status of

---

[9]*The Tacit Dimension*, cited in "Can We Say?" 158 (my emphasis). One
might cite as contemporary examples in the field of biblical studies the
continued effort of dedicated inquirers to determine the identity of the
Fourth Gospel's Beloved Disciple, or Mark's naked fugitive (Mark 14:52).

[10]*The Archaeology of Knowledge*, trans. A. M. Sheridan Smith (New
York: Pantheon Books, 1972) 50.

"being a doctor" is a development of the late eighteenth century; it is not ontologically given, and claims to its exclusive appropriateness are under constant (though largely unsuccessful) dispute from chiropractors, homeopaths, acupuncturists, and others. The ground for a doctor's status is the doctor's participation in an institution devised by doctors to accredit only those who behave in determined ways; deviants from a professional norm are weeded out from the beginning, and expelled if they fall from grace after having attained medical authority. In like manner, modern New Testament theologians ignore works they *know* to diverge from modern standards.

There are good reasons for experts being treated as experts, and it should be noted that both Herrnstein Smith and Kermode are eminent literary theorists (not excluded victims of institutional oppression). At the same time, the benefits that disciplinary exclusion offers (freedom from the responsibility to consider absolutely every interpretation that comes down the road, a sense of a shared task, and so on) are not ideologically neutral; the voices modern New Testament theology refuses to hear are not only those of cranks and "fundamentalists."[11]

## • Disciplines and Autonomy •

The privilege interpretive experts claim, is justified by the disciplinary knowledge at their disposal. New Testament scholars are

---

[11]The Westar Institute is an interesting version of this phenomenon in reverse in biblical studies. One expressed purpose for forming this body of scholars has been to publicize the conclusions of modern scholarship, to counterbalance the media presence of right-wing interpreters. Among their projects are an edition of Jesus' sayings color-coded to the degree of probability that Jesus said them (according to the seminar members) and a new edition and translation of the Bible called "The Scholar's Version." Whereas Kermode and Herrnstein Smith are questioning the exclusionary character of institutional interpretation, the Westar Institute is questioning the exclusive media presence of noncanonical interpreters in the name of the exclusive academic interpretive framework.

presumably better informed about the text of the New Testament and its "legitimate" interpretation than are any other people; therefore, others ought to listen to what these scholars say. The problem with this assumption is not that it is groundless, but that it builds the edifice of disciplinary expertise on too narrow a foundation. A degree in New Testament will always require expertise in historical scholarship, but may include only relatively superficial acquaintance with hermeneutical problems, or sociological analysis, or Christian theology; "history" is the key reference point for the discipline.

There is, of course, nothing inherently wrong with specialization and expertise; these contribute conceptual clarity and enable deeper and more detailed research on subjects of common interest. The sharp focus that disciplined historical studies have brought to bear on New Testament interpretation is welcome. Once again, however, there are hazards that go with these benefits. Since "disciplines" are never pure, since their practices and interests are always alloyed with extradisciplinary practices and interests, the principal hazard is that a given discipline—in this case, historiography—may begin to treat the criteria and methods it has established for its own field as authoritative *outside* that field, as though historiography provided the *only* reliable criteria and methods. Standards that are voluntarily recognized by colleagues who share interpretive interests are thereby imposed on interpreters who are not committed to the same interests.

The appeal to historiographic standards has been particularly attractive to New Testament theology operating with modern assumptions, since academic historiography satisfies the chronological interests and the concern for disciplinary autonomy characteristic of modernity, while divorcing New Testament theology from its past ties to pietism and to orthodox Protestant dogmatics.

Disciplinary purity is not an unalloyed blessing, however. While Habermas can find hope for redemptive communicative rationality only in the careful division of labor among the autonomous spheres of science, morality, and art, guided by experts,[12] there is ample reason to believe that the tidy world of value spheres overlooks or conceals the critical impasses and ineradicable intertwinings of the spheres that complicate Habermas's vision. Moreover, the institution of the value-sphere or discipline may always be ideologically overdetermined; Western culture has tended to define the value-spheres on its own terms, and even within Western culture, it has been unusual for women or people of color to be accorded serious attention. Disciplines whose discourses have been defined and refined by middle-class Euro-American men tend to treat these men's criteria and interests as self-evidently valid.

Jean-François Lyotard has attacked the vision of a communicative rationality based on discrimination among rationalized discourses at a number of points. First, he raises the question of the role of reason in such a vision. Habermas regards philosophy's role in such a system as that of the modest, self-critical custodian of rationality, but Lyotard questions the possibility of a philosophy sufficiently purified of ideological overdetermination to fill that role.[13] Once a particular construal of rationality attains a position of dominance, it becomes "the institution of will into reason,"[14] with opposing construals immediately relegated to the status of "irrationality" and disordered communication—which Lyotard regards as an intellectual politics of terror. A dispute takes place between two parties—in this case two ways of reasoning—that cannot be resolved except on the principles of one or the other

---

[12]Cf. "Questions and Counterquestions," trans. James Bohman, in *Habermas and Modernity*, ed. Richard J. Bernstein (Cambridge MA: MIT Press, 1985) 196.

[13]Habermas harbors no illusions about the possibility of actually attaining conditions of discursive purity, but holds up the ideal quality of the "ideal speech situation" as a sufficient milepost by which a philosophy grounded in formal pragmatics may orient itself for properly exercising its custodial function.

[14]"Rules and Paradoxes and Svelte Appendix," *Cultural Critique* 5 (1986): 216.

party; so one of the parties is both plaintiff and judge.[15] Under such circumstances, dominant discourses make certain ideas "unpresentable"; they do not fit into the discourses available for expressing them.[16] Lyotard proposes that we avoid terror by cultivating more and more projects that defy the regimes of reason as instituted in Habermas's vision of harmonized value spheres; "Let us wage war on totality; let us bear witness to the unpresentable; let us activate the differences, and save the honor of the name."[17] Lyotard shows the conceptual repression that is the price we must pay for the benefits disciplinary autonomy offers, and points toward a philosophical framework that acknowledges itself as an interested party in the disputes it participates in.

## • Time and Determination •

Modernity has a compelling interest in time. For modernity, time is not simply another medium in which we think and move and have our being, but is a decisive matrix for determining human existence. Anthony Giddens has argued persuasively that the commodification of time that enabled the shift of labor relations from agricultural to industrial production—enshrined in the capitalist axiom "time is money"—has fundamentally shaped the discourse of time for those who live under cultural conditions

---

[15]Cf. "A Memorial for Marxism," trans. Cecile Lindsay in *Peregrinations: Law, Form, Event* (New York: Columbia University Press, 1988) 60-61; *The Differend*, trans. Georges Van Den Abbeele (Minneapolis: University of Minnesota Press, 1988); and "The *Différend*, the Referent, and the Proper Name," trans. Georges Van Den Abbeele, *Diacritics* 14 (1984): 4-14.

[16]One might think of the status of "the historical Jesus" before the interpretive developments described in Hans Frei's *Eclipse of Biblical Narrative* (New Haven: Yale University Press, 1974); there was simply no space for the notion that the referent of "the historical Jesus" might differ from the Jesus whom the West knew up to that point.

[17]"Answer to the Question: What Is Postmodernism?" trans. Régis Durand, in *The Postmodern Condition* (Minneapolis: University of Minnesota Press, 1984) 82; translation modified here.

governed by advanced capitalism.[18] Likewise, Baudrillard has claimed that modernity is shaped by a tripartite relation to time: a measured and abstract time that makes possible the division of labor and that modernity substitutes for the rhythm of festivals and seasons; a linear time that implies the constitution of the past, always separated from the present by the unvarying vector of time's flow; and a historic time that serves as a transcendental reference point for modernity.[19] The specific relation of modernity to time is implicated in aspects of modern New Testament theology that have presented problems to some of the theological critics cited above; this contingent construal of temporality, like the conceptions of disciplinary autonomy and professional expertise, must be displaced for an alternative approach to New Testament theology to blossom.

Michel de Certeau has pointed out the extent to which the sharp division of past from present is peculiar to the modern West. Whereas familiar historiography posits an initial discontinuity between "present" and "past," and recapitulates this division by creating historical epochs like "the Middle Ages," and "the Renaissance," some peoples appropriate their past in very different ways. De Certeau cites Indian society, wherein "a 'process of coexistence and reabsorption' is a cardinal fact," as an example. Other attitudes toward the past include taking "the past [as] a treasure placed in the *midst* of the society that is its memorial, a food intended to be chewed and memorized" (the Merina culture of Madagascar), or as a message from upriver (the Fô of Dahomey).[20]

---

[18]"Modernism and Postmodernism," *New German Critique* 22 (1981): 15-16.

[19]"Modernité," in the *Encyclopædia Universalis*, vol. 11 (Paris: Encyclopædia Universalis France, 1968) 140.

[20]Michel de Certeau, *The Writing of History*, trans. Tom Conley (New York: Columbia University Press, 1988) 3-4. The internal quotation in the first quoted phrase comes from Louis Dumont's "Le Problème d'Histoire," in *La Civilisation indienne et nous* (Paris: Colin, Coll. Cahiers des Annales, 1964) 31-54. While we should beware of staking too much on any particular alien "concepts of history" mediated to us by our fellow

I will not analyze here the pernicious effects of commodified time. They are less directly complicit in the travails of New Testament theology;[21] they are perhaps most problematic in the propensity to speculative periodization. When a New Testament theology must be conceived on the basis of a chronological development (as in the Baur tradition, reiterated in Wrede) that depends upon the same construal of the texts that the theology then explicates, the modern concern for temporality writes itself into its criteria of justification. I will not address the linearity of modern time, either; this would involve me in the protracted argument over "biblical ideas of time."[22]

The modern fascination with the phenomenon of history, however, involves pivotal claims of modern New Testament theology and its dissenters. Whereas Baudrillard describes history as modernity's transcendental reference point, this canonized orientation toward an absolute history has become increasingly problematic. It is problematic in the field of New Testament theology because it focuses attention not on the New Testament text but on events

---

Western intellectuals, the point that ours is not self-evidently the reasonable (or "natural" or "necessary") relation of a social group to its forebears seems indisputable.

[21]Heidegger's treatment of the temporality of *Dasein* in §65 of *Being and Time* implies some of the critical problems of the commodified time constitutive of modernity. Modern time, commodified time, defies the prospectivity (on the one hand) and thrownness (on the other hand) of *Dasein*, and especially their interpenetration; even more important, the key concept "repetition" (or "retrieval" or "recovery"—"*Wiederholung*") depends upon a nonmodern relation of *Dasein* to time. Cf. John Caputo, *Radical Hermeneutics* (Bloomington: Indiana University Press, 1987) 82-92, and passim.

[22]The cardinal documents in connection with this debate are Oscar Cullmann's *Christ and Time*; Thorlief Boman's *Hebrew Thought Compared with Greek*; and James Barr's *Semantics of Biblical Language* and *Biblical Words for Time*. Now see also Bruce J. Malina, "Biblical Time: Swiss or Mediterranean?" *Catholic Biblical Quarterly* 51 (1989): 1-31, who suggests that the entire debate is shaped by modern presuppositions about time.

and ideas, and because the history that can be recaptured and fit into the overarching chronological scheme is not necessarily the history scholars want to find (cf. problems concerning the resurrection, and concerning the role of women in the early Christian communities). More fundamentally, however, close examination undermines the assumption that "history" exists in a way that can justify its functioning as a critical principle. Modern New Testament theology has appealed to the discourse of history as a discourse that will tell the truth about the subjects of the New Testament writings; scientific historiography is authorized to dictate the proper referents and contexts for interpreting texts from which current readers have supposedly become separated in the name of a privileged relationship to the real, to the absolute history that is modernity's transcendental reference point. But critical examination of the practice of historical discourse has opened up the possibility that, to the contrary, the discourse of modern historiography is no better equipped to avoid ideological overdetermination than is the discourse of theology, or the New Testament's discourse of historiography.

In this context, it is important to attend to three possible referents of the term "history." First, we often use this term to designate the actual events of the past as they happened, which (ideally) would provide the measure of our efforts to identify and reconstruct those events. Second, "history" is used to refer to the discipline by which the past is reconstructed. Third, "history" is what historians produce; Bultmann's analysis of the synoptic tradition is a history in this sense, without regard to whether it is an accurate reflection of the processes it claims to represent. Therefore, "history" is, in different senses, simultaneously the subject, the producer, and the product. Yet only the first of these could carry the freight modern New Testament theology (and, according to Baudrillard, modernity in general) loads onto the term. Only as the transcendental signified of all truthful discourse can history (in the first sense) provide New Testament theology with an authority it otherwise lacks; only as a discourse of the Real can the discipline of history impose its own authority upon the discourse of New Testament theology.[23]

This distinction implies, however, that although modernity craves history of the first kind, it has access only to history of the third kind. Where the Original is sought, only reproductions can be found. It is the first sense of "history" that provides the validation for discourses which appeal to historical investigation; as de Certeau puts it, "in effect, every authority bases itself on the notion of the 'real,' which it is supposed to recount. It is always in the name of the 'real' that one produces and moves the faithful."[24] Moreover, the original has no abiding existence *except* in reproductions.[25] "By definition, all that is past does not exist. To be accurate

---

[23]This tripartite distinction is heuristic for the following section of the argument. I do not want to underwrite the Platonic assumptions it reflects; instead of positing a Real History that stands over against various (mere) interpretations, I would prefer to stress the extent to which various consensuses contest particular interpretations, and the way historical interpreters can always find elements within a consensus that provide a basis for internal contestation.

Arguments in defense of the necessity of history generally lack conceptual clarity in their use of the term "history." To take but one example, John McGrath ("The Rights and Limits of History," *The Downside Review* 108 (1990): 20-36) argues that "history is vital to Christianity and inherent to its nature," since "it is the way we come to know God," in this case apparently referring to history of the first kind, *real* history. But "the complexity of human knowledge . . . requires the freedom of history," here referring to the second, *disciplinary* use of "history." McGrath finally qualifies his insistence on "history" by imposing restrictions on the scope of historical reasoning that few historians would accept as legitimate (e.g., McGrath regards the authority of the Catholic church as a sound limit for historical investigation).

[24]"History: Science and Fiction," in *Heterologies: Discourse on the Other*, trans. Brian Massumi (Minneapolis: Univ. of Minnesota Press, 1986) 203.

[25]Such reproductions need not be "historical accounts." One might think, e.g., of the persistence of Eucharistic table-fellowship as a complex reproduction of an "original."

the object of history is whatever is *represented* as having hitherto existed."[26]

One may claim that these representations are adequate substitutes for the original history (or that, *faute de mieux*, we must content ourselves with admittedly flawed reproductions). This claim, however, begs the question by eliding the authority of the indisputable truth (of "history" of the first kind) with the authority of one among many interpretations of the truth. On what basis can it be claimed that a twentieth-century historian's version of the events in the first-century Mediterranean basin is truer than Luke's version (or Augustine's)? Only on a basis laid by the twentieth-century discipline of historical inquiry whose authority is in question. In this case—as in the question of interpretive expertise—the self-implication of criteria points toward the criteria's ideological overdetermination.

Mark Cousins has described the claims of historical investigation with relation to their warrants in "The Practice of Historical Investigation."[27] Cousins debunks the notion that historical investigation can protect us from anachronistic impositions of current conceptual categories upon data from antiquity—which notion lies at the heart of the modern attachment to history.

The initial, devastating thrust of Cousins's short essay cuts to the methodological heart of historiography. "[Historical investigation] must deal with questions of identity and difference."[28] Certain phenomena are the same as others in certain respects; other phenomena differ from them. The differences mark off the space of the particular: the male, Galilean, Jewish, apocalyptic preacher named Jesus, and so on. But the work of distinguishing must be counterbalanced by a process of identifying: like other

---

[26]Barry Hindess and Paul Q. Hirst, *Pre-Capitalist Modes of Production*, as quoted in Ann Wordsworth, "Derrida and Foucault: Writing the History of Historicity," in *Post-Structuralism and the Question of History*, ed. Derek Attridge, Geoff Bennington, and Robert Young (Cambridge: Cambridge University Press, 1987) 116.

[27]In *Poststructuralism and the Question of History*, 126-36.

[28]"Historical Investigation," 128.

apocalyptic preachers, like other Jews, like other human beings, like other men, like other charismatic figures of legend. The particularity of each moment, individual, and event must be correlated and compared (as in Troeltsch's principles), so that the result is not the evermore-nuanced distinction of one thing from everything else, nor the abstract course of general traits, but an account incorporating and ordering both tendencies.

> Historical writing is then caught up in a play of representing differences through identities which differ from each other. The point is not criticism of historical investigation but it underlines the fact that *there is a level of irreducible theoretical decision within historical writing*. What sorts of objects can be referred to, what objects have a sufficient difference to be considered different objects, what objects have a sufficient identity to be considered the same objects—all these issues will crucially affect the product of historical investigation but will not themselves be part of that product.[29]

Cousins suggests that one may respond to the necessity of prior theoretical decision either by adopting a general philosophy of history (be it Hegelian, Marxist, or scientific-evolutionary) or by eschewing the philosophy of history in favor of a disciplined practice of historiography.[30] The former is problematic for those who do not subscribe to the chosen philosophy of history, and the latter rests upon a problematic distinction between "the facts" and the subsequent interpretation.

> What seems to be at stake in this judgement is that whatever philosophical or political preferences the individual historian may exercise, they have nothing to do with the practice of historical

---

[29]"Historical Investigation," 12; my emphasis.

[30]Cousins's dichotomy seems to provide insufficient space for the situation into which (as I would judge) most current historians fit. They are indeed disciplined practitioners of an investigative discourse; but this discourse is underwritten, in at least an attenuated way, by the evolutionary/emancipatory metanarrative of modern liberalism.

investigation itself. The core of that practice is held to be one which neither requires nor supports any general conception of History at all. There is, quite simply, the past which can be known through its representations. Historical investigation may be modestly proposed as the discovery of the past through a range of techniques and standards of evidence.[31]

The conviction that evaluation of the past can bypass political and philosophical reflection, however, masks the necessary moment of theoretical decision which enables historians to specify and relate the identities and differences which are the constituents of historiographic discourse.

This maneuver creates the illusion that—whatever divergent conclusions historians reach—the discourse of history at least *begins* with appeals to uncontroversial documentary and archaeological evidence. These are the primary sources to which historians must always return, presumably because they are closer to their objects; they reflect their objects with fewer of the distortions introduced by mediation.[32] Once historical investigation is described this way, it shows a close and illuminating parallel with case law (wherein the highest rank is accorded eyewitness evidence, and secondhand testimony—hearsay—is excluded). In each case, rules of evidence and procedure govern proceedings that reach conclusions that have validity with respect to those rules and procedures, though not necessarily outside those conventions. Both discourses *make* truth. Just as, strictly speaking, there is no such thing as a "miscarriage of justice," so there is no such thing as a "miscarriage of historiography"; any point can always be reconsidered on appeal, provided the appeal falls within the bounds established by the rules of the discourse. Qualification, however, always haunts these discourses, for they pronounce verdicts that have ontological weight ("guilty," "innocent," "true," "false") but that are valid

---

[31]"Historical Investigation," 130.

[32]Here, however, is a paradox; for the historian also believes that her own account of the primary source's object is truer than that source's account (otherwise, the historian would be redundant).

only within the discipline. This points to what Cousins calls "the particular blind spot of historical investigation," "the blindness to the fact that its truth claims are established ultimately only within a definite practice which is not without its own conditions."[33]

Cousins warns that when history is taken as the key to interpretive problems, "as the one and only proper court for the enactment of a truthful discourse on what has existed,"[34] it overreaches the boundaries of its own situation as an interpretive practice. Granted that history always proceeds from prior theoretical decisions, decisions that cannot be called into question within the practice of historical investigation, any claim to epistemological or interpretive privilege is ill founded. Cousins dismisses such a claim as "fantasy" as he asserts that the historical mode is only one of the possible modes of the existence of objects, that historical investigation is only one of the ways of telling the truth about the past.[35]

This does not by any means imply that historical investigation is altogether unnecessary. One could hardly interpret the New Testament, for example, without relying on the painstaking philological and textual research that has produced the standard grammars, lexicons, critical editions, and translations. On the other hand, this inevitable reliance upon historical scholarship does not necessitate *exclusive* or even *primary* status for historical investigation. The role of historical judgment is not summed up by a binary choice of "aye or nay." Even the most rigorously ascetic historians are involved in the selection and suppression of evidence, and in the construction of persuasive accounts to defend their versions of history. In these (non-"historical") activities, historians elaborate a dialogical relation between the strictly historical aspect of their work and various rhetorical, fictive, and ideological aspects.

The historian cannot, after all, be obliged to limit oneself to the work of reproduction of the actual past; otherwise the historian would be chained to the prospect, reminiscent of Borges, of putting

---

[33]"Historical Investigation," 130.
[34]"Historical Investigation," 135.
[35]"Historical Investigation," 135.

together a replica universe that corresponds to this in every detail. At some point, the historian has done *enough* of the research and correlation by which we define the historian's vocation; the historian's task then is to arrive at conclusions, to display their coherence with some commonly held beliefs about the past (the "facts"), and to present his or her case in a compelling way.

The first of these supplementary tasks is inescapably ideological. It can be explicitly ideological, as when historians are explicitly propounding an apologetic argument for some prior philosophical commitment; such cases include, for example, many current analyses of the recent events in Eastern Europe (alleged to demonstrate the evolutionary supremacy of liberal democratic capitalism), or hypothetical resolutions of the so-called contradictions in scripture (alleged to salvage the literal inerrancy of the biblical text). Most of the time, however, the ideological underpinnings of historical argument are implicit, hidden in the very ideas of what *might* be true—ideas that are in many cases specific to the historiographic endeavor, and which thus fall outside the authorizing domain of historical investigation.

One example of the ideological problem immanent in the historical project comes from Jane Tompkins's efforts to learn about the relations between Native Americans and settlers in colonial America.[36] Tompkins undertook her studies in an effort to learn the truth about how the Puritans and Native Americans got along. She began with standard "secondary" texts, but soon found them unacceptably tainted with racial prejudice against Indians;[37] secondary texts sympathetic to Native Americans either patronized their subjects by accounting for them as underdeveloped or undertook an explanation of Native American behavior in their own

---

[36]"Indians: Textualism, Morality, and the Problem of History," *Critical Inquiry* 13 (1986): 101-19. Tompkins uses the language of "primary" and "secondary" sources, which—I have tried to show—is itself a distinction that underwrites modern assumptions.

[37]One source cited with approbation John Winthrop's description of a storm that "through God's mercy . . . did no hurt, but only killed one Indian with the fall of a tree" ("Indians," 105).

categories, which categories were so remote from the conventions of modern historiography that this interpretation could not clarify but only contrast with other sources. Tompkins's research into "primary" texts was no more helpful, but only emphasized the extent to which the firsthand accounts of the encounter between Europeans and Native Americans were themselves ideologically constructed. While she felt that accusations of massacre and genocide, on the one hand, and torture and kidnapping, on the other, demanded some judgment on her part, she saw no reliable grounds for condemning or condoning anyone; all the witnesses were interested parties. This is not the point of her essay, however. Her claim is that it was precisely her ideological determinations that led her to construct the historical impasse she saw: as a poststructuralist predisposed to the idea that "facts" are always theory-dependent, she found what she was looking for. And when she resumed her reflection on European-Native American relations, she did so not in the effort to find or provide a disinterested account, but to piece together an account that met her (ideologically determined) criteria for responsible historical narration.

Just as the historical interpreter is always entangled in ideological nets, so he or she also is hemmed in by the rhetorical and fictive aspects of historical discourse. As Hayden White has argued, claims about history necessarily involve questions of selection and emplotment;[38] historical discourse edits out information it deems irrelevant to the events in question, and situates those events in a narrative context that shows the events' appropriate precedents and their subsequent outcome.

The question of selectivity points to the problem of when a historical account is adequate. Exactly how much need one consider? White cites as an example the *Annals of Saint Gall.*[39] During the

---

[38]Cf. *Metahistory* (Baltimore: Johns Hopkins University Press, 1973); *Tropics of Discourse* (Baltimore: Johns Hopkins University Press, 1978); "The Value of Narrativity in the Representation of Reality" and "The Narrativization of Real Events," in *On Narrative*, ed. W. J. Mitchell (Chicago: University of Chicago Press, 1981) 1-24 and 249-54.

[39]"The Value of Narrativity," 7-16.

period between 709 and 734, the annalist provided a dozen clipped entries, including "Flood everywhere" in 712 and "Charles fought against the Saracens at Poitiers on Saturday" in 732; fifteen years have no entries whatever. The principle of selectivity with which the annalist operated is entirely obscure; why is the Battle of Poitiers mentioned, but not the Battle of Tours? Why was the day of the week worth notice, but not the month and day? But however idiosyncratic the annalist's choice of entries may seem, White stresses that we must not dismiss the annalist as a poor historian. Instead, White suggests that the annalist had criteria of his own, criteria by which the *Annals of Saint Gall* is a quite satisfactory record. This point is amplified by Marilyn Robinson Waldman in a response to White's essay;[40] Waldman points out that unfavorable judgments about the quality of the *Annals* assume that the annal is a failed effort to achieve what is only really attained with modern narrative historiography. She supports Barbara Herrnstein Smith's alternative view that historiography (of whatever kind) is, like fiction, a response to specific circumstances—and that

> the extent to which a narrator takes or claims responsibility for the veridicality of his tale will serve different interests and, accordingly, have a different sort of value for himself and for his audience depending on the nature and constraints of the transaction between them and, conversely, that different situations and structures of motivation will elicit and reward different *kinds and degrees* of truth claims.[41]

In other words, the adequacy of historical statements depends on the narrator's and reader's motivations and interests. A simple historical narrative might be suitable for introducing elementary schoolchildren to the gross outline of events; a somewhat more detailed narrative might serve as background for a novelist; neither would be useful to a professional historian.

---

[40]"'The Otherwise Unnoteworthy Year 711': A Reply to Hayden White," in *On Narrative*, 240-48.

[41]Barbara Herrnstein Smith, "Narrative Versions, Narrative Theories," in *On Narrative*, 231; as quoted in Waldman, 248.

Historical narrative is not only necessarily selective; it is also necessarily rhetorical. It is, of course, rhetorical inasmuch as historical articles aim to persuade their audience; but Hayden White has pointed out that the rhetorical character of historiography runs much deeper. A historical narrative, he argues, will eventually take one of four shapes—each corresponding to one of the classical rhetorical tropes: metaphor, metonymy, synecdoche, or irony.[42] The dominant trope provides a pattern by which the historian (usually unconsciously) sorts and arranges data into narrative form. A tendency to see history metaphorically impels historians to emplot their narratives in the form of romance; synecdoche, toward the comic; metonymy, toward the tragic; and irony, toward the satiric. "In short, 'interpretation' in historical thought would consist of the formalization of the phenomenal field originally constituted by language itself on the basis of a dominant tropological wager."[43] Historiographic interpretation is formed and informed by tropes; there is no "real history" in historiography, only ideologically grounded narrative.[44]

These profound criticisms of the discipline of history do not effect the dissolution of the enterprise, or reveal it to be vain or self-deluded; on the contrary, they simply show a number of reasons to doubt that historical investigation is a generally applicable way of solving problems. Interpreters who posit "history" as a privileged context for interpretation, then appeal to history as a ground for their interpretation, have to face these probing ques-

---

[42]White argues this thesis at exhaustive length in *Metahistory*, and in a condensed version in "Interpretation in History," *Tropics of Discourse*, 51-80.

[43]"Interpretation in History," 74.

[44]White consistently runs the risk of reinstating the Platonic dualism of "real history" and "interpreted history" in reverse; where conventional historiographers have sought to minimize the interpretive aspect of their work in favor of presenting bare facts, White's emphasis on the tropological construction of history often suggests a realm of "real history" which awaits variegated rhetorical appropriations. Once again I reject the dichotomy.

tions about the ideological, rhetorical, and fictive aspects of history—questions which may well be no easier to answer than were the questions that impelled a turn to history in the first place. If modernity situates history as a Supreme Court of interpretive inquiry (to continue Cousins's judicial metaphor), it will do so at the cost of silencing these contestatory voices; but for those who are suspicious of the ideology or rhetoric of historiography, it is not necessary to employ historical investigation as a final arbiter of interpretation.

All this being said, some will persist in defending historical interpretation on the basis that current cultural conditions require that intelligible (or, in Van Harvey's case, "intellectually honest") discourse reflect modernity's interest in historicity. In connection with the project of demythologizing (not, admittedly, in explicit connection with the hermeneutics of historical inquiry) Bultmann occasionally writes this way: "It is impossible to use electric light and the wireless and to avail ourselves of modern medical and surgical discoveries, and at the same time to believe in the New Testament world of spirits and miracles."[45] It is certainly true that there are people who will insist upon historical foundations for New Testament theology; they may do so, and may criticize others who prefer other approaches, but they will have to recognize the difficulties which their adherence to the standards of modernity brings them.

Other interpreters—represented at the most sophisticated level by Ernst Käsemann—ground their insistence on historical interpretation on the claim that the orthodox interpretation of the Incarnation requires a painstaking search for the facts about Jesus of Nazareth (and the early communities), lest Christianity slip into

---

[45]"New Testament and Mythology," in *Kerygma and Myth* [vol. 1], ed. Hans Werner Bartsch, trans. Reginald H. Fuller (London: SPCK, 1960; New York: Harper & Row, 1961) 5. If I were performing *Sachkritik* upon Bultmann, I would de-emphasize this sentence in favor of the benign claim that historical interpretation is incumbent upon modern people— which claim leaves open the possibility that a reluctance to rely on historical interpretation may simply imply that the interpreter is not "modern."

Docetism.[46] Such a claim assumes that historical investigation comes closer to "truth" and "facts" than other sorts of discourse, a claim the scholars cited above have rendered problematic. By the same token, Käsemann's position may not be the only way of resisting Docetism; indeed, exclusive attention to the *actual* Jesus, accessible to historical investigation, runs a grave risk of nurturing Ebionism. Nonetheless, it should be noted that Käsemann's argument rests primarily upon theological warrants (and only secondarily on the assumption that historical investigation is the only way of regaining contact with ancient truth); to the extent that his argument is theologically motivated, it is not distinctively modern and therefore escapes some of the force of my counterargument.[47]

## • Ancients and Moderns •

The distinction that brought "modernity" into existence—the contrast between "Ancients" and "Moderns"—has unambiguously favored the latter term for hundreds of years; this is, after all, "the modern age." The opposition between "ancient" and "modern" is not static, however; as Jean-François Lyotard points out, "the very idea of modernity is narrowly correlated with the principle that it is possible and necessary to break with tradition and to found a manner of living and thinking that is absolutely new."[48] What was modern in 1900 will look quite antique in 2000; its essential quality

---

[46]"Vom theologischen Recht historisch-kritiker Exegese," *Zeitschrift für Theologie und Kirche* 64 (1967): 279-80.

[47]It must be acknowledged that Käsemann's essays "Blind Alleys in the 'Jesus of History' Controversy" (in *New Testament Questions of Today*, trans. W. J. Montague [Philadelphia: Fortress Press, 1969] 22-65) and "The Problem of the Historical Jesus" (in *Essays on New Testament Themes*, trans. W. J. Montague [London: SCM, 1964; Philadelphia: Fortress Press, 1982] 15-47) show an extraordinarily subtle grasp of the problem of historical investigation as a discourse of the Real. Still, he insists that "A New Testament theology is . . . of necessity a historical discipline" ("The Problem of a New Testament Theology," *New Testament Studies* 19 [1973]: 242).

[48]*Le Postmoderne Expliqué aux Enfants* (Paris: Éditions Galilée, 1986) 121.

of "newness" would have worn off. Therefore, modernity entails a continual cycle of surpassing what has been modern until now. It is just this endless drive to surpass that makes problematic modernity's social and epistemological privilege.[49]

In the first place, this ensures that modernity's status as an "incomplete project" (Habermas) is not the result of a wrong turn at the Hegelian or Marxian crossroads; rather, incompleteness is built into the modern project. It will always be incomplete, precisely because it will never be modern *enough*. An illustration drawn from the sphere of New Testament theology would be the conflict between the insistence that New Testament theology be built upon the foundations of historical investigation, and the inevitably ephemeral quality of those results; a modern New Testament theology is outdated shortly after it is published.[50] (Of course, being outdated is both the great danger of modern scholarship and its inevitable fate.)

Modernity may choose to legitimate its cultural dominance by appealing to the great progress it has brought. Though Blumenberg's monumental justification of modernity's "human self-assertion" operates at a highly sophisticated level, his argument is

------

[49]In this connection, Lyotard submits that modernity does not so much surpass the tradition as it represses it (*Postmoderne Expliqué*, 121). Thus, for him, the prefix "post-" is not intended to reinscribe the "postmodern" in the endless cycle of surpassing ("even *better* than modern"), but is closer to the prefix "ana-", in the sense of "analysis, anamnesis, anagogy, and anamorphosis, which elaborate an 'initial forgetfulness'" (126); Lyotard's postmodernity strives to remind modernity of what it has forgotten/repressed.

[50]Indeed, given the delays characteristic of the publishing industry, a N.T. theology is fortunate not to be out of date *before* it is published. This is *not* to argue that the continually shifting character of critical scholarship's conclusions alone makes those conclusions a methodologically or theologically inadequate basis for N.T. theology; rather, I am simply arguing that a N.T. theologian may have good reason to be hesitant to build her work on such foundations, particularly if there are other sites available—as I will argue below.

effectively similar to this. Yet every available claim to progress is two-edged; progress has brought world wars, totalitarianism, the exploitation that has brought wealth to the Northern Hemisphere at the expense of the Southern Hemisphere, unemployment and urban poverty, education crises, and so on.[51] The defense of progress must focus on specific fields, and ignore the regressive social costs of that progress.

One critique of modernity's self-consuming drive to surpass will provide a key concept for the ensuing discussion. Gianni Vattimo's resistance of modernity identifies modernity's need to surpass, to overcome, with Heidegger's *Überwindung* (cf. chap. 1, above). Vattimo proposes we give up the endless cycle of *Überwindung* in favor of *Verwindung* (convalescence, resignation). This *Verwindung* does not indicate "surpassing" but "learning-to-live-with."[52] Modernity cannot be overcome; in a paradox worthy of the Sophists, if you overcome modernity, modernity wins. Instead, one can only free oneself of the modern cycle of *Überwindung* by accepting it and going along. What is more, *Verwindung* can also mean "twisting" or "torsion."[53] One who is *verwunden* to modernity does not simply accept modernity as it is, but turns it to a different end. If one builds a New Testament theology on historical foundations, the foundations may shift and the walls cave in; if one recognizes that the historical aspects of the theology will flex as historical construals of the text change, then one may choose not to assign to history the role of foundation.

---

[51]The list is from Lyotard, *Postmoderne Expliqué*, 130.

[52]*The End of Modernity*, 39-40, 52, 171-80. "We know from what Heidegger told the French translators of *Vorträge und Aufsätze*, where the term appears in an essay concerning the *Überwindung*—overcoming—of metaphysics, that it indicates a going-beyond that is both an acceptance and a deepening" (172).

[53]Vattimo acknowledges that this is only a peripheral aspect of the word's semantic range (172); at the same time, the point is not that the word does the conceptual work, but that the word can emblematize that work.

In short, the opposition between modernity and antiquity is inscribed into modernity itself, and is not a necessary opposition. On this account, one does not escape this opposition by ascribing it to an unfortunate previous era (or "paradigm") which we have now surpassed.[54] One can escape modernity's "ancient/modern" opposition by dwelling within it, decentering it and turning it. Thus, this final aspect of modernity's physiognomy is not binding—at least not in the way modern New Testament theologians have claimed—upon the New Testament theologian who is dissatisfied with the great divorce separating one from the "ancient" interpreters.

## • Conclusion •

In response to the critics of New Testament theology's modernity, I have marshalled the testimony of philosophers and theoreticians to make a case that the problem in question may not simply be a matter of fine-tuning modern New Testament theology, but one of changing course from procedures and criteria that derive their authority from assumptions embedded in modernity. I suggest that these critics give up trying to divert the vast momentum of modern New Testament theology into paths more agreeable to *them*, and instead undertake the project of imagining New Testament theology in a different way. My final chapter constitutes an initial schematic proposal toward that end.

---

[54]One of the grave problems of much "postmodern" discourse is its relegation of "modernity" to an ashcan, proudly boasting of our "postmodern era." It should go without saying that I reject such a flat interpretation of what "postmodernity" entails. My thesis in this book is that there are alternatives to modernity, not that modernity is bad and needs to be abandoned.

# Chapter 6

# Prospects for Nonmodern New Testament Theology

*Nothing opposes historical investigation as such; nothing denies its importance; nothing undervalues its humane pleasures. All that is opposed here is the claim that such investigations can resolve problems within the human sciences.* —Mark Cousins

The starting point for an approach to interpretation without the imperatives of modernity, a hermeneutic that can open up a richer field for discontented New Testament theologians, is the very simple observation that interpretation is something people do with things. It is something very complicated, and I will not short-circuit that complexity by appealing to the (indisputable) fact that people interpret constantly, without fretting about it.[1] Instead, I will treat interpretation as the practice of "making sense" of things—in this case, making sense of the New Testament.[2] My shadow interlocutor throughout this section will be the hermeneutics of *Verstehen*, of "understanding," that seeks to establish and

---

[1]John Caputo enlists the later Heidegger (among others) in formulating a radical hermeneutics of "keeping the difficulty of life alive" and "keeping its distance from the easy assurances of metaphysics and the consolations of philosophy." *Radical Hermeneutics* (Bloomington: Indiana University Press, 1987) 3.

[2]This starting point, which I have been working with for several years, is adumbrated in a short article by Jonathan Culler: "Making Sense," *20th Century Studies* 12 (1974): 27-36.

regulate legitimate interpretation on criteria which inhere to the posited nature of "understanding" or "textuality"—an interpretive categorical imperative.[3]

### • Making Sense of New Testament Theology •

The phrase "making sense" points to the active role of the interpreter who strives to subsume the interpretand (be it a writing, a gesture, an utterance, an artifact)[4] under categories with which the interpreter is already familiar. As Jonathan Culler puts it, the phrase "making sense" "links meaning with an active, creative process and thus frees us from the lapsarian theoretical postulate which makes interpretation a guilt-ridden and nostalgic attempt to recover an original meaning which time and the human condition have obscured."[5] As such, interpretation depends to a great extent upon the categories the interpreter can deploy, the relative importance of those categories to the interpreter, and the interpreter's imagination in deploying them. Culler illustrates this with the sentence, "Colorless green ideas sleep furiously." At first glance, the sentence is utterly nonsensical; but we can quickly *make* sense of it by labelling it "an example of a nonsensical sentence." Further, Culler suggests this might be a poetic assertion that "bland and as yet unripe ideas . . . lead a life of furious dormancy, repressed because of their blandness and able to accede to their potential fury only if they are awoken by an imaginative infusion

---

[3]The phrase "interpretive categorical imperative" is Jeffrey Stout's, from "The Relativity of Interpretation," *The Monist* 69 (1986): 114. Some scholars treat interpretation as subject to a natural law, so that those who disregard historical context (or authorial intention) become the hermeneutical equivalent of cannibals. The burden of my argument in this chapter will be that anarchic interpreters—like cannibals—seem to be legendary projections of fearful Western minds.

[4]Hereafter I will refer to the interpretand as "the text," without prejudice as to the character of the posited text.

[5]"Making Sense," 29.

of life and color."[6] Hypothetical senses of the sentence could be multiplied indefinitely, but the point is that an interpreter can make sense of even a deliberately nonsensical and self-contradictory statement. In short, sense is something *ascribed to* the text, not a property that the text *has*.

The text, on this account, marks the place of an absence of sense where we, as interpreters, want to establish sense. Such an account stands in diametric opposition to attempts to treat texts as sites or containers of the presence of sense.[7] We have seen implicit appeals to this approach in the imperative to hear the text's own voice, to read the text on its own terms, or to exegete ("read out from") rather than eisegete ("read into") the text. The difficulty with the claims for present sense contained in the text is that the sense that is present is never present *enough*; and it is the sensible *interpreter* who helpfully offers to tell us what the text's own voice sounds like, or what its own terms are, or what is in the text to be read out. Then, however, the authoritative scene of present sense is not the text, but the interpreter's account of the text in the context of the extratextual information the interpreter deems appropriate.

Richard Rorty illuminates the suggestion that we treat interpretation as "making sense" of textual objects as he proposes that we transgress the disciplinary divide that separates the "hard sciences" from textual interpretation.[8] Just as the scientist strives to make sense of a lump based on principles of science in which the scientist has been trained, so a reader seeks to make sense of a text on the basis of hermeneutical principles in which the reader has

---

[6]"Making Sense," 29.

[7]Lakoff and Johnson offer a highly pertinent discussion of the power of the "conduit metaphor" of meaning over hermeneutical discourse in their *Metaphors We Live By* (Chicago: University of Chicago Press, 1980) 10-11; cf. also 29-30.

[8]Cf. "Texts and Lumps," *New Literary History* 17 (1985): 1-16, and "Science as Solidarity," in *The Rhetoric of the Human Sciences*, ed. John S. Nelson, Allan Megill, and Donald McCloskey (Madison: University of Wisconsin Press, 1987) 37-52.

been trained. In both cases, the interpreter may (or may not) be open to the possibility that the principles he or she has been taught do not answer the needs of the interpretive problem; but the interpreter will never be able to solve his or her problems by referring to a theory of legitimate interpretation (or "understanding"), since this is exactly what is in question when interpretation is a problem.

"Making sense" also provides the advantage of suggesting the important question of motivation, because "making sense" does not imply a particular context in relation to which the interpreter will locate the problematic text. *Why* is the interpreter trying to make sense of this text, and with relation to what? The interpreter may not defuse the question by claiming simply to be seeking the truth; the point of the question is not whether the interpreter is seeking to mislead the audience, but *why* the interpreter has chosen to interpret this text in the first place. Why *this*, rather than another text; why *interpret* it, rather than simply repeating it? The follow-up question, "Why in this context rather than another?" declines the opportunity to treat one particular context as natural or given. Once again, the interpreter avoids no problems by claiming that one can understand a text only by setting it in a specific context.

At the same time, the interpretive approach that foregrounds "making sense" directs attention to the interpreter's interests. What does the interpreter hope to end up with? Interpretation always has some purpose, and this purpose determines the sort of interpretation one devises—though not the particular interpretation itself. An interpreter who expects to use a text as evidence in a historical argument may reach a different interpretation from an interpreter who is building a case concerning archetypes and the collective unconscious. Jeffrey Stout has in several articles shown the extent to which "interests" and "purposes"—rather than any posited "nature of meaning"—determine the appropriate basis for interpreting a text.[9]

---

[9]Notably, "What Is the Meaning of a Text?" *New Literary History* 14

Marxists will say that the meaning of a text is a matter of its position in a context defined by the history of class struggle. A Freudian will say that the real meaning is a matter of personality and family romance as construed by the devices of psycho-analytic theory.[10]

At one point, Stout even specifically suggests that a religious community would have good reason for interpreting its canonical texts without primary regard for authorial intention:

> An apostle of a religious movement writes a letter that is later canonized. You may be interested in constructing a picture that explains what the apostle was up to. If so, you will map the letter onto your language accordingly. But you may be interested instead in the letter as a scriptural book, in the relations its words and sentences take on in its canonical setting, and in its use as a normative document some centuries after it was authored. In that case, you will probably want an interpretation you can ascribe to the community for which the letter functions as scripture, thereby helping to explain the community's behavior under circumstances unlike the author's own.[11]

Stout suggests it is misguided to claim that given readings fail to reflect the *real meaning* (or fail to understand) the text. In the first place, he argues, "meaning" functions simply as a placeholder for the practices of a theory of interpretation; and in the second place, if there were some universally accessible "real meaning," it would simply displace disagreement about the meaning to disagreement about what to do about the meaning. He has no use for either hermeneutics (in the sense of the search for *understanding*, "the quest for *the* method of interpretation"[12]) or a privileged

---

(1982): 1-12; "The Relativity of Interpretation." *The Monist* 69 (1986): 103-18; and "A Lexicon of Postmodern Philosophy," *Religious Studies Review* 13 (1987): 18-22.

[10]"What Is the Meaning," 5.

[11]"Relativity," 110.

[12]"Lexicon," 21. Stout allows for hermeneutics in the "good sense" of

method ("a self-sufficient set of rules for performing some task; what students of religion would like to discover by reading philosophy . . . perfectly captured in this sentence from Camus: *Quand on n'a pas de caractère, il faut bien se donner une méthode*"[13]). For Stout, interpretation is good or bad, valid or invalid, but these judgments are made with respect to the interests and purposes of the interpreter, not the text itself.[14]

Such an account of interpretation fits well with the Heideggerian description of interpretation given in §32 of *Being and Time*. Heidegger connects interpretation with "understanding" here, but in so doing he veers from the tradition that sees understanding as the end of interpretation. Instead, Heidegger posits understanding as the *precondition* of interpretation: "interpretation is grounded existentially in understanding."[15] Interpretation happens when that which is customarily unproblematic (*zuhanden*) is rendered problematic (*vorhanden*); we resort to interpretation to overcome the alienness of the *vorhanden* text. But we can do so only in terms of what is already *zuhanden* to us. We do not restate an alien text in equally alien terms, but in unproblematic, easily grasped terms. As Gerald Bruns points out, this suggests that "the structure of inter-

---

"the art of enriching our language in conversation with others; also, reflection designed to raise this art to self-consciousness without reducing it to a set of rules; the assumption that any successful attempt at rational commensuration is likely to be temporary" (21).

[13]"Lexicon," 20. There is likewise an "innocuous sense" of method: "rules of thumb for performing a task; not a substitute for *phronesis* and tact" (20).

[14]Cf. Robert Morgan's observation that "texts, like dead men and women, have no rights, no aims, no interests. They can be used in whatever way readers or interpreters choose": *Biblical Interpretation* (Oxford: Oxford University Press, 1988) 7. Stephen Fowl draws out the implications of Stout's claims in the context of biblical criticism in his essay, "The Ethics of Interpretation or What's Left Over after the Elimination of Meaning," *Society of Biblical Literature Seminar Papers* (1988): 69-81.

[15]*Being and Time*, trans. John MacQuarrie and Edward Robinson (New York: Harper & Row, 1962) 242.

pretation is figural, rather than, say, intentional."[16] Bruns takes allegorical interpretation as a positive example of what Heidegger is implying; in allegorical interpretation, we rationalize the text into a world of familiar concepts and entities, we translate the *vorhanden* into the *zuhanden*. And in this sense, all interpretation is allegorical interpretation:[17] modern New Testament interpretation dwells in a world of historiographically approved reference points, and maps the New Testament texts onto those points, but this is not formally different from the Patristic proclivity for mapping the text onto reference points approved by dogmatic theology.

One implication of this approach is that the problem of "special hermeneutics"—a problem Benjamin Jowett thrust into the spotlight in England with "On the Interpretation of Scripture" (his contribution to *Essays and Reviews*[18])—dissolves. Each hermeneutical situation is defined both by its proper interests and purposes, and by the audience that will authoritatively receive or reject an interpretation. The fact that most hermeneutical situations pose no challenge to our interpretive capacities does not provide a lever called "general hermeneutics" which takes precedence over the distinct context in which particular interpretations take place. Stanley Fish has correctly shown that "normal circumstances, literal language, direct speech acts, the ordinary, the everyday, the obvious," and "what goes without saying" are themselves instances of

---

[16]Gerald Bruns, "On the Weakness of Language in the Human Sciences," in *The Rhetoric of the Human Sciences*, ed. John S. Nelson, Allan Megill, and Donald McCloskey (Madison: University of Wisconsin Press, 1987) 243.

[17]This is the thrust of Morton Bloomfield's excellent "Allegory as Interpretation," *New Literary History* 3 (1972): 301-17. See also A. K. M. Adam, "The Future of Our Allusions," *Society of Biblical Literature Seminar Papers* (1992): 5-13.

[18]Of course, the question had been considered at some length in German hermeneutical discourse; cf. Friedrich Schleiermacher's *Hermeneutics: The Handwritten Manuscripts*, ed. Heinz Kimmerle, trans. James Duke and Jack Forstman, AAR Texts and Translation Series 1 (Missoula MT: Scholars Press, 1977).

special hermeneutics: "language does not have a shape independent of context, but since language is only encountered in contexts and never in the abstract, it always has a shape, although it is not always the same one."[19] Whereas Pat Kelly (an outfielder for the Baltimore Orioles) understood his athletic accomplishments as a sign of divine favor, an interviewer could only make sense of them "on strictly a baseball level."[20] Readers make sense of mystery novels, theology essays, operas, grocery lists, funerary inscriptions, and the Bible in *specific* ways. Indeed, Daniel Boyarin has made this aspect of interpretation a keynote of his recent analysis, *Intertextuality and the Reading of Midrash*.[21] Boyarin takes the circumstantial determination of interpretation as a thematic device that enables him to get beyond sterile disputes over "objectivity" and "subjectivity," and thereby to treat midrash as a way of coping on the one hand with the underdetermination of the biblical text and, on the other hand, with the impossibility of formulating an overarching explanation of the ways in which midrashic interpreters resolve that underdetermination.[22] Just as there is no extrinsic rule that could compel Pat Kelly to talk about hanging curve balls instead of the power of the Spirit, so there is no extrinsic rule that restricts making sense of the Bible by treating

---

[19]"Normal Circumstances, Literal Language, Direct Speech Acts, the Ordinary, the Everyday, the Obvious, What Goes without Saying, and Other Special Cases," *Is There a Text in This Class?* (Cambridge MA: Harvard University Press, 1979) 268-92; the quotation is from Fish's introduction to the article on 268.

[20]"Normal Circumstances," 270.

[21]Bloomington: Indiana University Press, 1990.

[22]Cf. esp. *Intertextuality*, 18-19, and the quotation from Gerald Bruns: "Midrash is not only responsive to the Scriptures as a way of coping with the text's wide-ranging formal problems; it is also responsive to the situations in which the Scriptures exert their claim upon human life" (18). The citation is from Bruns's "Midrash and Allegory," in *The Literary Guide to the Bible*, ed. Robert Alter and Frank Kermode (Cambridge MA: Harvard University Press, 1987) 629.

it in the same way as "any other book."[23] There is no *sacrificium intellectus* in undertaking a special hermeneutical approach when *every* hermeneutic is a special hermeneutic.

There are several distinct advantages of the foregoing approach to interpretation. First, it avoids reference to a standard that is itself contested. After all, critics who share a commitment to understand the text often disagree vehemently over what that understanding entails. Under such circumstances, the term "understanding" can only be the projected image of the interpreter's own ideological stance. Helmut Koester and F. F. Bruce both seek to understand the resurrection narratives, but each would claim that the other fails to understand; and the dispute hinges not on a matter of interpretation, but on the conflict of the ideologies that are put into play in the process of interpretation.

This impasse points to a second advantage of this approach to hermeneutics: its explicit acknowledgment of the social character of interpretation. If one accepts the proposition that the validity of interpretation is an active "making sense" which is at the same time ineluctably enmeshed with the interests and purposes of the interpreter (and the interpreter's audience), one sees the social aspect of interpretation not as a categorical imperative of communicative action, but as the responsibility of the interpreter to a particular group of readers. Several critics have analyzed this phenomenon under varying rubrics: Stanley Fish, as the role of the

---

[23]So Ernst Käsemann's defense of historical criticism rests upon a fallacious dichotomy when he says that "[L]esen wir . . . die Bibel nicht als ein vom Himmel gefallenes Buch, dessen Verständnis übernatürliche Erleuchtung voraussetzt. Verstehen kann hier jedermann unter den gleichen Schwierigkeiten, wie sie andere antike Schriften bereiten, falls er sich darum Mühe gibt" ("Vom theologischen Recht historisch-kritischer Exegese," *Zeitschrift für Theologie und Kirche* 64 [1967]: 264). There are not two alternatives, "a book fallen from heaven, requiring supernatural illumination to be understood" and "any other ancient writing"; the possible approaches to making sense of the New Testament are innumerable. The vast number of options defeats Käsemann's defense of the theological authority of historical criticism by dissolving the "either/or" he offers.

"interpretive community" in interpretation; Frank Kermode, as "institutional control of interpretation"; and Tony Bennett, as the constructive role of "reading formations."[24] The burden of these studies is the insight that interpretation is not a homogeneous practice with logically dispensable specific texts, contexts, and audiences, but that the context, the audience, the text, and the reader are bound together in the act of interpretation. This thesis is also related to Habermas's ethics of communicative behavior, though these scholars eschew Habermas's interest in positing a universal and necessary status for interpretation. All of these critics, however, press the case for seeing interpretation not as a matter between an individual and a text, but as a much more populous affair. The individual does not interpret the text in isolation from the social groups of which she is a part; instead, the social groups jostle for priority in impressing their interpretive agenda on the individual. Since much in contemporary culture is strongly influenced (if not ruled) by the assumptions characteristic of modernity, modern New Testament theologians are reasonable in arguing that their audience must acknowledge the power of their interpretive dicta. The pivotal question here, however, is not whether there is good reason for pursuing New Testament theology as a distinctly modern enterprise; the question is whether any other sort of New Testament theology is legitimate. The answer to that question is, "Yes, for those interpreters who do not grant primary allegiance to the imperatives of modernity." Quite bluntly, there are no transcendent rules or criteria for judging interpretations.

In other words, if Walter Wink is more committed to the psychological well-being of his audience than he is to his audience's harmony with modern culture, then he is well justified in proposing that that audience feel free to interpret the Bible in nonmodern

---

[24]*Is There a Text in This Class?*; Frank Kermode, "Institutional Control of Interpretations" (and other relevant essays) in *The Art of Telling* (Cambridge MA: Harvard University Press, 1983) 168-84; Tony Bennett, "Texts in History," in *Post-Structuralism and the Question of History*, ed. Derek Attridge, Geoff Bennington, and Robert Young (Cambridge: Cambridge University Press, 1987) 63-81.

ways. If Elisabeth Schüssler Fiorenza is more certain that gender equality is the basis of any sound relation between Christians and their Bible than she is of the necessity of modern hermeneutical laws, then she may rightly reject modern readings that limit the theme of sexual equality to the margins of the Bible. Such readings will appear troublesome to interpreters whose primary hermeneutical loyalty is to characteristically modern approaches. Modern readers will lament the anachronistic tendentiousness with which Matthew might be made into an evangelist of women's liberation, or the Revelation represented as an archetypal journey to individuation. They will accuse nonmodern interpreters of importing agendas that are alien to the disciplinary role of New Testament studies, especially if those interpreters have interests and purposes oriented toward dogmatic theology. They will warn that, if the constraints on interpretation are social rather than disciplinary, then *just anyone* can propound legitimate New Testament theology. These ominous consequences do not, however, show the necessity of modern New Testament theology; instead they mark out the intellectual and social limits of the jurisdiction of the rules of modern New Testament theology. If—as I have argued here—there are not transcendent criteria for interpretation, but only local customs and guild rules, the reluctance modern New Testament theologians express about admitting the possible legitimacy of other appropriations of the New Testament is an expression of cultural imperialism and intellectual xenophobia.

Third, treating interpretation as "making sense" of a text, and so stressing the social dimension of interpretation, encourages a less exclusively intellectual conception of interpretation. That is, if legitimate interpretation concentrates on excavating buried past meaning from a text, the debate over interpretation will persistently revert to the intellectual question of whether the origins have been assessed correctly; any subsequent use of the text (as in Nicholas Lash's treatment of "performing the Scriptures"[25]) will

---

[25]In *Theology on the Way to Emmaus* (London: SCM Press, 1986) 37-46. The entire second section of *Theology on the Way to Emmaus* spins out the

wait upon the power of the exegete to effect his or her interpretation of the text's origins. One need not wait upon the exegete, however, to make sense of the text; and one may well argue that a correct theological interpretation of the New Testament is a fundamentally practical, *enacted* phenomenon. On this account, St. Francis's *enacted* New Testament theology is as worthy of consideration as any modern interpreter's *conceptualized* New Testament theology.

"Making sense of New Testament theology" would then consist in formulating an interpretation that begins with the sense one makes of the New Testament and then restates it in a different way. It is a repetition of the New Testament, to the extent that it partakes simultaneously of identity and difference. Like Althusser's interpretation of Marx, or Lacan's of Freud, the New Testament theologian's interpretation would continue the discourse of the canonized text in keeping with the theologian's (and the audience's) sense of the New Testament.[26] The interpretation will rest in part on historical grounds, but also in part on various other grounds, and there is no extrinsic rule by which the correct proportions of ingredients can be determined. But, freed from what Culler called the "guilt-ridden and nostalgic attempt to recover an original meaning that time and the human condition have obscured," the interpreter will not be embarrassed or over-confident about recovering the treasure hidden in the locked chest. Instead, "placing himself at the exterior of the text, he constitutes a new exterior for it, writing texts out of texts";[27] he will go forward to interpret with παρρησία.

---

implications of Lash's "performative" hermeneutic. Stephen Fowl and Gregory Jones address this at greater length in *Reading in Communion: Scripture & Ethics in Christian Life* (Grand Rapids: Eerdmans, 1991).

[26]I owe this perspective on Lacan and Althusser to Catherine Belsey, *Critical Practice* (London: Methuen, 1980).

[27]Michel Foucault, on the role of the commentator; "The Discourse of History," *Foucault Live*, trans. John Johnston, ed. Sylvère Lotringer, Foreign Agents Series (New York: Semiotext(e), 1989) 21.

One final reservation concerning my proposal for "understanding-free" interpretation: Does not historical criticism uniquely provide an avenue for discerning the specificity and particularity of the text? Does not my proposal disrespect the otherness of the text, and increase the likelihood of poor judgment in interpretation? My response is simply this: no *method* insures respect for the otherness of the text. If the otherness of the text is among the interpreter's interests, the interpreter will accord the text a corresponding degree of respect, whether the interpreter appeals to psychological or theological or historical warrants for her interpretations.[28] An interpreter who poorly understands priorities, authoritative audience, and one's own arguments will generally produce poor interpretations—once again, whether the interpreter is a historical critic or not. One cannot ensure well-formed interpretation by restricting the bases of interpretations.

### • Criteria for Nonmodern New Testament Theology •

The absence of any transcendental criteria of legitimacy for New Testament theology does not in any way imply the absence of all criteria. My claims do not imply a hermeneutical dystopia where intellectual arm-twisting settles interpretive disputes, nor that each New Testament theology is as good as any other. On the contrary, since interpretation is always social, and is always involved in particular interests and purposes, it would be impossible for there *not* to be criteria. The problem that arises when one dominant set of criteria falls from dominance is *recognizing* other criteria.

There are manifold criteria by which one may evaluate New Testament theologies. In fact, once modernity's criteria are dislodged from their preeminence, a great variety of other criteria can be seen more clearly. Of course, such criteria are always specific to

---

[28]Indeed, the historical-critical effort to allow the otherness of the text to speak most often (if not always) results in a sort of self-effacing ventriloquism, where we are asked to believe that the text itself is speaking, but we always hear the interpreter's voice.

the critic and the critic's audience;[29] but this does not prevent one from describing certain criteria that do not rely on modern presuppositions for their validity. For example, one may outline several categories of criteria in order to illuminate fields to which the critic may look for guidance. One may also suggest criteria that are held by the various general and specific audiences of New Testament theology. I will suggest several grounds—which I will call "general" to mark their status as less than universal, but more than regional in scope—for judging New Testament theologies. Among these categories of criteria one may begin with criteria that inhere in the name "New Testament theology"; others include aesthetic criteria, ethical/political criteria, and theological criteria.[30]

I begin with the suggestion that New Testament theology may reasonably be expected actually to bear some manifest relation to the wider discourse of theology and to the New Testament (as distinct from other bodies of early Christian literature). That is, I propose reversing Wrede's judgment on the field of New Testament theology: if it seems that what we are talking about is not "New Testament theology," but rather "the history of early

---

[29]Remember, too, that some audience-specific criteria are specific to so vast an audience that they are virtually universal. The nearer the criteria approach to universality, however, the more trivial they are (except, of course, when an interpreter transgresses them). Consider simple grammatical criteria, at the point closest to universality; at a less trivial level, interpretations on behalf of exotic or unfamiliar theological/philosophical systems (say, an anthroposophical interpretation of Matthew) may be rejected out of hand by most New Testament theologians.

[30]It is certainly true, and not at all comfortable for my thesis, that the modern division of value-spheres lies at the root of contemporary distinctions between "ethical" and "aesthetic" criteria. (Here Foucault's treatment of sexual behavior in antiquity, specifically his suggestion that the ethical ideal was simultaneously an aesthetic ideal, provides an illuminating reminder that the distinction with which we work is not a *necessary* distinction.) I will discuss aesthetic and ethical criteria separately here, not because I find a rigorous distinction between them, but because the vocabulary for treating them as a single field is not readily available.

Christian religion," then perhaps we ought not to pursue the latter under the name of the former.[31] (The capacity to make the distinction depends, of course, on a prior notion of what a "New Testament theology" might be; but I would argue that there is something surprising about finding neither theology nor a concentration on the New Testament in a "New Testament theology.") When I open a book entitled *The Oxford English Dictionary* and find therein nothing but Mother Goose rhymes, I do not suppose that I have been wrong about dictionaries all along; I simply assume that somehow the book of nursery rhymes was incorrectly categorized. If modern New Testament theologians are inclined to write books about the history of early Christian religion, that is all right, but that leaves open the possibility of writing something different called a "New Testament theology."

Audiences who find this suggestion persuasive may follow it up in a number of ways. They may look for a concentration on the writings of the New Testament, rather than noncanonical or hypothetical documents. Such communities would frown on theologies founded on the writings of the Apostolic Fathers or the Gospel of Thomas, or on Q, or *ur*-versions of the canonical gospels, or purported sayings of the historical Jesus (to the extent that they diverge from canonical versions of those sayings). They may likewise expect that the broad range of New Testament writings be included in the theology, without prejudice against "deuteroPauline" or "early Catholic" writings.

At the same time, this criterion points toward the *theological* character of New Testament theology.[32] (Here I am referring only to formal theological criteria; I will pursue material theological cri-

---

[31]Richard Hays called to my attention the oddness of Wrede's having suggested that the name "New Testament theology" was wrong in both its terms, but not going on to say that we simply ought to forget about New Testament theology in favor of the proper task of the history of early Christian religion.

[32]I take it that the importance of considering the biblical text (rather than a "historical background") and of addressing the theological import of that text are the cardinal issues at stake for Brevard Childs.

teria below.) The *Wredestrasse* leads to a New Testament theology conceived as history, explicitly opposed to dogmatic theology. While there are manifestly grounds for treating history as a cardinal category for New Testament theology, one may well wonder about the desirability, indeed, the *possibility* of divorcing biblical from dogmatic theology. Why, for example, ought one not arrange a New Testament theology by theological loci (as did Richardson, much to Keck's dismay)? The customary response—that doing so distorts the message of the New Testament by reading it in the light of categories and topics devised much later[33]—is not applicable unless one has a prior commitment to the historical determination of interpretation; if one begins from the perspective of "making sense" of the text, there is no theoretical obstacle to a topical approach to New Testament theology.[34]

New Testament theology may also appeal to general criteria of aesthetic judgment which extend beyond the confines of modern New Testament interpretation.[35] It is exceptionally difficult to produce a general catalogue of useful aesthetic criteria; examples provide an easier avenue to the latter. So, for example, particular theologies may be rich in detail and nuance, or they may be only superficial; they may be illuminating and evocative accounts of the

---

[33]Of course, the idea of "history" in the light of which modern N.T. theologians interpret the text is itself such an anachronistic category.

[34]It must be granted that the protest against topical theological interpretation grew to a great extent as a reaction against shoddy realizations of the project in Protestant Orthodoxy of the seventeenth century; but criticism of specific biblical theologies or N.T. theologies does not imply that their operating principles are invalid.

[35]One need not propose one particular æsthetic theory to flesh out this suggestion here; whether one endorses Vivas's aesthetic of "intransitive attention" or a Kantian æsthetic of the sublime, the point is that aesthetic criteria can be brought to bear upon N.T. theologies. While I concentrate on conceptual and stylistic evaluation in this section, it is important to remember that material aspects of a published work (design, typography, printing and binding) are relevant to that work's aesthetic impression—and are not infrequently so noted in reviews.

points under discussion, or they may be typically wooden discur-sive-academic prose. One particular aspect of aesthetic judgment that is particularly pertinent is the relation of the proposed theolo-gy to the New Testament. A given theology may homogenize dif-ferent voices that others would prefer to preserve as distinct, or may contrariwise insist too strenuously on distinctions others see no reason not to harmonize.

Harold Bloom's recent work on "the anxiety of influence"[36] provides a useful approach to aesthetic judgment of New Testa-ment theologies. The New Testament theologian is, after all, always in the position of the "ephebe," to adopt Bloom's terminol-ogy. Just as twentieth-century poets may be interpreted as continually looking over their shoulders at their great precursors, so New Testament theologians stand in the shadow of the ultimate precursor text. They may react by callow repetition of their precursor text; they may seek to preserve a posited "essence" or "heart" of their precursor while resetting it in another context; or they may stand in the place of the text they are interpreting, so that their discourse virtually eclipses the precursor text.[37] In this last instance, for example, the audience that reads Luther's exposition of Romans and Galatians is so impressed with the power of the theological insight that they may forget that Paul wrote his letters to a motley assortment of believers in ancient Mediterranean cities. The interpreter who thus makes the voice of the precursor text his or her own—whom Bloom calls a "strong misreader"—will generate fierce loyalty and determined opposi-

---

[36]Bloom has published a tetralogy on his Freudian analysis of literary production, but the first volume—*The Anxiety of Influence*, (Oxford: Oxford University Press, 1973)—sums up his position clearly, with less of what Frank Lentricchia calls "a terminology drawn from the periphery of rhetoric and from the religious periphery of occultist tradition" (*After the New Criticism* [Chicago: University of Chicago Press, 1980] 325).

[37]I refer here only to three of Bloom's "revisionary ratios." *The Anxiety of Influence* offers six ratios, specifying with varying degrees of clarity what distinguishes these "revisions" from other sorts.

tion, but usually exemplifies a high standard for what I propose as aesthetic criteria.

Ethical and political criteria provide another general basis for judging New Testament theologies. Theologies that offer a thoroughly theological consideration of the New Testament text, or that represent a compellingly strong (mis)reading, may still espouse a theological outlook that the reviewer could not commend. The complaints from feminist interpreters and the exegetes of liberation theology are prominent examples of ethical criteria. While one could reasonably propound a New Testament theology that insisted upon the subjugation of women, founded in plenteous New Testament texts, with appeals to theologoumena like "orders of creation," those who cannot accept the proclamation of a patriarchal gospel may equally reasonably reject such a theology.[38]

While the criteria that legitimate or invalidate a given theological construal of the New Testament may be fundamental to the group that shares the conviction, and thereby transcend the particularity of the individual interpreters who constitute that group, it would be a mistake to elevate the criterion that transcends the given group into a criterion that transcends all possible interpretive groups. A pro-apartheid Afrikaaner New Testament theology— however offensive it might be to non-Afrikaaners—is not methodologically illegitimate. At the same time, New Testament theologies that reflect the ethical priorities of the dominant groups in the practice of New Testament interpretation are not thereby removed from the field of ethical debate. It is, for example, much to Elisabeth Schüssler Fiorenza's credit that she has sought to bring the ethical implications of "normal discourse" in the Society of Biblical Literature to the foreground.[39]

---

[38]Parties to either side of such a dispute could appeal to "the text" for justification; situations like this underline the extent to which "what the text says" is not a useful category for adjudicating interpretive disputes.

[39]Particularly in her presidential address cited above, "The Ethics of Interpretation: De-Centering Biblical Interpretation," *Journal of Biblical Literature* 107 (1988): 3-17.

The final *general* criterion that I put forward here is a theological criterion. Certain theological options have been excluded by various bodies as heterodox; if a New Testament theology advocated an Arian Christology, this would constitute adequate reason for many interpreters to reject that work. The modern strictures against mixing disciplines carry little or no weight here, for despite Stendahl's warnings, it is impossible to separate biblical from dogmatic interests in New Testament theology (a fact which Käsemann's theological adherence to the importance of historical interpretation illustrates). From this point of view, then, Keck has erred in attacking Richardson for daring to label some New Testament theologies "orthodox" and others (specifically, Bultmann's) as "heretical"; Richardson's fault comes not from applying these categories in the first place, but (if indeed he is wrong) from applying them inappropriately.[40] Nor is Keck justified in criticizing Richardson for presenting Jesus with a distinctly Anglican slant; presumably if Richardson had thought that Jesus was more like a Southern Methodist, or a German Lutheran, he would have written his *Theology* that way.

The often-repeated claim that historical reconstruction is necessary, since it stands over against theological interpretation, is valid only to a point. In the first place, it assumes that historical inquiry constitutes a higher court of appeals than theological inquiry—an assumption the practice of New Testament interpretation in general simply does not support. Even apart from such obvious cases as the efforts of some Southern Baptists to ensure that only interpretations grounded in the doctrine of biblical inerrancy be taught in denominational seminaries, the "quest for the historical Jesus" has revealed again and again the extent to which historical conclusions reproduce prior convictions about God and humanity.[41] Arguments from historical investigation will often provide

---

[40]As Robert Morgan correctly notes; cf. "The Historical Jesus and the Theology of the New Testament," in *The Glory of Christ in the New Testament,* ed. L. D. Hurst and N. T. Wright (Oxford: Clarendon Press, 1987) 200n.15.

[41]Brandon Scott—now one of the leaders of the Westar Institute's

sufficient leverage to displace particular theological positions, but this does not by any means imply that one must always prefer historical hypotheses that cast doubt on a particular theological interpretation. As I said above, history must take a place among the various other interpretive interests jostling for influence on the interpreter, and sometimes it will attain more influence than others.

These general criteria—aesthetic, ethical-political, theological, and that of the definition of the enterprise—are not limits, but possibilities. They represent several broad approaches to judging New Testament theologies, approaches that are not intrinsically dependent upon modernity's assumptions. There are also *local* criteria for evaluating New Testament theologies; that is, within each distinct reading formation (to adopt Bennett's usage) there will be specific criteria associated with the distinctive character of that reading formation. For example, the criteria of modern New Testament theology—though they may not be universally applicable—are relevant to some extent to almost all interpretations produced within the academic study of the New Testament. To refer to a previous example, Alan Richardson's *Introduction to the Theology of the New Testament* purports to appeal to some of the criteria of modern New Testament theology; Richardson believes that his hypothesis that most of the distinctive ideas of the New Testament can be traced to Jesus' influence is the most reasonable historical explanation for those ideas. Likewise, he believes his particular interpretations are grounded in reliable historical-critical judgments; he would utterly repudiate the idea that his theses about New Testament theology might rest on prior theological

---

Jesus Seminar—rehearsed the course of the quest in his seminar paper "The New Synoptic Problem: The Convergence of Methods in the Quest," that concluded with a prophecy that contemporary historical-Jesus research would produce a Jesus who reflected the cultural ideals of late-twentieth-century Jesus scholars. Scott and the Jesus Seminar have gone on to enact just this prediction, creating a Jesus who is a cynic philosopher, who stands on the margins of society criticizing his culture to little effect; one might find a dozen or so mirror images of this Jesus in any good-sized faculty meeting in an American university.

commitments. In the preponderance of cases, the New Testament theology in question will explicitly appeal to these familiar criteria, and in such cases one would be perfectly justified in applying those criteria to evaluate the theology.

The criteria of modern New Testament theology would also be applicable to cases in which the proposed theology appeals to a modern audience without addressing the interpretive imperatives of modernity. A reviewer committed to modern New Testament theology, addressing a sympathetic audience, would justifiably advise the audience that a nonmodern theology is misguided and ill-founded—on the assumption that the audience shares the reviewer's modern commitments. When certain criteria are constitutive of a body of interpreters, as the criteria of modern New Testament theology are for a number of contemporary New Testament scholars, then there is nothing problematic about that body applying those criteria generally.

Granted, though, that the burden of this book is to open the field to alternatives to modern New Testament theology, what specific criteria might remain for judging nonmodern New Testament theologies? The various plaintiffs in the case against modern New Testament theology are obvious representatives of several different refigurations of interpretive priorities. Such interpretations of the dissenters will entail soft-pedalling their allegiance to modern interpretive rules, but this necessary (dis)torsion of their positions will help clarify what is at stake in the dispute over modern New Testament theology. In the following section, I will describe conflicts[42] between particular interpretive priorities and the criteria of modern New Testament theology (based upon, but not necessar-

---

[42]When in the paragraphs to follow I use the word "conflict" to describe the opposition of modern interpretive assumptions with possible alternatives, I use it in the same sense in which Lyotard uses the term "differend," i.e., to describe a dispute that one cannot resolve by appealing to criteria that transcend that dispute. Once again, cf. *The Differend*, trans. Georges Van Den Abbeele (Minneapolis: University of Minnesota Press, 1988) and "The *Différend*, the Referent, and the Proper Name," trans. Georges Van Den Abbeele, *Diacritics* 14 (1984): 4-14.

ily intended to mirror, the complaints of the theological dissenters discussed at the beginning of chap. 4, above). These conflicts will imply alternative sets of criteria, which I will sketch for each case.[43]

I will first consider the conflict represented by the Tübingen New Testament theologians (Stuhlmacher and others), for example, since they explicitly advocate a method of theological interpretation that strays only a little from the fold of modern New Testament interpreters. Their starting point might be expressed as follows: "The New Testament makes claims that modern New Testament theology is structurally maladapted to evaluate, and therefore modern New Testament theology tends either to bypass such claims or to transform them into claims that are more easily assimilated to modern assumptions. Moreover, the methodological skepticism modern interpretation practices (for disciplinary reasons) is antithetical to hermeneutics in the interest of faith." First, in other words, to the extent that specifically modern presuppositions restrict consideration of such theologoumena as a resurrection or an incarnation of God as a human being, modern criteria are inadequate for these interpreters. This proposition involves no animus against historical investigation as such, and sympathetic interpreters may hold to this axiom at the same time they claim that the very idea of incarnation implies the necessity of concrete historical investigation; they will simply add that when historical investigation comes upon an allegation it is unsuited to evaluate (such as "Jesus Christ was God incarnate,"), it ought not to continue its work by a historical reduction (to "Some people thought Jesus Christ was God incarnate") without making room

---

[43]Each case below will treat the suggested conflicts in isolation, but it is to be expected that some nonmodern N.T. theologians will work with more than one of these hypothetical operating assumptions. That is, while some feminist theologians derive considerable interpretive leverage from such extracanonical texts as the *Acts of Paul and Thecla*, a feminist theologian might well restrict her N.T. theology to canonical texts. (In such cases the relative precedence of these alternative principles will vary: Is she more certain of her feminist premises or of her obligation to respect the N.T. canon? Is there even necessarily a conflict?)

for the possibility that the allegation in question is true.[44] Second, New Testament theologians ought to shift the burden of proof in their historical investigations; the theologian will not feel obliged to mount an argument that will win over a skeptical observer, but only to present a reasonable case for the possibility of his or her position.[45]

The criteria that develop from this position will vary according to the theologian's judgment of historical probability, but they ought in principle to remain fairly close to modern criteria. Their principal difference from the criteria of modern New Testament theology is a negative difference—certain points are declared "out of bounds" for interpretation on the basis of modernity's assumptions. Theologians who are committed to this axiom will produce theologies that tend closely to resemble current conservative theologies, though without the need for aggressive apologetics (since historical skeptics will no longer be the audience addressed, but rather sympathetically inclined believers).

A second alternative principle for interpretation is the hypothetical feminist claim, "A patriarchal interpretation of the message of the New Testament falsifies that very message; valid interpretations of New Testament theology will uphold the liberation of the oppressed from the social constructions that oppress them." The fundamental truth, for this community, is that all humans are in principle equal, and that any interpretation that undermines that equality, or that enforces distinctions with positive/negative poles, is therefore invalid. This position finds modern New Testament theology culpably negligent of its political determination. It is not enough to seek out "how things were," nor to profess in the name of disciplinary autonomy that the task of redressing perceived

---

[44]Some interpreters, of course, will want to uphold a fairly extensive list of allegations which are to be believed without historical confirmation; the argument which this might instigate is clearly not an argument over "legitimate New Testament theology," but an argument over the necessary content of Christian belief.

[45]"A reasonable case" will, clearly, be defined differently by differing audiences in differing contexts.

wrongs is not our department. Valid interpretation depends—on this account—upon participating in the effort to dismantle patriarchal oppression.

The implicit criterion here is fairly obvious, though it is not always deployed *in opposition to* modern interpretive criteria; it is more common to see efforts to effect the aims of feminist discourse within the confines of modern interpretation. Scholars repudiate the ancient institution of patriarchy, point out the extent to which the texts of antiquity are bound to their social and historical setting, and pursue a strictly historical basis on which to found antipatriarchal practices. A feminist interpreter who places the antipatriarchal criterion above the criteria of modernity need not feel obliged to follow this pattern; her commitment to the disruption of patriarchal structures justifies her deviation from modern criteria. Modernity's posited chronological abyss, after all, swallows up the deplorable continuity of patriarchal oppression. A nonmodern feminist theology, then, might trace out the isomorphisms between the situation of women (and male Gentiles) in the New Testament and women (and male minority-group members) in our own culture. At times, such a theology might ignore or contradict conclusions of modern scholars—perhaps concerning the trustworthiness of the Acts of Paul and Thecla—in the interest of illustrating avenues of resistance to patriarchy. Of course, if the feminist theology is addressed to a modern audience in order to persuade that audience to convert from patriarchal to egalitarian attitudes, the warrants that support the theology will need to be determined (at least to some extent) by the audience, not by the theologian's own interpretive commitment.

A third alternative guiding principle for a theological interpretation of the New Testament is a concern for the specifically psychological benefits of biblical interpretation.[46] One might make a

---

[46]Modern N.T. interpretation has with few exceptions steered sharply away from any interest in psychological aspects of biblical interpretation; twenty years ago, Dan Via wrote that "fifty years or more is really long enough for 'psychology' to have been a dirty word in biblical studies" ("A Quandary of Contemporary New Testament Scholarship: The Time

principle, for example, of the claim that "A theology of the New Testament is legitimated only by its orientation toward interpreters' psychological well-being."[47] Whereas modern New Testament theologians aim to present the development of early Christian religion (perhaps on the basis that "the truth" is necessarily salutary for their audience), the psychological interpreter expounds the New Testament in the light of his or her understanding of psychological structures and tendencies. Such an interpreter might lay out the theology of the New Testament as a reader's journey toward individuation, or treat the New Testament as a reflection in concrete terms of psychological truths. Or that interpreter might involve the reader more actively; he or she might choose not to provide a vademecum for New Testament theology, but instead to suggest symbols, myths, anecdotes, and so on in order to enrich the readers' relation to the New Testament through amplification (the process of handling dreams wherein interpretation is encouraged for its own sake, the analyst simply providing supplementary material which the dreamer may or may not use as interpretive context for the dream).

Whatever the specific psychological relation to the New Testament, it is clear that the standards for a psychologically relevant New Testament theology need have relatively little to do with modern New Testament theology's criteria. The psychological interpreter will have certain theory-specific criteria: orthodox Freudian, Lacanian, Jungian, developmental. Beyond this, the psychological New Testament theology will concentrate more on the truths provided by psychological insight than on those attained by any of the critical methods characteristic of modernity; where the latter are applied, they will serve the former. Thus the

---

between the 'Bultmanns'," *Journal of Religion* 55 [1975]: 459), and matters have changed hardly at all since his words appeared.

[47]I will not specify the content of the idea of "psychological well-being" here. Obviously the goal of psychological work differs in different approaches to the task; the particular interpreter would be responsible for her presentation of psychological interpretation as well as the way she works that idea out in her New Testament theology.

psychological New Testament theologian, like the Tübingen and feminist theologians, may transgress the boundaries set by modern New Testament theology in the interests of expounding truths that cannot be expressed within those boundaries.

I will conclude this roster of possible sets of local criteria for New Testament theology by considering the axiom that a New Testament theology ought to accord principal emphasis to interpretation within the bounds of the biblical canon. This claim might be framed as: "Inasmuch as it is the New Testament—rather than extracanonical or hypothetically reconstructed texts—that the church reads, proclaims, and interprets, and inasmuch as the New Testament is itself an inadequate guide for faith without the Old Testament, therefore a legitimate New Testament theology will ground its interpretations in the final form of the biblical text, and will emphasize intertextual relations of biblical texts to one another." Such a theology places the practice of New Testament theology squarely within an ecclesiastical context (since the canon of the New Testament is an ecclesiastical creation), and relegates other interests to the background. It does not imply that the canon cannot be critically interpreted; the church has always interpreted the canon critically (though the criteria have changed). It does imply, however, that the criteria brought to bear on the canonical text should themselves be based on another canonical text (as when Gal 3:28 is cited as warrant for criticizing canonical texts that authorize patriarchal social structures).

A New Testament theology constructed along these lines might well bear a strong formal resemblance to the biblical theologies of the past. The canonical principle, after all, is not an innovation but a deliberate effort to recapture the vitality with which biblical theology flourished before the "crisis" which Childs posits.[48] The canonical principle does not require that a New Testament theolo-

---

[48]Of course, there is considerable dispute over whether there actually was such a crisis (cf. James Smart's *The Past, Present, and Future of Biblical Theology* [Philadelphia: Westminster Press, 1979]), but this does not affect the fundamentally nostalgic motivation for the canonical approach.

gy be conservative or retrospective, however; one might well combine canonical with feminist/liberation interests on the basis that it is the church's canon—not the critic's historical setting or reconstructed urtext—that marginalized interpreters read.[49]

The local criteria for interpretation that I have sketched here exemplify several alternatives to the modern construal of New Testament theology. In no case is historical criticism banished; in each case, however, the particular situation (the interests of the interpreter, the interpreter's audience, and their respective circumstances) may relegate the criteria proper to modern New Testament theology to secondary importance. Such nonmodern New Testament theologies are not inherently invalid or illegitimate, but may be valid workings out of the interpretive principles belonging to a nonmodern reading formation. In the closing section of this chapter, I will propose a thought experiment in which Bultmann's magisterial *Theology of the New Testament* provides an example of what such a nonmodern New Testament theology might look like.

### • *The Theology of the New Testament* in a Nonmodern Key •

In the third chapter, I described a particular widespread interpretation of Rudolf Bultmann's theology in which emphasis is put on the specifically modern aspects of his work. At the time, I acknowledged that such a view was problematic, and offered later to propose another interpretation of Bultmann's New Testament theology. The following section makes good on that promise, though (once again) it is presented not as Bultmann's own interpretation of his New Testament theology, but as a reading of that work as if it were conceived along the lines I have advocated in this chapter.[50]

---

[49]Cf. James Dawsey's "The Lost Front Door into Scripture: Carlos Mesters, Latin American Liberation Theology, and the Church Fathers," *Anglican Theological Review* 72 (1990): 292-305.

[50]This caveat is intended not to suggest that I think mine *is not* Bultmann's own understanding of his task; indeed, Gareth Jones's ingenious

To begin with, then, I will posit as the work's overriding interpretive principle the effort to make sense of the New Testament on the basis of the conviction that Jesus' purpose makes some present demand upon human existence.[51] That purpose must—for both theological and philosophical reasons—be eschatological. That is, first, the New Testament proclaims Jesus "to be God's eschatological act of salvation";[52] and at the same time, it is the eschatological point of view that permits some continuity between the New Testament and contemporary interpreters, since both first-century believers and twentieth-century Christians are in similar positions with relation to God. Any other interpretive axiom is subsidiary to this; the truth in which we are interested here concerns the New Testament as a record of the unfolding of believing self-understanding, not (necessarily) the conclusions of historical analysis of the New Testament writings.

(The point at which I diverge most sharply from Bultmann's own estimation of his task is the extent to which we believe that historical criticism is necessary for intellectually honest contemporary interpreters.[53] It is one of Bultmann's cardinal points that his-

---

interpretation depicts Bultmann's understanding of his N.T. theology in a way fundamentally amenable to the account provided here. E.g., "the historical-critical study of the New Testament is a part of the task of faithful existence, even though it can never be its basis" (*Bultmann: Toward a Critical Theology* [London: Polity Press, 1991] 40). Likewise, Bultmann himself states that in his interpretation of N.T. theology, the historical work serves the theological interests, not vice versa (*Theology of the New Testament*, vol. 2, trans. Kendrick Grobel [New York: Charles Scribner's Sons, 1951] 251).

[51]The phrase "makes some present demand upon human existence" alludes to Bultmann's *Jesus and the Word*, trans. Louise Pettibone Smith and Erminie Huntress Lantero (New York: Charles Scribner's Sons, 1934; [2]1958) 8: "Attention is entirely limited to what [Jesus] *purposed*, and hence to what in his purpose as a part of history makes a present claim on us."

[52]Bultmann, *Theology of the New Testament*, 1:1.

[53]This is a different point from the claim noted above that historical investigation has a purely pedagogical role in Bultmann's theology. From

torical criticism is necessary, and so his *Theology* employs histori-cal-critical interpretations at every step of the way. I do not find any intellectual culpability in making sense of the New Testament on other-than-historical bases, so I will downplay Bultmann's his-torical-critical *apologiai* and highlight his hermeneutical decisions as aspects of his primary interpretive commitment.)

The first chapter of Bultmann's *Theology* sets out the cardinal presupposition of New Testament theology: the preaching of Jesus. This is a presupposition, not a part of New Testament theology, for the basis for New Testament faith is not Jesus' own message, but the message *about* Jesus. Bultmann's interest in Jesus here extends as far as Jesus warrants the kerygma, and no further.[54] Jesus justi-fies the kerygma principally by virtue of his eschatological message: "The dominant concept of Jesus' message is the *Reign of God*."[55] The imminent advent of God's reign implies the necessity of decision for or against Jesus. Jesus' message demands the whole of a person's life, obedience without reserve: "fulfillment of God's will is the condition for participation in the salvation of His Reign."[56]

---

a theological point of view, historical criticism is not necessary a priori, but only as a pedagogical device; but in practice, Bultmann regularly privileges historical interpretation various ways. Sometimes it is the avenue of "appropriate" preunderstanding, or "genuine understanding," ("The Problem of Hermeneutics," in *New Testament and Mythology*, ed. and trans. Schubert Ogden [Philadelphia: Fortress Press, 1984] 79); some-times it is taken for granted as the basis of interpretation. The practical evidence for the effective primacy of the historical in Bultmann's *Theology* is his constant appeal to historical-critical warrants in justifying his inter-pretations.

[54]Jones appositely suggests that Bultmann affirms a pedagogical value for "the historical Jesus," in that this academic phantasm teaches us how little we need know about the man from Nazareth in order to be saved by the Christ.

[55]*Theology of the New Testament*, 1:4.

[56]*Theology of the New Testament*, 1:20.

The second chapter of Bultmann's *Theology* moves from Jesus himself to the earliest church's image of Jesus. Bultmann proposes that the earliest communities showed no interest in the *personality* of Jesus, nor in his extraordinary nature, but only in his meaning as eschatological occurrence. The proclaimer became the proclaimed in the sense that Jesus, the preacher of God's eschatological demand, was subsequently interpreted as the agent of that demand. By the same token, the earliest community saw itself as the eschatological congregation, the chosen ones who joined themselves to Christ in baptism and eucharist. They submit to the Messiah who rules them, as they await the Son of Man who will deliver them. They preach a kerygma of faith in the God who raised Christ from death, and who will likewise raise up all who follow Christ.

Bultmann's exposition of Paul continues in the same vein. Bultmann takes words that recur in Paul's preaching (σῶμα, ψυχή, πνεῦμα, ζωή, σάρξ) and makes of them anthropological *termini technici*.[57] Σῶμα, for example, expresses the human capacity for self-transcendence: "Man is called soma in respect to his being able to make himself the object of his own action or to experience himself as the subject to whom something happens."[58] Paul expresses the obverse of σῶμα in terms such as ψυχή and πνεῦμα (which indicate human purposiveness, intentionality). "Flesh" (σάρξ) and "sin" (ἁμαρτία) can become powers which can enslave people. Once enslaved by sin, people are in the thrall of death, in the realm of this world (κόσμος)—the very opposite of God's Realm.

In a similar way, Bultmann organizes Paul's positive anthropological terms into a systematic exposition of life "under faith."

---

[57]Bultmann treats Paul's occasional discussions of human existence in ways similar to those theological analyses that provoked Wrede's denunciations of "doctrinal concepts" theologies; often the exposition is more weighty than the usage that supports it. My thesis, of course, *supports* the boldness with which Bultmann provides Paul a systematic structure which the apostle himself does not display clearly.

[58]*Theology of the New Testament*, 1:195.

Δικαιοσύνη indicates preparation for, openness to the possibility of life.[59] It is a possibility that is God's gift to those who have died with Christ and who hope to be raised again. This possibility is made known in the crucifixion-resurrection of Jesus, which is the salvation-occurrence; but the cross and resurrection of Christ constitute the salvation-event only in the sense that they express the demand for obedience, and "faith" that is merely assent to propositions that assert the salvific effect of Jesus's death and resurrection falls short of expressing the full dimension of the salvation-event. Therefore, once again, the *character* of the one crucified is of secondary interest; the primary emphasis falls on the proclamation that "God has made a crucified one Lord."[60] The full and appropriate dimensions of faith are manifest in obedience. The life of obedient faith reorients one's entire existence, down to one's daily meals, to that freedom (from the world, the powers, even from death) which God gives.

Bultmann—following Wrede—deems John and Paul the only noteworthy theologians in the New Testament, and Bultmann's interpretation of the former is as nuanced and rich as is his interpretation of the latter. Bultmann stresses Paul's focus on the cross and resurrection; in his volume 2, he stresses John's interest in the character of John's Jesus, who comes not as a rabbi, nor as a personality, but as the Revealer, and his revelation is only that he *is* the revealer.

Jesus's existence as the Revealer is significant not in terms of normative sayings or acts to be repeated (so John diverges from Gnostic traditions with their divinely authorized hermetic doctrine, and likewise from the sacramental interest of other early Christian groups). Instead, John juxtaposes Jesus' status as revealer with the dualism characteristic of the Johannine writings. The Revealer, once he is recognized as such, explodes the possibility of authentic existence on the human pole of John's dichotomies (divine/*human*, light/*darkness*, life/*death*): "The Revelation is represented as the

---

[59]*Theology of the New Testament*, 1:270.
[60]*Theology of the New Testament*, 1:303.

shattering and negating of all human self-assertion and all human norms and evaluations."[61] When the Revealer confronts the world, the encounter is the world's judgment (κρίσις); his advent is the eschatological event.[62]

One can recognize the Revealer, and thereby attain true life, only through faith.[63] Whereas Paul discussed faith as the way *to* salvation, John treats faith as the way *of* salvation; it entails overcoming the scandal of the particular incarnation of Jesus, participating in eschatological existence, and abiding in the Revealer (as he abides in the faithful ones).[64] Faith is the way of living in freedom, peace, truth, and joy. This way of life derives its strength from the Holy Spirit, the "Spirit of Truth," which increases the community's knowledge (which knowledge, in turn, the community disseminates: "[the Paraclete] will bear witness to me; you also bear witness," John 15:26-27).

Bultmann's exposition concludes with a section on "The Development toward the Ancient Church."[65] He clearly looks on this development with regret (there are no Pauls or Johns in this period, though Ignatius earns qualified praise[66]). In this period, the church begins to coalesce into an institution rather than an eschatological community; it loses its vivid dialectic of present and future realization as the future is pushed back for an indefinite interval, it shifts from charismatic to official leadership, it falls into the legalism the original communities rejected. The Synoptic Gospels

---

[61] *Theology of the New Testament*, 2:68.

[62] *Theology of the New Testament*, 2:37.

[63] *Theology of the New Testament*, 2:69.

[64] *Theology of the New Testament*, 2:75, 78, 84.

[65] *Theology of the New Testament*, 2:95-236.

[66] Cf. *Theology of the New Testament*, 2:113: "But when this Pauline-Johannine dialectic is missing and the knowledge is lost that the future so qualifies the present that believers already exist existentially now, understanding for the paradoxical quality of the Christian situation . . . gradually disappears"; and 2:198: "Ignatius, in contradistinction to all other writers of early Christianity after Paul and John, is a figure having originality."

domesticate the radical demand of the salvation event by transmuting the kerygma about Jesus into biography and history. The later New Testament writers worry about orthodoxy and about differentiating the nascent church from any of the various competing Hellenistic cults. Most important, the developing church forgets that faith involves a radical conversion of one's life (as in Paul and John); the future is no longer treated as impinging directly upon the present. Instead, the church develops a sacramental and liturgical system designed to address the needs of a people counting upon only a future salvation. To the extent Bultmann can salvage insights and refinements upon the Pauline-Johannine theology from the later canonical literature, these texts merit his commendation; but these highlights are relatively rare. No longer is there a radical tension between the indicative and the imperative; instead, the imperative note in the kerygma hardens into a new law. Bultmann's concluding section shows how all the early Christian texts apart from John and Paul function to show the truest gospel as it is expressed in John and Paul.[67]

The foregoing description outlines high points of Bultmann's *Theology*, but it treats these as claims that rest upon their theological plausibility, rather than upon historical verification. On this account, the first section of Bultmann's *Theology*—"Presuppositions and Motifs of New Testament Theology"—does not so much constitute a catalogue of ideas that are in or behind the New Testament text as it reflects the conceptual tools by which Bultmann will make sense of the whole. The claim, "The dominant concept of Jesus' message is the *Reign of God*,"[68] need not be true historically;[69] it is an axiom, not a conclusion (though it is an axiom well

---

[67]I omit discussion of Bultmann's epilogue (*Theology of the New Testament*, 2:237-51) here, since the epilogue is a methodological excursus whereas I am here concentrating on the theological exposition.

[68]*Theology of the New Testament*, 1:4.

[69]Indeed, Burton Mack has argued that *none* of the kingdom-sayings in Mark is authentic ("The Kingdom Sayings in Mark," *Forum* 3 [1987]: 3-47).

grounded in the text of the New Testament). The eschatological message, the call to decision that Jesus represents, is a rule by which Bultmann *makes sense* of the New Testament. In other words, from this point of view, the arguments "But that's not what Jesus really said" or "That's not what 'Reign of God' implies historically" carry no weight; the eschatological character of Jesus' preaching is a presupposition for Bultmann's *Theology of the New Testament* theology rather than an aspect of that theology itself.

Likewise the fact that Bultmann posits a Jewish legalism that cannot be supported with reference to first-century Jewish sources is not hermeneutically fatal. Bultmann can cite New Testament texts to make a case for a Jesus who stands against *any* legalism; one need not project this legalism onto actual first-century Pharisees in order for Jesus' stand to be distinct and compelling. Moreover, the point Bultmann tries to establish here—that God makes a demand upon the entirety of human life in a way that allows no appeal to presumed legal limits to that claim—remains amply justified.

If one reads the remainder of Bultmann's introductory section—dealing with Jesus' conception of God and with Jesus' Messianic consciousness—without assuming the need to justify the claims therein at the bar of historical criticism, one will get the impression that Bultmann is here offering an interpretation of the New Testament material that most moderate-to-liberal Christians would find generally plausible. It is an interpretation that requires him to downplay or reject those portions of the New Testament that seem to ascribe messianic status and consciousness to Jesus, but this obligation is counterbalanced by the coherence with which Bultmann connects the New Testament testimony about Jesus to his (Bultmann's) theological theme. The Jesus of chapter 1 is a prophetic herald warning all who have ears to hear that each individual in the world stands near to God in a continual relation of judgment, and that under the circumstances, everyone ought to recognize the radical demand such a relation implies. Such a Jesus makes a comprehensible demand upon contemporary existence—whether he is justified by the work of historical reconstruction or not.

The earliest communities—like Bultmann himself, and like an audience that shares Bultmann's modern sensibilities—showed no interest in the *personality* of Jesus, nor in his extraordinary nature, but only in his meaning as eschatological occurrence. The preacher became the proclaimed in the sense that Jesus, the preacher of God's eschatological demand, was subsequently interpreted as the agent of that demand. Such an image of Jesus complements Bultmann's modern interpretation; as Bultmann notes, the image of Jesus as "coming eschatological Son of Man" effects no essential change in the content of the message, for the radical demand remains the decisive aspect of the proclamation. The theological weight of these interpretations can readily be transferred to the modern believer; we, too, can recognize ourselves as part of the eschatological congregation, proclaiming the Proclaimer whose significance was that of eschatological event.[70]

Bultmann's exposition of Paul leans heavily upon a tremendous amount of etymological and comparative analysis, by which Bultmann legitimates his premise that Paul meant what Bultmann is saying. These warrants have not all fared well over the years since Bultmann composed his theology; if Bultmann's word studies are not currently convincing, however, his existential appropriation of Pauline thought is still impressive. By the same token, one need not subscribe to Bultmann's reconstruction of John's Gospel to appreciate the power with which Bultmann limns Johannine faith. If we were to explode Bultmann's source theory—and with it, the *Ur*-Gospel's antisacramental tendency and its unambiguous realized eschatology—we could still acknowledge Bultmann's theological interpretation. And though scholars may demur from Bultmann's deprecatory remarks about "early catholicism," his powerful theological interrogation of efforts to disarm or domesti-

---

[70]Likewise the *modern* believer can sit loose to questions about "how [the disciples' decision to reaffirm their commitment to following Jesus] took place in detail, how the Easter faith arose in individual disciples" (*Theology of the New Testament*, 1:45).

cate Jesus' radical demand upon those who would follow in the way of the cross is not diminished.

One could perform such an exercise upon most New Testament theologies. To the extent that they are theologies at all, rather than simply narrative accounts of what successive communities of early Christians believed, the theological foundation will consistently stand (or fall) apart from the issue of whether the historical foundations are built upon rock or sand. After all, no historical foundations *are* built upon bedrock; theologies that lean most heavily upon their historical warrants are soonest discarded, as the particular historical consensuses shift.

This does not imply, however, that theological interpretation of the New Testament is utterly independent of historical interpretation. Once again, there are cogent reasons for attending to the results of historical-critical inquiry when undertaking a theological interpretation. The most important of these is the social character of interpretation. Social constraints are often unrelated to historical or scientific warrants, but this does not make them any less binding. A reader who wants to interpret the New Testament theologically, but who utterly ignores historical criticism (let us say the reader uses only *The Living Bible* as a basis for his or her ruminations), will be in the position of one who feels free to forego silverware at a presidential banquet. Such things simply *aren't done,* and an interpreter will have to behave more conventionally in order to gain a hearing in the biblical guild.

On the other hand, manners do change from time to time. They are sometimes changed by contingent circumstances, but at other times they yield to deliberate reform. Just to this extent, New Testament theologians have an opportunity to reconsider the manners that posit the historical criterion as the absolute norm for judging New Testament theology. Since there seems to be considerable interest in reforming the endeavor of New Testament theology (cf. chapter 4, above), this may be an auspicious time to take alternative criteria for New Testament theology seriously.

Thus, although I have tried to show that we need not reject Bultmann's New Testament theology even if its historical warrants no longer hold up, I have yet to show how it fares against other criteria. I earlier referred to criteria relative to the identity of the New Testament theology, æsthetics, politics, and theology; Bultmann's explicit philosophical interests justify judging his theology by philosophical criteria.[71] These provide ample basis for evaluating New Testament theology. Moreover, they illuminate the qualities of Bultmann's theology in a fascinating way.

One strong count against Bultmann's theology is its overwhelming reliance on just two voices in the New Testament. There is reason to hesitate before accepting the assertion that a theology of Paul and John (a purified theology of Paul and John as well, since Bultmann has used *Sachkritik* to strain out any divergent theological notes)—with corroborating exempla drawn from other New Testament sources—ought to count as a *New Testament* theology. Where Paul and John are the criterion against which other canonical texts are judged, significant aspects of the New Testament are silenced.[72]

Ought not a *New Testament Theology* offer substantive discussion of such historically and theologically important texts as the Letter to the Hebrews? Bultmann devotes slightly more than two pages of his two-volume *Theology* to the exposition of Hebrews.[73] Indeed, Bultmann uses most of this space to explaining why Hebrews falls short of the Pauline ideal. For example: despite Hebrews' emphasis on the theme of "faith" (with special reference to Abraham, among others), its reference to the Pauline proof text

---

[71]This ought not be taken to imply that philosophical criteria are unjustified when the N.T. theologian does not thematize philosophical reflection; I simply propose the particular appropriateness of applying this criterion to Bultmann.

[72]The methodological epilogue appended to vol. 2 of Bultmann's *Theology of the New Testament* defends this selective procedure by claiming that it is in the theology (Bultmann uses the singular here) of Paul and John that the relation of believing self-understanding to the kerygma is amenable to direct analytical clarification (*Theology*, 2:251).

[73]I refer here to the discussion of "Christology and Soteriology" in *Theology of the New Testament*, 2:166-68.

"The righteous one shall live by faith," and its demand for radical commitment, Bultmann discounts Hebrews because "the dialectic relationship between imperative and indicative has been lost from sight" so that "salvation is only future."[74] When texts from outside the Pauline and Johannine collections receive such short shrift, one may fairly complain that Bultmann's theology is not so much a *New Testament Theology* as a *Theology of John and Paul*.

While Bultmann's selectivity has irritated many critics, even his detractors recognize the majesty of his *Theology* and the attraction it commands. Bultmann is probably the outstanding "strong (mis)reader" of John in the twentieth century, and his reading of Paul is challenged only by Barth's electrifying commentary on Romans. Bultmann's patient, painstaking outline of the way the New Testament presents its theme of authentic existence in the presence of God is a remarkable achievement in close reading. Bultmann unfolds an interpretation of the New Testament that reveals hitherto hidden aspects of the texts, which invites the reader to consider the New Testament in a unique light. The harmonies between Paul and John are carefully constructed, and they constitute finely balanced twin pillars for Bultmann's theology. The aesthetic quality of Bultmann's interpretation makes it easier to explain why New Testament theologians continue to feel Bultmann's influence despite their disagreement with his historical-exegetical conclusions.

The political implications of Bultmann's theology are more problematic. As he himself observes, his engagement with socio-political matters has never been more than indirect; he refers to his activities in the Confessing Church, but only to his efforts to ascertain that "free scientific work retained its proper place" therein.[75]

---

[74]*Theology of the New Testament*, 2:168.

[75]"Autobiographical Reflections," in *Existence and Faith*, 288. Cf. the alternate version of the same essay included in *The Theology of Rudolf Bultmann*, ed. Charles Kegley (New York: Harper & Row, 1966), wherein Bultmann observes: "I have never directly and actively participated in political affairs" (xxii).

By the same token, in a personal letter he professes to have been unmoved by the First World War:

> Of course, the impact of the war has led many people to re-vise their concepts of human existence; but I confess that that has not been so in my case. Perhaps I am going too far towards the other extreme, but I must be frank; the war was not a shattering experience for me. Of course there were a great many individual things, but not the war as such. I am quite clear about this, and I once defended my case in numerous conversations, that war is not so different from peace; a shipwreck, an act of meanness, the sort of thing that happens every day, confronts us with exactly the same questions as the heaping up of events in war. So I do not believe that the war has influenced my theology.[76]

To be sure, the letter in question was written before the rise of the Nazis, before Bultmann's brother was executed in a concentration camp;[77] it does suggest, however, that Bultmann is less than acute-ly sensitive to the political status of theological discourse. Dorothée Soelle and Gareth Jones bring just this charge against Bultmann: his theology reduces "the power of God for salvation" to the indi-vidual's capacity for authentic self-understanding.[78] As Bultmann banishes engagement with a particular construct of Jesus in favor of John's and Paul's reflections on the kerygma, he dismisses the concrete expectations that so impressed the early communities. The ethical aspect of New Testament theology surfaces first as rumina-

---

[76]Quoted from a letter to Erich Forster in Jones, *Bultmann*, 18.

[77]On the other hand, his "The Task of Theology in the Present Situation" (in *Existence and Faith*, 158-65) is a comparatively mild critique of Nazism (cf. esp. the three examples of "wrongdoing" that Bultmann cites: changing the names of thoroughfares, encouraging an atmosphere of mistrust (a point he also specifies retrospectively in his "Autobiograph-ical Reflections," 285), and smearing German Jews (he is "well aware of the complicated nature of the Jewish problem in Germany," but wishes it to be resolved honestly rather than by slander, 165).

[78]Jones, 186; Soelle, *Political Theology*, trans. John Shelley (Philadelphia: Fortress Press, 1974) chap. 4.

tions on "the understanding of the imperative";[79] even when Bultmann addresses "the content of the ethical demand," he shows a consistent proclivity to slip toward general, abstract descriptions like "the demand for sanctification," rather than "feeding the hungry."[80]

Jones—himself a great admirer of Bultmann's theology—observes that the phenomenological approach which is Bultmann's greatest strength needs to be supplemented by a keen attention to the material conditions within which theology takes its shape. "An event theory in itself is insufficient. A genuine theology must give the event theory work to do."[81] Though Bultmann—commendably—refuses to split the act of thinking from the act of living, his theology addresses the act of living not in terms of distinct deeds or choices, but in thematic generalizations about "freedom." Thus, while Bultmann's theology succeeds on æsthetic grounds, it is open to forceful criticism on political grounds.

There remains the question of whether Bultmann's New Testament theology is theologically acceptable. Clearly Alan Richardson believed it was not, since, as noted above, he refers to Bultmann's theology as heretical;[82] the Evangelical Church likewise debated Bultmann's orthodoxy. Since the Evangelical Church found no conclusive error in Bultmann's teaching, and since Richardson's evaluation has been largely ignored, it is probably more pertinent to

---

[79]*Theology of the New Testament*, 2:203-18.

[80]Bultmann discusses the problems concerning Christian use of material assets in one paragraph (*Theology of the New Testament*, 2:229-30).

[81]Jones, 190. In a succeeding paragraph, Jones reflects on Bultmann's observation that "it suffices to recognize that faith in God and nationality stand in a positive relation, insofar as God has placed us in our nation and state" (from "The Task of Theology in the Present Situation," 159). Where Bultmann would have us accept our nationality as God's will, Jones urges us to adopt an always critical stance *over against* nationality, *in the name of* God (190).

[82]Richardson, *An Introduction to the Theology of the New Testament* (London: SCM Press, 1958) 14.

pose the question of the extent to which Bultmann's theology is *sound*.

There are countless dead ends into which we might run in answering such a question. I propose that we short-circuit them by observing immediately that one cannot deny that Bultmann's theology may be edifying for the faithful. The emphases in Bultmann's work open up certain risks (to which Jones and Soelle have alerted us), but theology always involves taking risks; Bultmannians are not peculiar in that regard. It is not insignificant that both Söelle and Jones criticize Bultmann not to bury him, but to reconstruct Bultmannian theology in a key more suitable to their priorities.

By now it should be quite clear that there is no danger of anarchy if New Testament theology abandons its fundamental reliance upon historically reconstructed authority. If one could somehow pass a law forbidding the use of historical-critical categories for judging New Testament theologies, that law would neither silence book reviewers nor wreak havoc upon the theological world. Instead, it would direct our attention to the myriad of critical resources that are currently subordinated to history.

The threat of anarchy ebbs all the more rapidly when one considers that I do not propose that one eliminate historical judgment from all New Testament theological reflection (as though that were possible). Instead, I want to stress that historical criteria provide only one among many approaches to judging a New Testament theology.

The point is simply this: reliance upon historical criteria is required neither by the nature of interpretation, nor by that of New Testament theology, but by the nature of modernity. It is a *social* and *institutional* necessity, not a methodological or theological necessity. Nonmodern New Testament theologians may sacrifice institutional benefits that are reserved for more conventionally modern interpreters, and the institution will probably rationalize excluding them on the basis that they are not sufficiently sensitive to the necessity of historical method. As I have shown, though, the modern interpretation is no less insensitive to its own ideological, patriarchal, academic overdetermination than nonmodern interpreters are insensitive to history.

New Testament theology is not properly thought of as "the history of early Christian religion," nor as ascertaining "what it meant," but as *making theological sense of the New Testament*. To the extent that an interpreter is modern, that interpreter will make theological sense of the New Testament by establishing historical warrants and reasoning from them. To the extent the interpreter is free from the priorities characteristic of modernity, he or she may make sense of the New Testament by establishing theological (or ideological, or psychological) warrants, and reasoning from them. No critic (or reviewer) can adjudicate the conflict between these two approaches without allying with one or the other; that is the way Lyotard defines the *differend*.[83] This impasse does not imply that only one of these approaches is acceptable, or that just any approach is acceptable. Instead, it means that the definition of what is acceptable always depends upon where one stands. The *Wredestrasse* is the main street of modern New Testament theology, but those who opt for roads less traveled may have good reasons.

---

[83]"One side's legitimacy does not imply the other's lack of legitimacy." *The Differend*, xi.

# Conclusion

*. . . la verdad, cuya madre es la historía. . . .*     —Pierre Menard

This book began with John Collins's dismal warning that biblical theology was in decline. It ends by suggesting that the decline in theological interpretation is not inevitable, and that a wealth of alternatives await exploration. The paths to these alternatives are impeded, however, by the barricades erected by several generations of New Testament theologians, and by warning signs that advise the venturesome interpreter that he or she risks entering a chaotic realm of irresponsible nihilists, or a tyrannical dictatorship where intellectual freedom has been outlawed in favor of doctrinal orthodoxy, or some other such chimerical badlands. These barricades and signs testify to a genuine concern, but it is a misguided and self-serving concern. It is a concern that both grows from and underwrites the presuppositions of one school of New Testament theology. This dominant school has borne no party label, and has presented its claims as necessarily true. This has tended to conceal the extent to which the characteristic presuppositions and interests of this school are themselves local and particular.

I have suggested here that the postulates that currently govern the production of New Testament theologies are not transcendent or necessary, but are closely comparable to the cultural imperatives of modernity. The four marks of modernity I isolated for consideration were the Renaissance humanists' claim to stand over against the Classical tradition, the compulsory power that time exercises over modern consciousness, the pivotal importance of disciplinary autonomy and specialization, and the distinction in kind between an expert's knowledge of a subject and a commoner's knowledge.

The history of biblical theology reflects an increasing stress on just these points. Gabler, Wrede, and Stendahl unanimously proclaim the necessity of breaking free from tradition (which they define as an obstacle, rather than an aid, to understanding). They insist upon historical inquiry as an indispensible guide to legitimate interpretation of the ancient Bible. They urge biblical theologians rigorously to enforce the boundaries that separate their discipline from dogmatic or systematic theology, lest biblical theology lose its distinctive role. They underline the difference between simple, unsophisticated believers and authoritative theologians, which involves both the the biblical sources and contemporary interpreters.

The power of the modern vision in New Testament theology must not be denied. All of these characteristics of modernity have positive sides. When modern scholars oppose the modern and the ancient, they provide leverage for innovative positions. When they fix their attention upon the chronological aspect of social determination, they honor one aspect of the text's particularity. When they distinguish their task from other similar disciplines, they gain a certain clarity about their goals and methods. When they insist on the expert's priority over the lay interpreter, they claim a respect the scholars have earned by enriching interpretation with their intensive researches. The *Wredestrasse* has helped many interpreters find their way out of oppressive situations; it has drawn attention to aspects of New Testament theology that previous generations had missed. It has been, and remains, the right way for many readers to formulate their New Testament theologies.

But, as we have seen, various estimable interpreters are frustrated by the limitations of modern New Testament theology. The strictures that constitute New Testament theology as a modern discourse rule out certain theological, or political, or psychological approaches to the endeavor. Not all interperters are in a hurry to separate interpretive moderns from their ancient forebears. Some interpreters are concerned that the disciplinary purity that modern New Testament theology seeks out costs the discipline its theological relevance. Others note the ways that the experts' exclusive authority over interpretation has persistently excluded interpreters who did not have equal access to venues of accreditation. Moreover, it has become increasingly clear that there are serious difficulties in the modern project itself. These may arise from moderni-

ty's incompleteness or (more likely, in my judgment) from structural blind spots which are the cost of so ambitious and powerful
a theoretical apparatus. There is no necessary gap between ancients
and moderns; it was constructed by the moderns as a tactical
maneuver in their struggle to win a hearing for their case. No
more is time the indispensible horizon for ascertaining meaning.
Privileged expertise and disciplinary purity are likewise highly
problematic postulates. It is clear, therefore, that readers who are
more committed to interests that conflict with modern imperatives
than they are to modernity are well justified in turning aside from
the *Wredestrasse*.

When interpreters take this turn away from modernity, they
will probably falter and stumble more often than they have on the
well-paved road of modern New Testament theology. Such clumsiness is not evidence that these interpreters' efforts are miscon-
ceived, any more than the faults of particular modern New
Testament theologies invalidate that approach. On the contrary,
this clumsiness simply follows from the fact that these nonmodern
approaches are unfamiliar, and that the first attempts to formulate
self-consciously nonmodern New Testament theologies are awk-
ward. If the possibility of nonmodern New Testament theologies
comes more clearly into view, however, efforts to sketch different
theologies will look less ungainly. As such efforts to formulate
nonmodern New Testament theologies receive increasing social
support, this support will coalesce into reading formations. These
reading formations will be defined by shared commitment to
certain goals, certain methods, and certain first steps in interpretation. As the reading formation covers more aspects of interpretation, its constituent interpreters will become more assured, and
may spend more time investigating the intricacies of its hermeneutical task than finding how to begin.

In the current critical environment, someone might take my
proposal to imply that I advocate "pluralism." On the contrary: I
do not by any means support pluralism for its own sake. I do, however, recognize that there will always be a plurality of interests in
interpretation, which plurality ought not be diminished by coer-
cion. I urge New Testament theologians to resist the desire to con-

trol interpretation. Disputes over the propriety of one or another sort of interpretation should be settled not by peremptory claims that one set of methods is innately superior, or uniquely suited to provide understanding, but by arguments concerning the interests that motivate interpreters to adopt particular methods.

My thesis thus has two conclusions. First, the modern approach to New Testament theology cannot justify claims that its own premises are necessary and exclusively valid (without circular reference to its own presuppositions). And second, those New Testament theologians who feel unreasonably constrained by the imperatives modern New Testament theology requires should look for legitimation from the particular reading formations that motivate their discomfort with modernity, not from the modernity that constrains them.

# Bibliography

Adam, A. K. M. *What Is Postmodern Biblical Criticism?* Guides to Biblical Scholarship. Minneapolis: Fortress Press, 1995.

_____. "The Future of Our Allusions." *Society of Biblical Literature Seminar Papers* (1992): 5-13.

Adorno, Theodor. *The Jargon of Authenticity.* Translated by Knut Tarnowski and Frederic Will. Evanston IL: Northwestern University Press, 1973.

Anderson, Perry. "Modernity and Revolution." *New Left Review* 144 (1984): 96-113.

Ankersmit, F. R. "Historiography and Postmodernism." *History & Theory* 28 (1989): 137-53.

Attridge, Derek, Geoff Bennington, and Robert Young, eds. *Post-Structuralism and the Question of History.* Cambridge: Cambridge University Press, 1987.

Baron, Hans. "The *Querelle* of the Ancients and Moderns as a Problem for Modern Scholarship." *Journal of the History of Ideas* 20 (1959): 3-22.

Barr, James. "Biblical Theology, Contemporary." In *The Interpreter's Dictionary of the Bible*, Supplementary Volume, ed. Keith Crim, 104-11. Nashville: Abingdon, 1976.

_____. "Exegesis as a Theological Discipline Reconsidered and the Shadow of the Jesus of History." In *The Hermeneutical Quest*, ed. Donald G. Miller, 11-45. Allison Park: Pickwick Publications, 1986.

_____. "Story and History in Biblical Theology." *Journal of Religion* 56 (1976): 1-17.

_____. "The Literal, the Allegorical, and Modern Biblical Scholarship." *Journal for the Study of the Old Testament* 44 (1989): 3-17.

_____. "The Theological Case against Biblical Theology." In *Canon, Theology, and Old Testament Interpretation*, ed. Gene M. Tucker, David L. Petersen, and Robert R. Wilson, 3-19. Philadelphia: Fortress Press, 1988.

_____. "Trends and Prospects in Biblical Theology." *Journal of Theological Studies* 25 (1974): 265-82.

_____. *Old and New in Interpretation.* London: SCM Press, 1966.

_____. *The Semantics of Biblical Language.* Oxford: Oxford University Press, 1961.

Barth, Karl, "Fifteen Answers to Professor von Harnack," and "An Answer to Professor von Harnack's Open Letter." In *The Beginnings of Dialectic Theology*, ed. James M. Robinson, trans. Keith R. Crim, 167-70 and 175-85. Richmond: John Knox Press, 1968.

_____. *Protestant Thought from Rousseau to Ritschl.* Translated by Brian Cozens. Repr. Salem: Ayer Company, 1971.

_____. *The Epistle to the Romans.* Translated by Edwyn C. Hoskyns. Repr. Oxford: Oxford University Press, 1976.

Baudelaire, Charles Pierre. *Œuvres Complètes.* Edited by Marcel A. Ruff. Paris: Éditions du Seuil, 1968.

Baudrillard, Jean. "Modernité." In *Encyclopædia Universalis.* Paris: Encyclopædia Universalis France, 1968.

Baur, Ferdinand Christian. *Vorlesungen über neutestamentliche Theologie.* Edited by F. F. Baur. Darmstadt: Wissenschaftliche Buchgesellschaft, 1973.

Beker, J. Christiaan. "Reflections on Biblical Theology." *Interpretation* 24 (1970): 303-20.

Belsey, Catherine. *Critical Practice.* London: Methuen, 1980.

Bendix, Reinhard. "Tradition and Modernity Reconsidered." *Comparative Studies in Society and History* 9 (1967): 292-346.

Benhabib, Seyla. "Epistemologies of Postmodernism: A Rejoinder to Jean-François Lyotard." *New German Critique* 33 (1984): 103-26.

Berger, Peter. *Facing Up to Modernity.* New York: Basic Books, 1977.

Berman, Marshall. *All That Is Solid Melts into Air.* New York: Simon & Schuster, 1982.

_____. "The Signs in the Street: A Response to Perry Anderson." *New Left Review* 144 (1984): 114-23.

Beyschlag, Willibald. *New Testament Theology.* Two volumes. Second English edition. Translated by Neil Buchanan. Edinburgh: T. & T. Clark, 1899.

Bleicher, Josef. *Contemporary Hermeneutics.* London: Routledge & Kegan Paul, 1980.

Bloom, Harold. *The Anxiety of Influence.* Oxford: Oxford University Press, 1973.

Bloomfield, Morton W. "Allegory as Interpretation." *New Literary History* 3 (1972): 301-17.

Blumenberg, Hans. *The Legitimacy of the Modern Age.* Translated by Robert M. Wallace. Cambridge MA: MIT Press, 1983.

Boers, Hendrikus. *What Is New Testament Theology?* Guides to Biblical Scholarship. Philadelphia: Fortress Press, 1979.

Bonhoeffer, Dietrich. *Creation and Fall* (translated by John C. Fletcher) and *Temptation* (edited by Eberhard Bethge, translated by Kathleen Downham). New York: Macmillan, 1959.

_____. *The Cost of Discipleship*. Revised edition. Translated by R. H. Fuller. New York: Macmillan, 1959.

Boyarin, Daniel. *Intertextuality and the Reading of Midrash*. Bloomington: Indiana University Press, 1990.

Brubaker, Rogers. *The Limits of Rationality*. Controversies in Sociology 16. London: George Allen & Unwin, 1984.

Bruns, Gerald L. "Midrash and Allegory: The Beginnings of Scriptural Interpretation." In *The Literary Guide to the Bible*, ed. Frank Kermode and Robert Alter, 625-46. Cambridge MA: Harvard University Press, 1986.

_____. "On the Weakness of Language in the Human Sciences." In *The Rhetoric of the Human Sciences*, ed. John S. Nelson, Allan Megill, and Donald McCloskey, 239-62. Madison: University of Wisconsin Press, 1987.

Bultmann, Rudolf. *Faith and Understanding*. Volume 1. Translated by Louise Pettibone Smith. New York: Harper & Row, 1969.

_____. *The Gospel of John*. Translated by G. R. Beasley-Murray (general editor), R. W. N. Hoare, and J. K. Riches. Oxford: Basil Blackwell; Philadelphia: Westminster Press, 1971.

_____. *History of the Synoptic Tradition*. Translated by John Marsh. Oxford: Basil Blackwell; New York: Harper & Row, 1963.

_____. "Is Exegesis without Presuppositions Possible?" In *Existence and Faith: Shorter Writings of Rudolf Bultmann*. Edited and translated by Schubert Ogden, 289-96. Living Age Books/Meridian Books. Cleveland: World Publishing, 1960.

_____. *Jesus and the Word*. Translated by Louise Pettibone Smith and Erminie Huntress Lantero. New York: Charles Scribner's Sons, 1934; ²1958.

_____. "New Testament and Mythology." In *Kerygma and Myth: A Theological Debate*, [volume 1,] ed. Hans Werner Bartsch, trans. Reginald H. Fuller, 1-44. London: SPCK; New York: Harper & Row, 1960.

_____. "The Problem of a Theological Exegesis of the New Testament." In *The Beginnings of Dialectic Theology*, ed. James M. Robinson, trans. Keith R. Crim, 236-56. Richmond: John Knox Press, 1968.

_____. "The Problem of Hermeneutics." In *The New Testament and Mythology and Other Basic Writings*, ed. and trans. Schubert Ogden, 69-93. Philadelphia: Fortress Press, 1984.

_____. *Theology of the New Testament*. Translated by Kendrick Grobel. Two volumes. New York: Charles Scribner's Sons, 1951, 1955.

Calinescu, Matei. *Five Faces of Modernity*. Second edition. Durham: Duke University Press, 1987.

Caputo, John D. *Radical Hermeneutics*. Bloomington: Indiana University Press, 1987.

Carroll, David, ed. *The States of "Theory."* New York: Columbia University Press, 1990.

Cartwright, Michael. "Practices, Politics, and Performance." Ph.D. diss., Duke University, 1988.

Cascardi, Anthony J. "Genealogies of Modernism." *Philosophy and Literature* 11 (1987): 207-25.

Certeau, Michel de. "History: Science and Fiction." In *Heterologies: Discourse on the Other*, trans. Brian Massumi. Minneapolis: University of Minnesota Press, 1986.

_____. *The Writing of History*. Translated by Tom Conley. New York: Columbia University Press, 1988.

Childs, Brevard. *Biblical Theology in Crisis*. Philadelphia: Westminster Press, 1970.

_____. "Interpretation in Faith: The Theological Responsibility of an Old Testament Theology." *Interpretation* 18 (1964): 432-49.

_____. *The New Testament as Canon*. Philadelphia: Fortress Press, 1985.

_____. *Old Testament Theology in a Canonical Context*. Philadelphia: Fortress Press, 1986.

_____. "The Sensus Literalis of Scripture: An Ancient and Modern Problem." In *Beiträge zur Alttestamentlichen Theologie*, ed. H. Donner, R. Hankart, and R. Smend, 80-93. Göttingen: Vandenhoeck & Ruprecht, 1977.

_____. "Some Reflections on the Search for a Biblical Theology." *Horizons in Biblical Theology* 4 (1982): 1-12.

Collins, John J. "Is a Critical Biblical Theology Possible?" In *The Hebrew Bible and Its Interpreters*, ed. William Henry Propp, Baruch Halpern, and David Noel Freedman, 1-17. Biblical and Judaic Studies 1. Winona Lake IN: Eisenbraun's, 1990).

Craig, Clarence T. "Biblical Theology and the Rise of Historicism." *Journal of Biblical Literature* 62 (1943): 281-94.

Culler, Jonathan. "Making Sense." *20th Century Studies* 12 (1974): 27-36.

Cullmann, Oscar. "La Nécessité et la fonction de l'exégèse philologique et historique de la Bible." *Verbum Caro* 3 (1949): 2-13.

Dahl, Nils. "Rudolf Bultmann's *Theology of the New Testament*." In *The Crucified Messiah*, 90-128. Minneapolis: Augsburg, 1974.

Dawsey, James. "The Lost Front Door into Scripture: Carlos Mesters, Latin American Liberation Theology, and the Church Fathers." *Anglican Theological Review* 72 (1990): 292-305.

de Man, Paul. *Allegories of Reading*. New Haven CT: Yale University Press, 1979.

_____. *Blindness and Insight*. Second edition. Minneapolis: University of Minnesota Press, 1983.

Derrida, Jacques. "Différance." In *Speech and Phenomena*, trans. David B. Allison, 129-60. Evanston IL: Northwestern University Press, 1973.

_____. "Structure, Sign, and Play in the Discourse of the Human Sciences." In *Writing and Difference*, trans. Alan Bass, 278-93. Chicago: University of Chicago Press, 1978.

Dilthey, Wilhelm. "The Rise of Hermeneutics." Translated by Fredric Jameson. *New Literary History* 3 (1972): 229-44.

Eagleton, Terry. "Capitalism, Modernism, and Postmodernism." *New Left Review* 152 (1985): 60-73.

_____. *Literary Theory*. Minneapolis: University of Minnesota Press, 1983.

Ebeling, Gerhard. "Hermeneutik." In *Die Religion in Geschichte und Gegenwart*, 3rd ed., vol. 3, cols. 242-62. Tübingen: J. C. B. Mohr (Paul Siebeck), 1962.

_____. "The Meaning of 'Biblical Theology'." In *Word and Faith*, trans. James W. Leitch, 79-97. London: SCM Press; Philadelphia: Fortress Press, 1963; German orig. 1960.

Englezakis, Benedict. *New and Old in God's Revelation*. Crestwood: St. Vladimir's Seminary Press, 1982.

Fish, Stanley. *Is There a Text in This Class?* Cambridge MA: Harvard University Press, 1979.

Ford, David. *Barth and God's Story*. Second edition. Frankfurt: Verlag Peter Lang, 1985.

Fosdick, Harry Emerson. *The Modern Use of the Bible*. Lyman Beecher Lectures on Preaching 1923–1924. Repr. New York: Macmillan, 1941 (1924).

Foster, Hal. "(Post)Modern Polemics." *New German Critique* 33 (1984): 67-78.

Foucault, Michel. *The Archaeology of Knowledge*. Translated by A. M. Sheridan Smith. New York: Pantheon Books, 1972.

_____. *Foucault Live*. Translated by John Johnston. Edited by Sylvère Lotringer. Foreign Agents Series. New York: Semiotext(e), 1989.

Fowl, Stephen. "The Ethics of Interpretation or What's Left Over after the Elimination of Meaning." *Society of Biblical Literature Seminar Papers* (1988): 69-81.

Fowl, Stephen E., and L. Gregory Jones. *Reading in Communion: Scripture & Ethics in Christian Life*. Grand Rapids: Eerdmans, 1991.

Frei, Hans. *The Eclipse of Biblical Narrative*. New Haven CT: Yale University Press, 1974.

_____. *The Identity of Jesus Christ*. Philadelphia: Fortress Press, 1975.

_____. "The 'Literal Reading' of Biblical Narrative in the Christian Tradition: Does It Stretch or Will It Break?" In *The Bible and the Narrative Tradition*, ed. Frank McConnell, 36-77. Oxford: Oxford University Press, 1986.

Freyne, Sean. "Our Preoccupation with History: Problems and Prospects." In *Proceedings of the Irish Biblical Association* 9 (1985): 1-18.

Frisby, David. *Fragments of Modernity*. Cambridge MA: MIT Press, 1986.

Froelich, Karlfried. "Biblical Hermeneutics on the Move." *Ex Auditu* 1 (1985): 1-13.

Fuller, Reginald H. "Sir Edwyn Hoskyns and the Contemporary Relevance of 'Biblical Theology'." *Ex Auditu* 1 (1985): 25-35.

Gabler, Johann Philipp. "On the Proper Distinction between Biblical and Dogmatic Theology." Translated by John Sandys-Wunsch and Laurence Eldredge. *Scottish Journal of Theology* 33 (1980): 133-58.

_____. (Untitled article). *Journal für theologische Literatur* 18 (1801): 363-413.

Gadamer, Hans Georg. *Truth and Method*. Translated by G. Barden and J. Cumming. New York: Seabury, 1975.

_____. "The Universality of the Hermeneutical Problem." Translated by David Linge. In *Contemporary Hermeneutics*, ed. Josef Bleicher, 128-40. London: Routledge & Kegan Paul, 1980.

Gese, Hartmut. *Essays on Biblical Theology*. Translated by Keith Crim. Minneapolis: Augsburg, 1981.

Giddens, Anthony. "Modernism and Postmodernism." *New German Critique* 22 (1981): 15-18.

Gilkey, Langdon. "Cosmology, Ontology, and the Travail of Biblical Language." *Journal of Religion* 41 (1961): 194-205.

_____. "The Roles of the 'Descriptive' or 'Historical' and of the 'Normative' in Our Work." *Criterion* 20 (1981): 10-17.

Gillot, Hubert. *La Querelle des Anciens et des Modernes en France*. Nancy: Crépin-Leblond, 1914.

Glebe-Möller, Jens. *Jesus and Theology*. Translated by Thor Hall. Philadelphia: Fortress Press, 1989.

Grässer, Erich. "Offene Fragen im Umkreis einer Biblischen Theologie." *Zeitschrift für Theologie und Kirche* 77 (1980): 200-21.

Green, Garrett, ed. *Scriptural Authority and Narrative Interpretation*. Philadelphia: Fortress Press, 1987.

Habermas, Jürgen. "The Entwinement of Myth and Enlightenment." *New German Critique* 26 (1982): 13-30.

_____. "Modernity versus Postmodernity." Translated by Seyla Ben-Habib. *New German Critique* 22 (1981): 3-14.

_____. *The Philosophical Discourse of Modernity*. Translated by Frederick Lawrence. Cambridge MA: MIT Press, 1987.

_____. "Questions and Counterquestions." Translated by James Bohman. In *Habermas and Modernity*, ed. Richard J. Bernstein, 192-216. Cambridge MA: MIT Press, 1985.

Hahn, Ferdinand. *Historical Investigation and New Testament Faith*. Translated by Robert Maddox. Philadelphia: Fortress Press, 1983.

Hanson, Paul D. "The Future of Biblical Theology." *Horizons in Biblical Theology* 6 (1984): 13-24.

_____. "The Responsibility of Biblical Theology to Communities of Faith." *Theology Today* 37 (1980): 39-50.

Harnack, Adolf von. "Fifteen Questions to Those among the Theologians Who Are Contemptuous of the Scientific Theology," "An Open Letter to Professor Karl Barth," and "Postscript to My Open Letter to Professor Karl Barth." In *The Beginnings of Dialectic Theology*, ed. James M. Robinson, trans. Keith R. Crim, 165-66, 171-74, 186-87. Richmond: John Knox Press, 1968.

Harvey, Van. *The Historian and the Believer*. Philadelphia: Westminster Press, 1966.

Hasel, Gerhard. *New Testament Theology*. Grand Rapids: Eerdmans, 1978.

_____. "The Relationship between Biblical Theology and Systematic Theology." *Trinity Journal* 5 (1984): 113-27.

Hauerwas, Stanley, and Steve Long. "Interpreting the Bible as a Political Act." *Religion & Intellectual Life* 6/3-4 (1989): 134-42.

_____. *A Community of Character*. Notre Dame IN: University of Notre Dame Press, 1979.

_____. "From System to Story: An Alternative Pattern for Rationality in Ethics." In *Truthfulness and Tragedy*, 15-39. Notre Dame IN: University of Notre Dame Press, 1977.

_____. "Story and Theology." In *Truthfulness and Tragedy*, 71-81. Notre Dame IN: University of Notre Dame Press, 1977.

Heidegger, Martin. *Being and Time*. Translated by John Macquarrie and Edward Robinson. London: SCM Press; New York: Harper & Row, 1962.

Hempel, J. "Biblische Theologie und biblische Religionsgeschichte, I. AT." In *Die Religion in Geschichte und Gegenwart*, 3rd ed., vol. 1, cols. 1256-59. Tübingen: J. C. B. Mohr (Paul Siebeck), 1962.

Hengel, Martin. "Historische Methoden und theologische Auslegung des Neuen Testaments." *Kerygma und Dogma* 19 (1973): 85-90.

Hiers, Richard. "Eschatology and Methodology." *Journal of Biblical Literature* 85 (1966): 170-84.

Hirsch, E. D. *Validity in Interpretation*. New Haven CT: Yale University Press, 1967.

Hopko, Thomas. "The Bible in the Orthodox Church." In *All the Fulness of God*, 49-90. Crestwood NY: St. Vladimir's Seminary Press, 1982.

Hoy, David Couzens, ed. *Foucault: A Critical Reader*. Oxford: Basil Blackwell, 1986.

Huhn, Thomas. "Jameson and Habermas." *Telos* 75 (1988): 103-23.

Hunter, A. M. "Modern Trends in New Testament Theology." In *The New Testament in Historical and Contemporary Perspective*, ed. Hugh Anderson and William Barclay, 133-48. Oxford: Basil Blackwell, 1965.

Huyssen, Andreas. "Critical Theory and Modernity: Introduction." *New German Critique* 26 (1982): 3-11.

_____. "Mapping the Postmodern." *New German Critique* 33 (1984): 5-52.

Ingram, David. "Foucault and the Frankfurt School." *Praxis International* 6 (1986): 311-27.

_____. *Habermas and the Dialectic of Reason*. New Haven CT: Yale University Press, 1987.

_____. "The Postmodern Kantianism of Arendt and Lyotard." *Review of Metaphysics* 42 (1988): 51-77.

Jameson, Fredric. Introduction to *The Postmodern Condition*, by Jean-François Lyotard. Minneapolis: Minnesota University Press, 1984.

_____. "Marxism and Postmodernism." *New Left Review* 176 (1989): 31-45.

_____. *The Political Unconscious*. Ithaca: Cornell University Press, 1981.

_____. "The Politics of Theory: Ideological Positions in the Postmodernism Debate." *New German Critique* 33 (1984): 53-65.

_____. "Postmodernism, or the Cultural Logic of Late Capitalism." *New Left Review* 146 (1984): 53-92.

_____. "Regarding Postmodernism—A Conversation with Fredric Jameson." Interview with Anders Stephanson. In *Universal Abandon? The Politics of Postmodernism*, ed. Andrew Ross, 3-30. Minneapolis: University of Minnesota Press, 1988.

Jauss, Hans Robert. "Ästhetiche Normen und geschichtliche Reflexion in der 'Querelle des Anciens et des Modernes'." Introduction to *Parallèles des Anciens et des Modernes*, by Charles Perrault. Repr. Munich: Eidos Verlag, 1964.

_____. "The Literary Process of Modernism From Rousseau to Adorno." *Cultural Critique* 11 (1988/1989): 27-61.

Jay, Martin. "Habermas and Modernism." In *Habermas and Modernity*, ed. Richard J. Bernstein, 125-39. Cambridge MA: MIT Press, 1985.

Jeanrond, Werner G. "The Theological Understanding of Texts and Linguistic Explication." *Modern Theology* 1 (1984): 55-66.

Jones, Gareth. *Bultmann: Toward a Critical Theology*. London: Polity Press, 1991.

Jones, Richard Foster. *Ancients and Moderns*. Second revised edition. St. Louis: Washington University Studies, 1961.

Josipovici, Gabriel. *The Book of God*. New Haven CT: Yale University Press, 1988.

Kähler, Martin. "Biblical Theology." In *The New Schaff-Herzog Encyclopedia of Religious Knowledge*, ed. Samuel Macauley Jackson, 183-86. Repr. Grand Rapids: Baker Book House, 1958.

_____. *The So-Called Historical Jesus and the Historic, Biblical Christ*. Translated by Carl E. Braaten. Philadelphia: Fortress Press, 1964.

Kant, Immanuel. *The Conflict of the Faculties*. Translated by Mary J. Gregor. New York: Abaris Books, 1979.

Käsemann, Ernst. "The Problem of a New Testament Theology." *New Testament Studies* 19 (1973): 235-245.

_____. *Essays on New Testament Themes*. Trans. W. J. Montague. London: SCM Press, 1964; Philadelphia: Fortress Press, 1982.

_____. *New Testament Questions of Today*. Trans. W. J. Montague. London: SCM Press; Philadelphia: Fortress Press, 1969.

_____. "Vom theologischen Recht historisch-kritischer Exegese." *Zeitschrift für Theologie und Kirche* 64 (1967): 259-81.

Keck, Leander. "Problems of New Testament Theology." *Novum Testamentum* 7 (1964/65): 217-41.

Kegley, C. W., ed. *The Theology of Rudolf Bultmann*. New York: Harper & Row, 1966.

Kermode, Frank. *The Art of Telling*. Cambridge MA: Harvard University Press, 1984.

_____. "The Modern." In *Modern Essays*, 39-70. London: Fontana, 1971.

Kolakowski, Leszek. "Modernity on Endless Trial." *Encounter* 66 (March 1986): 8-12.

Kolb, David A. *The Critique of Pure Modernity*. Chicago: University of Chicago Press, 1986.

_____. *Postmodern Sophistications*. Chicago: University of Chicago Press, 1990.

Kraus, Hans-Joachim. *Die Biblische Theologie: Ihre Geschichte und Problematik*. Neukirchen-Vluyn: Neukirchener Verlag, 1970.

Krentz, Edgar. *The Historical-Critical Method*. Guides to Biblical Scholarship. Philadelphia: Fortress Press, 1975.

Kümmel, Werner Georg. "Bibelwissenschaft des NT." In *Die Religion in Geschichte und Gegenwart*, 3rd ed., vol. 1, cols. 1236-51. Tübingen: J. C. B. Mohr (Paul Siebeck), 1962.

_____. *The New Testament: The History of the Investigation of Its Problems*. Translated by S. MacLean Gilmour and Howard Clark Kee. Nashville: Abingdon Press, 1972.

LaCapra, Dominic. "Criticism Today." In *The Aims of Representation: Subject/Text/ History*, ed. Murray Krieger, 235-55. Columbia Univ. Press, 1987.

_____. *History & Criticism*. Ithaca NY: Cornell University Press, 1985.

_____. *Rethinking Intellectual History*. Ithaca NY: Cornell University Press, 1983.

Lakoff, George, and Mark Johnson. *Metaphors We Live By*. Chicago: University of Chicago Press, 1980.

Lash, Nicholas. *Theology on Dover Beach*. London: Darton, Longman, and Todd, 1979.

_____. *Theology on the Way to Emmaus*. London: SCM Press, 1986.

Lawler, Justus George. "Theology and the Uses of History." *New Theology* 4, ed. Martin Marty and Dean Peerman, 147-61. New York: Macmillan, 1971.

Lentricchia, Frank. *After the New Criticism*. Chicago: University of Chicago Press, 1980.

Lessing, Gotthold E. *Lessing's Theological Writings*. Translated and edited by Henry Chadwick. Stanford CA: Stanford University Press, 1956.

Levenson, Jon D. "Why Jews Are Not Interested in Biblical Theology." In *Judaic Perspectives on Ancient Israel*, ed. Jacob Neusner, Baruch A. Levine, and Ernest S. Frerichs, 281-307. Philadelphia: Fortress Press, 1987.

Lindbeck, George. *The Nature of Doctrine*. Philadelphia: Westminster Press, 1984.

Löwith, Karl. *Meaning in History*. Chicago: University of Chicago Press, 1949.

Lyotard, Jean-François. *The Differend*. Translated by Georges Van Den Abbeele. Minneapolis: University of Minnesota Press, 1988.

_____. "The *Différend*, the Referent, and the Proper Name." Translated by Georges Van Den Abbeele. *Diacritics* 14 (1984): 4-14.

_____. *Peregrinations: Law, Form, Event*. New York: Columbia University Press, 1988.

_____. *The Postmodern Condition*. Trans. Geoff Bennington and Brian Massumi. Minneapolis: Minnesota University Press, 1984.

_____. *Le Postmoderne expliqué aux enfants*. Paris: Éditions Galilée, 1986.

_____. "Rules and Paradoxes and Svelte Appendix." *Cultural Critique* 5 (1986): 209-219.

_____. "The Unconcious, History, and Phrases: Notes on *The Political Unconscious*." Translated by Michael Clark. *New Orleans Review* 11 (1984): 73-79.

McGrath, John. "The Rights and Limits of History." *The Downside Review* 108 (1990): 20-36.

MacIntyre, Alasdair. *After Virtue*. Second edition. Notre Dame IN: University of Notre Dame Press, 1984.

_____. *Whose Justice? Which Rationality?* Notre Dame IN: University of Notre Dame Press, 1988.

Mack, Burton L. "The Kingdom Sayings in Mark." *Forum* 3 (1987): 3-47.

_____. *A Myth of Innocence*. Philadelphia: Fortress Press, 1988.

McKnight, Edgar. "A Biblical Criticism for American Biblical Scholarship." *Society of Biblical Literature Seminar Papers* (1980): 123-34.

_____. *Postmodern Use of the Bible*. Nashville: Abingdon Press, 1988.

Maier, Gerhard. *The End of the Historical-Critical Method*. Translated by Edwin W. Leverenz and Rudolph F. Norden. St. Louis: Concordia Publishing House, 1977.

Manson, T. W. "The Life of Jesus: Some Tendencies in Present-Day Research." In *The Background of the New Testament and its Eschatology*, ed. W. D. Davies and David Daube, 211-21. Cambridge: Cambridge University Press, 1956.

Margolis, Joseph. "Postscript on Modernism and Postmodernism, Both." *Theory, Culture, and Society* 6 (1989): 5-30.

Martin, Ralph P. "New Testament Theology: Impasse and Exit." *Expository Times* 91 (1980): 264-69.

Megill, Allan. *Prophets of Extremity*. Berkeley: University of California Press, 1985.

Merk, Otto. *Biblische Theologie des Neuen Testaments in ihrer Anfangszeit*. Marburg: N. G. Elwert Verlag, 1972.

Mesters, Carlos. *Defenseless Flower*. Translated by Francis McDonagh. Maryknoll NY: Orbis Books, 1987.

_____. "The Use of the Bible in Christian Communities of the Common People," in *The Bible and Liberation*, ed. Norman K. Gottwald, 119-33. Maryknoll NY: Orbis Books, 1983.

Meyer, Ben F. "Conversion and the Hermeneutics of Consent." *Ex Auditu* 1 (1985): 36-46.

_____. "The Primacy of Consent and the Uses of Scripture." *Ex Auditu* 2 (1986): 7-18.

Meyer, Paul W. "Faith and History Revisited." *Princeton Seminary Bulletin* 10 (1989): 75-83.

Michalson, Gordon E., Jr. "Faith and History: The Shape of the Problem." *Modern Theology* 1 (1985): 277-90.

_____. *Lessing's "Ugly Ditch": A Study of Theology and History*. Philadelphia: Pennsylvania State University Press, 1985.

_____. "Pannenberg on the Resurrection and Historical Method." *Scottish Journal of Theology* 33 (1980): 345-59.

_____. "Theology, Historical Knowledge, and the Contingency-Necessity Distinction." *International Journal for Philosophy of Religion* 14 (1983): 87-98.

Milbank, John. "'Postmodern Critical Augustinianism': A Short Summa in Forty Two Responses to Unasked Questions." *Modern Theology* 7 (1991): 225-37.

Minear, Paul. "Christian Eschatology and Historical Methodology," in *Neutestamentliche Studien für Rudolf Bultmann*, ed. Walther Eltester. Berlin: Alfred Töpelmann, 1954.

_____. "Ecumenical Theology—Profession or Vocation?" *Theology Today* 33 (1976): 66-73.

_____. "Gospel History: Celebration or Reconstruction?" In *Jesus and Man's Hope*, ed. Donald G. Miller and Dikran Y. Hadidian, 13-27. A Perspective Book. Pittsburgh: Pittsburgh Theological Seminary, 1971.

_____. "The Transcendence of God and Biblical Hermeneutics." In *CTSA Proceedings of the Twenty-Third Annual Convention* 23 (1968): 1-19.

Mitchell, W. J. T., ed. *Against Theory*. Chicago: University of Chicago Press, 1985.

Morgan, Robert. "F. C. Baur's Lectures on New Testament Theology." *Expository Times* 88 (1977): 202-206.

_____. "Gabler's Bicentenary." *Expository Times* 98 (1987): 164-68.

_____. "The Historical Jesus and the Theology of the New Testament." In *The Glory of Christ in the New Testament*, ed. L. D. Hurst and N. T. Wright, 187-206. Oxford: Clarendon Press, 1987.

_____. *The Nature of New Testament Theology*. Naperville IL: Alec R. Allenson, 1973.

Morgan, Robert, and John Barton. *Biblical Interpretation*. Oxford: Oxford University Press, 1988.

Morgan, Robert, and Michael Pye, eds. *The Cardinal Meaning: Essays in Comparative Hermeneutics: Buddhism and Christianity*. Religion and Reason 6. The Hague: Mouton, 1973.

Nations, Archie L. "Historical Criticism and the Current Methodological Crisis." *Ex Auditu* 1 (1985): 125-32.

Nehemas, Alexander. *Nietzsche: Life as Literature*. Cambridge MA: Harvard University Press, 1985.

Niebuhr, H. Richard. *The Meaning of Revelation*. New York: Macmillan, 1941.

Nietzsche, Friedrich. *Beyond Good and Evil*. Translated, with commentary, by Walter Kaufmann. Vintage Books. New York: Random House, 1966.

_____. *The Birth of Tragedy* and *The Case of Wagner*. Translated, with commentary, by Walter Kaufmann. Vintage Books. New York: Random House, 1967.

_____. *On the Genealogy of Morals* and *Ecce Homo*. Translated, with commentary, by Walter Kaufmann. Vintage Books. New York: Random House, 1967.

_____. *The Portable Nietzsche*. Edited and translated by Walter Kaufmann. Viking Portable Library. New York: Viking Press, 1954; repr. Harmondsworth: Penguin Books, 1968.

_____. *Untimely Meditations*. Translated by R. J. Hollingdale. Texts in German Philosophy. Cambridge: Cambridge University Press, 1983.

O'Leary, Joseph. "Theology on the Brink of Modernism." *boundary* 2 13 (1985): 145-56.

Oden, Robert A., Jr. "Hermeneutics and Historiography: Germany and America." *Society of Biblical Literature Seminar Papers* (1980): 135-57.

Ogden, Schubert. Review of Gareth Jones, *Bultmann: Towards a Critical Theology. Modern Theology* 8 (1992): 215-17.

Ollenburger, Ben C. "Biblical and Systematic Theology: Inventing a Relationship." Typescript, 1990.

_____. "Biblical Theology: Situating the Discipline," in *Understanding the Word*, ed. J. T. Butler, E. W. Conrad, and B. C. Ollenburger, 37-62. JSOT Supplement Series 37. Sheffield: JSOT Press, 1982.

_____. "What Krister Stendahl 'Meant': A Normative Critique of 'Descriptive Biblical Theology'." *Horizons in Biblical Theology* 8 (1986): 61-98.

Pältz, E. H. "Gabler, Johann Philipp." In *Die Religion in Geschichte und Gegenwart*, 3rd ed., vol. 2, col. 1186. Tübingen: J. C. B. Mohr (Paul Siebeck), 1962.

Perrin, Norman. "The Challenge of New Testament Theology Today." *Criterion* 4 (1965): 25-34.

_____. "Jesus and the Theology of the New Testament." *Journal of Religion* 64 (1984): 413-31.

_____. "The Wredestrasse Becomes the Hauptstrasse: Reflections on the Reprinting of the Dodd Festschrift." *Journal of Religion* 46 (1966): 296-300.

Pippin, Robert B. "Nietzsche and the Origin of the Idea of Modernity." *Inquiry* 26 (1983): 151-80.

Prabhu, Joseph. "The Tradition of Modernity." In *Religious Pluralism*, ed. Leroy S. Rouner, 77-93. Boston University Studies in Philosophy and Religion 5. Notre Dame IN: University of Notre Dame Press, 1984.

Räisänen, Heikki. *Beyond New Testament Theology*. Philadelphia: Trinity Press International, 1990.

Rajchman, John. "Habermas's Complaint." *New German Critique* 45 (1988): 163-91.

Rasmusson, Arne. "Bibeln och den Kristna Församlingen." *Tro och Liv* 47/6 (1988): 20-27.

Ray, S. Alan. *The Modern Soul*. Harvard Dissertations in Religion 21. Philadelphia: Fortress Press, 1987.

Reisenfeld, H. "Biblische Theologie und biblische Religionsgeschichte, II. NT." In *Die Religion in Geschichte und Gegenwart*, 3rd ed., vol. 1, cols. 1259-62. Tübingen: J. C. B. Mohr (Paul Siebeck), 1962.

Reiss, Timothy J. *The Discourse of Modernism*. Ithaca NY: Cornell University Press, 1982.

Reventlow, Henning Graf. *Problems of Biblical Theology in the Twentieth Century.* Philadelphia: Fortress, 1986.

Richardson, Alan. "Biblical Theology and the Modern Mood." *Theology* 39 (1939): 244-52.

_____. "Historical Theology and Biblical Theology." *Canadian Journal of Theology* 1 (1955): 157-67.

_____. *Introduction to the Theology of the New Testament.* London: SCM Press, 1958.

_____. "What Is New Testament Theology?" *Studia Evangelica* 6, ed. Elizabeth A. Livingstone, 455-65. Berlin: Akademie-Verlag, 1973.

Riches, John. "Biblical Theology and the Pressing Concerns of the Church." *The Modern Churchman* 30 (1988): 6-12.

Rigault, Hippolyte. *Histoire de la Querelle des Anciens et des Modernes* In *Oeuvres Complètes*, vol. 1. Paris: Librairie de L. Hachette et Cie., 1859.

Robinson, James M. "The Future of New Testament Theology," *Religious Studies Review* 2 (1976): 17-23.

Rollmann, Hans. "From Baur to Wrede: The Quest for a Historical Method." *Studies in Religion/Sciences Religieuses* 17 (1988): 443-54.

Rorty, Richard. "Habermas and Lyotard on Postmodernity." In *Habermas and Modernity*, ed. Richard J. Bernstein, 160-75. Cambridge MA: MIT Press, 1985.

_____. "Science as Solidarity." In *The Rhetoric of the Human Sciences*, ed. John S. Nelson, Allan Megill, and Donald McCloskey, 37-52. Madison: University of Wisconsin Press, 1987.

_____. "Texts and Lumps." *New Literary History* 17 (1985): 1-16.

Russell, Letty M., ed. *Feminist Interpretation of the Bible.* Philadelphia: Westminster Press, 1985.

Saebø, Magne. "Johann Philipp Gablers Bedeutung für die Biblische Theologie." *Zeitschrift für alttestamentliche Wissenschaft* 99 (1987): 1-16.

Said, Edward. *The World, the Text, and the Critic.* Cambridge MA: Harvard University Press, 1983.

Scalise, Charles J. "The 'Sensus Literalis': A Hermeneutical Key to Biblical Exegesis." *Scottish Journal of Theology* 42 (1989): 45-65.

Schlatter, Adolf. "Ätheistische Methoden in der Theologie." In *Beiträge zur Förderung christlicher Theologie* 9/5 (1905): 229-50. (Gütersloh: Bertelsmann, 1905.)

_____. "The Theology of New Testament and Dogmatics," trans. Robert Morgan. In *The Nature of New Testament Theology*, 117-66. Naperville IL: Alec R. Allenson, 1973.

Schneiders, Sandra. *The Revelatory Text*. San Francisco: HarperSanFrancisco, 1991.

Schüssler Fiorenza, Elisabeth. *Bread Not Stone*. Boston: Beacon Press, 1984.

_____. "Emerging Issues in Feminist Biblical Interpretation." In *Christian Feminism: Visions of a New Humanity*, ed. Judith L. Weidman, 33-54. New York: Harper & Row, 1984.

_____. "The Ethics of Interpretation: De-Centering Biblical Interpretation." *Journal of Biblical Literature* 107 (1988): 3-17.

_____. *In Memory of Her*. New York: Crossroad, 1983.

_____. "Lk 13:10-17: Interpretation for Liberation and Transformation." *Theology Digest* 36 (1989): 303-19.

_____. "The Politics of Otherness: Biblical Interpretation as a Critical Praxis for Liberation." In *The Future of Liberation Theology*, ed. Marc H. Ellis and Otto Maduro. Maryknoll NY: Orbis Books, 1987.

_____. *But She Said*. Boston: Beacon Press, 1992.

_____, ed. *Searching the Scriptures*. New York: Crossroads, 1993.

Scott, Bernard Brandon. "The New Synoptic Problem: The Convergence of Methods in the Quest." Typescript, 1986.

Scroggs, Robin. "Can New Testament Theology Be Saved? The Threat of Contextualisms." *Union Seminary Quarterly Review* 42 (1988): 17-31.

Sloterdijk, Peter. "Cynicism—The Twilight of False Consciousness," trans. Michael Eldred and Leslie A. Adelson. *New German Critique* 33 (1984): 190-206.

Smart, James. *The Past, Present, and Future of Biblical Theology*. Philadelphia: Westminster Press, 1979.

Smend, Rudolf. "Johann Philipp Gablers Begründung der biblischen Theologie." *Evangelische Theologie* 22 (1962): 345-57.

Smith, Barbara Herrnstein. *Contingencies of Value*. Cambridge MA: Harvard University Press, 1988.

_____. "Narrative Versions, Narrative Theories." In *On Narrative*, ed. W. J. Mitchell, 209-32. Chicago: University of Chicago Press, 1981.

Soelle, Dorothée. *Political Theology*. Translated by John Shelley. Philadelphia: Fortress Press, 1974.

Stanton, Graham N. "Interpreting the New Testament Today." *Ex Auditu* 1 (1985): 63-73.

Steinmetz, David. "The Superiority of Pre-Critical Exegesis." *Theology Today* 37 (1980): 27-38.

Stendahl, Krister. *The Bible and the Role of Women*. Translated by Emilie T. Sander. Facet Books 15. Philadelphia: Fortress Press, 1966.

_____. "The Bible as a Classic and the Bible as Holy Scripture." *Journal of Biblical Literature* 103 (1984): 3-10.

_____. "Biblical Theology, Contemporary." *Interpreter's Dictionary of the Bible,* ed. George Buttrick, A-D:418-32. Nashville: Abingdon Press, 1962.

_____. *Meanings. The Bible as Document and as Guide.* Philadelphia: Fortress Press, 1984.

_____. "Method in the Study of Biblical Theology." In *The Bible in Modern Scholarship,* ed. J. P. Hyatt, 196-216. Nashville: Abingdon, 1965.

_____. *Paul among Jews and Gentiles.* Philadelphia: Fortress Press, 1976.

_____. "The Art of Preaching." Lyman Beecher Lectures on Preaching. Yale Divinity School. 1984.

Stout, Jeffrey. "A Lexicon of Postmodern Philosophy." *Religious Studies Review* 13 (1987): 18-22.

_____. "The Relativity of Interpretation." *The Monist* 69 (1986): 103-18.

_____. "What Is the Meaning of a Text?" *New Literary History* 14 (1982): 1-12.

Strecker. Georg, ed. *Das Problem der Theologie des Neuen Testaments.* Darmstadt: Wissenschaftliche Buchgesellschaft, 1975.

_____. "William Wrede." *Zeitschrift für Theologie und Kirche* 57 (1960): 67-91.

_____. "Wrede, William." In *Die Religion in Geschichte und Gegenwart,* 3rd ed., vol. 6, col. 1822. Tübingen: J. C. B. Mohr (Paul Siebeck), 1962.

Stuhlmacher, Peter. "Adolf Schlatter's Interpretation of Scripture." *New Testament Studies* 24 (1977/1978): 433-46.

_____. "The Ecological Crisis as a Challenge for Biblical Theology," trans. James M. Scott. *Ex Auditu* 3 (1987): 1-15.

_____. "*Ex Auditu* and the Theological Interpretation of Holy Scripture." *Ex Auditu* 2 (1986): 1-6.

_____. "The Gospel of Reconciliation in Christ—Basic Features of a Biblical Theology of the New Testament," trans. George R. Edwards. *Horizons in Biblical Theology* 1 (1979): 161-90.

_____. *Historical Criticism and the Theological Interpretation of Scripture.* Translated by Roy A. Harrisville. Philadelphia: Fortress Press, 1977.

_____. *Reconciliation, Law, and Righteousness.* Translated by Everett Kalin. Philadelphia: Fortress Press, 1986.

_____. *Vom Verstehen des Neuen Testament: Eine Hermeneutik.* Grundrisse zum Neuen Testament 6. Second edition. Göttingen: Vandenhoeck and Ruprecht, 1986.

Sturrock, John, ed. *Structuralism and Since*. Oxford: Oxford University Press, 1979.

Stylianopolis, Theodore. "Historical Studies and Orthodox Theology, or The Problem of History for Orthodoxy." *Greek Orthodox Theological Review* 12 (1967): 394-419.

Surin, Kenneth. *The Turnings of Darkness and Light*. Cambridge: Cambridge University Press, 1989.

Swift, Jonathan. *The Writings of Jonathan Swift*. Edited by Robert A. Greenberg and William B. Piper. Norton Critical Editions. New York: W. W. Norton & Co., 1973.

Theissen, Gerd. *Biblical Faith: An Evolutionary Approach*. Translated by John Bowden. Philadelphia: Fortress Press, 1984.

Thiemann, Ronald. *Revelation and Theology*. Notre Dame IN: University of Notre Dame Press, 1985.

Tompkins, Jane. "Indians: Textualism, Morality, and the Problem of History." *Critical Inquiry* 13 (1986): 101-19.

Troeltsch, Ernst. "Historiography." In *Encyclopedia of Religion and Ethics*, ed. James Hastings, 716-22. Repr. New York: Charles Scribner's Sons, 1959.

Tuckett, Christopher. "Christology and the New Testament." *Scottish Journal of Theology* 33 (1980): 401-16.

Ugolnick, Anton. "An Orthodox Hermeneutic in the West." *St. Vladimir's Theological Quarterly* 27 (1983): 93-118.

Vattimo, Gianni. "Bottle, Net, Truth, Revolution, Terrorism, Philosophy." *Denver Quarterly* 16/4 (1982): 24-34.

_____. *The End of Modernity*. Translated by Jon R. Snyder. Baltimore: Johns Hopkins University Press, 1988.

_____. "Metaphysics, Violence, Secularization," and "Toward an Ontology of Decline." Translated by Barbara Spackman. In *Recoding Metaphysics*, ed. Giovanna Borradori, 45-75. Evanston IL: Northwestern University Press, 1988.

Via, Dan O., Jr. *The Parables*. Philadelphia: Fortress Press, 1966.

_____. "A Quandry of New Testament Scholarship: The Time Between the 'Bultmanns'." *Journal of Religion* 55 (1975): 456-61.

Wagner, B. S. "'Biblische Theologien' und 'Biblische Theologie'," *Theologische Literaturzeitung* 103 (1978): 785-98.

Waldman, Marilyn Robinson. "'The Otherwise Unnoteworthy Year 711': A Reply to Hayden White." In *On Narrative*, ed. W. J. Mitchell 240-48. Chicago: University of Chicago Press, 1981.

Wallace, Robert M. "Progress, Secularization, and Modernity: The Löwith-Blumenberg Debate." *New German Critique* 22 (1981): 63-79.

Weber, Max. *From Max Weber: Essays in Sociology*. Translated and edited by H. H. Gerth and C. Wright Mills. Oxford: Oxford University Press, 1946.

_____. *The Protestant Ethic and the Spirit of Capitalism*. Translated by Talcott Parsons. New York: Charles Scribner's Sons, 1930; ²1958.

Weiss, Bernhard. *(Textbook on the) Biblical Theology of the New Testament*. Translated by David Eaton and James E. Duguid. Two volumes. Edinburgh: T. & T. Clark, n.d.; German orig. 1868, ET 1882–1883.

Wellmer, Albrecht. "On the Dialectic of Modernism and Postmodernism." *Praxis International* 4 (1985): 337-62.

West, Cornel. "Fredric Jameson's Marxist Hermeneutics." *boundary 2* 11 (1982/1983): 177-200.

_____. "Interview with Cornel West," by Anders Stephanson. In *Universal Abandon? The Politics of Postmodernism*, ed. Andrew Ross, 269-86. Minneapolis: University of Minnesota Press, 1988.

_____. *Prophesy Deliverance!* Philadelphia: Westminster Press, 1982.

White, Hayden. *Metahistory*. Baltimore: Johns Hopkins University Press, 1973.

_____. "The Narrativization of Real Events." In *On Narrative*, ed. W. J. Mitchell, 249-54. Chicago: University of Chicago Press, 1981.

_____. *Tropics of Discourse*. Baltimore: Johns Hopkins University Press, 1978.

_____. "The Value of Narrativity in the Representation of Reality." In *On Narrative*, ed. W. J. Mitchell, 1-24. Chicago: University of Chicago Press, 1981.

Wilder, Amos N. "New Testament Theology in Transition." In *The Study of the Bible Today and Tomorrow*, ed. Harold R. Willoughby, 419-36. Chicago: University of Chicago Press, 1947.

_____. "Norman Perrin and the Relation of Historical Knowledge to Faith." *Harvard Theological Review* 82 (1989): 201-11.

Williams, Raymond. "When Was Modernism?" *New Left Review* 175 (1989): 48-52.

Wink, Walter. *The Bible in Human Transformation*. Philadelphia: Fortress Press, 1973.

_____. *Transforming Bible Study*. Nashville: Abingdon Press, 1980.

Wittgenstein, Ludwig. *Philosophical Investigations*. Translated by G. E. M. Anscombe. Third edition. New York: Macmillan, 1968.

Wolin, Richard. "Modernism vs. Postmodernism." *Telos* 62 (1984/1985): 9-29.

Wrede, William. "On the Task and Methods of 'New Testament Theology'." Translated by Robert Morgan. In *The Nature of New Testament Theology*, 68-116. Naperville IL: Alec R. Allenson, 1973.

_____. *Paul.* Translated by Edward Lummis. London: Philip Green, 1907.

_____. *Über Aufgabe und Methode der sogenannten Neutestamentlichen Theologie.* Göttingen: Vandenhoeck und Ruprecht, 1897.

_____. *Vorträge und Studien.* Tübingen: J. C. B. Mohr (Paul Siebeck), 1907.

Yoder, John Howard. *The Politics of Jesus.* Grand Rapids: Eerdmans, 1972.

_____. *The Priestly Kingdom.* Notre Dame IN: University of Notre Dame Press, 1984.

# Index of Names